The View
from the Hill

Christopher Somerville

*For Jane, constant companion and
illuminator of these expeditions.*

First published in 2021 by
HAUS PUBLISHING LTD.
4 Cinnamon Row, London SW11 3TW

This paperback edition published in 2023

The right of Christopher Somerville to be identified as the author of this
work has been asserted in accordance with the Copyright, Designs and
Patents Act, 1988.

Some of these pieces first appeared in the following publications: *The Times,
Sunday Times, Financial Times, Daily Telegraph, Country Living, Saga Magazine,
Walk Magazine, Compass.*

ISBN 978-1-914982-03-3
eISBN: 978-1-909961-79-1

Typeset in Garamond by MacGuru Ltd

Printed in the United Kingdom by Clays Ltd (Elcograf S.p.A.)

A CIP catalogue for this book is available from the British Library

www.hauspublishing.com

Contents

Newly opened eyes   1

New Year into Spring   5

1   The putcher-maker   7
2   Nuttall bagging   9
3   Parson Hawker's Morwenstow   12
4   A is for Anger   15
5   Covidiots?   17
6   Walking in snow   19
7   Snowholing   22
8   Natural remedy   25
9   Dry stone wall   27
10   B is for Binoculars   29
11   Salt marsh   31
12   Ships' graveyard   33
13   Animal tracking   36
14   Blue prince of the mountains   39
15   C is for Curmudgeon Man   42
16   Forest floor   44
17   Digby in glory   46
18   New Forest in mist   48
19   The randy natterjack   50
20   Whatever happened to Lover's Lane?   53
21   D is for Drovers   55
22   Keep it simple, stupid   57

23	Death of the map	59
24	Gellius Philippus: who he?	62
25	Neatsfoot oil	65
26	Penwith granite	67
27	E is for Elephant	70
28	Summons soup with the Laird of Gight	72
29	Turncoats of the Peak	75
30	St Swithun's Way	78
31	F is for Flora and Fauna	81
32	Bempton Cliffs	83
33	Salmon on the Spey	85
34	G is for Green Man	88
35	Up the down and down the beach	90
36	Slutch	93
37	H is for Heroes	96
38	Google Translate	98
39	Greenham Common resurgent	100
40	Covid Spring: two walks	104
41	I is for Islands	107
42	Freemining in the Forest of Dean	109
43	Dawn chorus	111
44	Ladder of life	114
45	J is for Jollity	115
46	Dunes of delight	117
47	Apple confetti	120

Summer		123
48	The Garden of Sleep	125
49	Covid Summer: off-grid in Dragondown Wood	129
50	With Rupert Brooke through Grantchester Meadows	131
51	Gannets of the Bass Rock	134

52	Covid Summer: the crayfish of Ironmaster's Vale	137
53	The figurehead of our wild lands	139
54	The Ringing Stone of Tiree	142
55	K is for Kyrgyzstan	145
56	A proper Lakeland how-d'ye-do	147
57	Nightjars and moths of Arne Heath	149
58	Splatchers	152
59	Worldwide seed of a single English field	154
60	L is for Landlady	157
61	Brocton Camp	159
62	I got 99 problems and a tent ain't one	162
63	Orford Ness: a funny old place	164
64	South Wales Valleys: iron and coal	167
65	A message to mucky mankind	170
66	Howlin' Dog Jackson	174
67	Covid Summer: Russet Mere and Monk's Kitchen	176
68	Secret riches	178
69	M is for Music	181
70	Fanfare for the soldier	183
71	Three Peaks of Yorkshire: a long, sharp shock	185
72	Bye, Arnold!	189
73	The badgers of Little Stoke Woods	192
74	Shingle	195
75	N is for Notebook	197
76	Red squirrels of the Sefton Coast	199
77	Hampshire chalk stream	203
78	Soaked on Scafell Pike	206
79	Lammas meadows	208
80	O is for Ooooohhhh	212
81	Living on an island	214
82	Tidal landscape of Worm's Head	217
83	Dream island	220

84 Welcome to GB!   223
85 Hard hats and humorous shags   226
86 Betjeman eyes   229
87 P is for Poetry   232
88 Through Sloch na Marra to Rathlin Island   233
89 The Walls of Derry   236
90 Larks over Hubberholme   239
91 Salt marsh and mudflat: Cobnor peninsula   241
92 Bat-watching in Petworth Park   244
93 A stroll on the Goodwin Sands   247
94 Q is for Quagmire   250
95 Englyn on Snowdon   252

Autumn   255
96 Jays in the ilex   257
97 Big Meadow   258
98 Gassy Webcap, Bedstraw Smut and the dreaded
    Cramp Balls   261
99 The Great Ash Massacre   263
100 Covid Autumn: India in the Cotswolds   266
101 R is for Rights   268
102 Climbing irons   270
103 Heather moors   272
104 The lord of Inivae   275
105 PITAPAT   278
106 S is for Stick   280
107 Bummelty-kites and yoe-brimmels   282
108 An end-of-the-earth kind of place   285
109 Wild magic of the Sperrins   288
110 Solitary mooch with a beautiful killer   290
111 Ancient oak   293
112 Staving off the sea   294

113	Dunwich shore and Dingle Marshes	297
114	T is for Thermos	300
115	Stranger on the shore	302
116	Autumn on the Severn	305
117	Roasted crabs	307
118	Bolving, soiling and Jacobson's organ: courtship of the red stag	309
Winter		313
119	Innominate Tarn	315
120	Strid and strong beer	317
121	U is for Umbrella	320
122	Galoshes	322
123	My bedside Essex	324
124	Moody, muddy Dengie	326
125	Flint and clay	329
126	V is for Vixen	332
127	Song of the mermaids	334
128	Starling roar	337
129	Land of the dragon	340
130	A pot of bile	343
131	What's under the jacket	345
132	W is for Willy Knott	348
133	Covid Winter: Skirrid in the Sky	349
134	Fight for the footpaths	351
135	The rough embrace of winter	354
136	Snow bridge	357
137	X is for Xmas	359
138	With George Borrow to Castell Dinas Bran	361
139	Angling and quanting: the Norfolk Broads in winter	363
140	3,000 geese at full gabble	366

141 The unspeakable Stiperstones 369
142 Y is for Yer Tiz 372
143 Too much damn trouble 374
144 Covid Winter: sunrise at the long barrow 376
145 Boxing Day: go climb a hill 378
146 Z is for Zymurgy 381
147 What's the point? 382

Notes 391

Newly opened eyes

There's nothing like a lockdown for sharpening you up. It's strange to think, as I sit writing this at Christmas 2020, that a year ago I'd never heard the term 'lockdown', let alone 'coronavirus'. I've learned a lot since then. And the lesson that stands out above all is a simple one: taste life to the full while it's there.

In the early phase of the global coronavirus pandemic, people sickened and died all over the country. The airwaves were stiff with stern-faced scientists, with politicians exhorting and fumbling. Newspapers and social media rang with hysteria, pessimism and misinformation. Shops and pubs closed, neighbours got twitchy about social distancing (a clunky new concept). Gates and stiles, doorknobs and Amazon packaging were suspected of being deadly viral fomites (another new and sinister word). Handwashing became a Lady Macbeth-like national neurosis.

Daily walks in spring, just about the only thing we were allowed to do outside the house, took on a magical and transcendent quality. No vans roared up the steep lane to the hills or censed the verges with grey diesel fumes. No aeroplane trails seamed the blue sky. No helicopters clattered above the woods. Not a sound drifted from the main road skirting the village. Instead: birdsong, loud and sweet, everywhere at once. I was astonished to realise the extent to which extraneous mechanical noise had been swamping it.

1

When we ventured as far as the top of the hill from where we look down across the city, we had another shock. Where was the familiar smear of dirty lemon-coloured photochemical pollutants close above the houses? Gone with the absent cars and lorries. Down in the bowl where the city lies, we found we could breathe easy for the first time since we came to live there thirty years ago.

Back in the woods and fields around our village, every leaf and plant looked freshly cut and newly polished. The contrast between this timeless manifestation of nature resurgent and the ominous news – minute by minute, if you wanted it and could stand it, in one's ear and brain like a spiritual tinnitus – was breathtaking. All the senses felt sharpened as the days and weeks followed one another, unbelievably clear and warm, the finest run of beautiful spring weather anyone could remember. We went out walking every day for several hours at a stretch, more walking than we'd ever continuously done, looking for Solomon's seal and herb Paris in corners of woodland never before explored, finding an old green-skinned pond forgotten in the crease of a field boundary, hiding at sunset beside another to watch blackbirds and blackcaps ecstatically bathing the day's dust away.

The dipper came back to the roadside river, where I hadn't seen him for decades. Chiffchaffs shouted triumphantly from the sunny woods. Early purple orchids flooded the margins of coppices, large sweet violets sprouted in the treads of wooden steps. These things were not unique to this oddest of years, of course. The chiffchaff and the orchids had always returned with the spring. So why did they seem to grace this dislocated season so particularly? I thought about it and realised that I had got out of the habit, out of the way, of taking proper time to look and listen. Too many deadlines, too many projects. I had been yomping through my walks, barging through the landscape like a runner on a mission, notebook and pen and GPS in hand, scribbling like a maniac, missing so much and so much. What a hell of a realisation for someone who for most of his life had been writing about the slow rhythms of the countryside and the creatures that move and live and have their being there.

In my workroom is a case of shelves that holds about 450 notebooks. Almost every walk I've ever written up is annotated there in hasty spidery handwriting that only I can decipher. The pages are creased and stained with mud, blood, flattened insect corpses, beer glass rings, smears of plant juice and gallons of sweat. So many notes, so much researching and burrowing for facts – church dates, notable residents, quotes from rural writers, the names of fields, fourteen species of bats, forgotten medieval skirmishes, turn left at the oak tree, look for the yellow arrow by the barn. Why hadn't I trusted more to luck and the day, let myself just go with the flow, as I was doing now during this Covid spring? What on earth had I been scribbling so copiously about?

In the enforced idleness of the pandemic restrictions, unable to travel further than Shanks's pony could carry me, I took a good long look back. Let's see… Notebook 350, how about that? Ah yes, springtime in the north of Scotland, standing by the old icehouse at the mouth of the River Spey in full spate and watching an Atlantic salmon leaping through the waves. Magical moment! All right, Notebook 205, the Goodwin Sands. That had been a freakish afternoon in a long hot summer, an evening hovercraft ride out to the treacherous Kentish sandbank in the company of cricketers, potholers, seal fanciers and Jesus freaks – adventurers who had a precarious hour to perform whatever eccentric rituals they pleased before the rising tide turned the sands to soft sinking jelly once more. Another one, um, Notebook 193, that'll do. November in the north, by the looks of it, all pages sodden and blurred by rain. Teesdale and High Force, Blanchland up in the Durham Dales... ah, here we are. Something that catches absolutely the essence of winter walking in the Yorkshire Dales. Eleven miles in a day-long downpour along the River Wharfe, drenched to the skin, mist curling in the bare tops of alders and silver birches, and the rain-swollen river hurling itself in angry strength through the rocky narrows of the Strid, rumbling and shaking the ground. Respite further up the dale in the New Inn at Appletreewick, drying off my soaking rain gear, steaming by the fire and eyeing their exotic beer menu. Belgian cherry beer, Trappist ale, smoked beer; Samichlaus, the strongest beer in the world. Good God, how did I make it out of there alive?

Those hundreds of notebooks, their scribbles and stains, the dried leaf fragments that fall out of their pages, the quick sketches of umbellifers ('goatsbeard?') and birds ('??? yellow breast, a few dark stripes, bouncy flight, *pt-cheeew chip-chip!* ???') were the seedbed in which this book grew. An account of walking the landscape through the seasons of forty years in every corner of these islands, the wildlife, the people, the shapes and colours of weather and hills, and the changing nature of the British countryside over the working lifetime of one walker.

I hope you enjoy this armchair walking as much as I did during those curious months when every day seemed freighted with portentous significance, and all we could do about it was walk and look around with newly opened eyes.

NEW YEAR INTO SPRING

1

The putcher-maker

'I always loved the river,' says Dave Bennet, master putcher-maker. 'Been salmon fishing all my life.' With the fist that holds his New Year tot, he gestures towards a photograph of himself, a big Severn salmon in his hands, standing knee-deep in the estuary beside a long line of woven willow putchers. Dave is the last of the traditional makers of these six-foot-long trumpet-shaped fish traps, the only man left on either bank of the Severn with the proper feeling – and the patience – to carry on the art.

'I learned putcher-making from a nice old boy near here. He wouldn't teach me anything or take me on the river – I just had to pick it all up by watching him. A little drop of cider and a lot of talk.'

Sleet ticks against the windowpane, but Dave drags me out into his garden regardless. He's promised to make me a putcher.

'Down, Beauty! Down, Bumper, you little bugger, you,' he growls in his Gloucestershire rumble as his excited spaniels slap their muddy paws on his knees. With a billhook, he splits withy wands that he has gone out to cut especially for my putcher. 'Natural materials, these: that's the way we've always gone in this job.'

Dave's fingers twist, coax, pull and tighten the withies. He works with concentration, the movements of his hands lent a beauty of economy by half a century of practice. Stavings, meters, rods; middle rings, bench rings, nose rings. Mysteries of a craft as old as Christianity, now sliding into oblivion since the Severn's salmon have ceased to run as thickly as they used to, and today's local youngsters scorn to get their hands and feet wet.

The putcher-maker glances at me through the sleet from under his bushy eyebrows, and a sardonic grin dents his hollow cheeks. 'Better make this bastard a good 'un, eh?' The doctor gave him some bad news yesterday. The putcher now taking shape could well be his last. As things turn out, Dave Bennet does not even live to see the start of salmon fishing in mid-April. As I taste the seasons up and down the estuary, I will often find myself thinking of this cold, spitting afternoon in the putcher-maker's garden.

2

Nuttall bagging

'Bleaklow Head,' stated the great Alfred Wainwright in his *Pennine Way Companion*, 'is an inhospitable wilderness of peatbogs over which progress on foot is very arduous. Nobody loves Bleaklow. All who get on it are glad to get off.'

Well, all I can say is – Wainwright must have had the offest of off-days on Bleaklow. Or maybe it was raining mousers and mastiffs, as it's all too likely to do any day of the year up in the High Peak. The crusty old master would surely have dug something brighter out of his formidable locker of language if he had seen Bleaklow as I did early on New Year's Day, a crisp cold morning of cloudless blue sky with firm snow crunching underfoot and sparkling all the colours of the spectrum like a scatter of pantomime gems. Just the kind of day, in fact, to stride out and bag a pair of Nuttalls.

Crunching between frozen sedge clumps across Shelf Moss towards the cairn on Bleaklow Head, John and Anne Nuttall were pondering the genesis of their book *The Mountains of England and Wales*. It was Anne who introduced John to hill-walking while they were courting, back in the 1960s. John in turn introduced Anne to the rugged attractions of camping. (They still camp regularly on the summits of mountains, and they spent millennium night in a tent on Bleaklow Head.) The Nuttalls honeymooned in the Lake District, explored the Lakeland fells with the help of Alfred Wainwright's wonderful little handwritten walking guidebooks and moved on to bag around a hundred Munros. But with two young boys to look after at home in Congleton, and wage-slaving to be done (John was a manager in IT, Anne a hospital pharmacist), they couldn't keep trekking up to Scotland from Cheshire.

'We looked around for something nearer home,' Anne said, 'and found *Bridge's Tables*, an old listing of the two-thousand-footers. As we walked them, we found a lot of mistakes – the tables had been compiled from old maps, and the maps were wrong. But the Ordnance Survey was bringing out its new series of much more accurate metric maps. We'd written our first walking book by then, and we thought: why not do a book of the two-thousanders that actually gets it right?'

'We wanted to make it personal, too,' added John, 'to tell about some of the things that happened to us, put in an occasional drawing of ourselves and the boys, just to take it away from the dry factual approach that's so boring to actually use.'

Measuring the 439 summits demanded endless poring over 1:10,000 scale maps in a Manchester library, followed by surveying trips to each top. They used a spirit level and employed John as a moveable sighting rod. For basic measurements they used the unit of 'J' (John's height from sole of foot to eye level), nine Js equalling fifty feet. This DIY work was carried out in every imaginable condition of weather, ground and mood.

We reached the Bleaklow Head cairn (a new Nuttall for my personal bag) and turned for home by way of the Wain Stones and the wreck of a 1940s United States Air Force (USAF) bomber, landmarks known well by those who tramp these moors.

What kept the Nuttalls climbing summits?

'If I see a trig pillar,' Anne said, 'I have to go to it and touch it. I have to climb the hill. It's… I don't know, a feeling of achievement, of having got there – wherever "there" is.'

'For me,' said John, 'I think it's a spiritual thing, the same kind of uplift that people feel from getting close to God. Look where ancient man built all his burial cairns – right on the summits, right at the top. It's just a need we all have, to get to the top of the hill.'

3

Parson Hawker's Morwenstow

The north Cornwall village of Morwenstow, a clifftop set-tlement near the border with Devon, is gentle enough in atmosphere. In summer, with the gorse and campion in flower, the high-banked lanes and grey-and-white houses give out an air of contented permanence. In winter, the tune changes as stiff gales blow in from the Atlantic and whip the smoke from the chimneys. It's then that you see why the trees all grow to lean so extravagantly inland. Hearing the sea crashing at the feet of the cliffs, you get a taste of Morwenstow as it was in the rough old days. Until the mid-nineteenth century, to be shipwrecked here in a winter storm was as likely as not a ticket to an early grave. The Morwenstow locals, like the inhabit-ants of many a remote seaside place in the West Country, were reputed to plunder wrecks without a thought of helping the victims to shore and safety. The villagers weren't wreckers, swinging treacherous lanterns on the most dangerous cliffs to lure the ships to their doom. And they weren't murderers either, not deliberate ones. They just went for the salvage, first and last.

The man who brought order to this wild place could lay claim to have been the wildest individual of them all. Robert Stephen Hawker, vicar of Morwenstow from 1834 until his death in 1875, instilled the fear of the Devil and of himself into his wayward flock. His behaviour and attitudes scandalised the church authorities of his day and remain a byword for eccentricity around north Cornwall. But his parishioners came to respect and rely on him. He was a practical benefactor, who left far more members of his flock able to read, write and count than could do so before his forty-year-long ministry.

When Hawker was nineteen, he wed his forty-one-year-old godmother. They enjoyed forty years of happy marriage. When she died, the sixty-year-old clergyman took a twenty-year-old Polish girl as his bride and fathered three daughters. Parson Hawker would carry out his duties around Morwenstow wearing tall sea boots, a pink coat, a yellow cloak and rows of holy medals on his fisherman's jersey. He would throw himself prone on the church floor during services, and he pinched babies at the font to make them roar the Devil out. He designed each chimney of his vicarage to resemble one of the church towers of his previous incumbencies. He installed a ship's figurehead of a claymore-wielding woman among the churchyard graves. Once, he startled the stolid fishermen and farmers of Morwenstow by dressing as a mermaid with a wig of seaweed.

It's hard to guess the wellspring of all this eccentric behaviour. Hawker felt subservient to no one; he was a genuine maverick who loved to pull the noses of the church authorities, and in strait-laced nineteenth-century England it was easy to get up those sanctified noses with the kind of antics he performed. Probably he just had a lot of fun doing what he did, being a highly intelligent man in a lonely backwoods setting. Maybe the copious amounts of opium he smoked had something to do with it too.

Like many wild men, Parson Hawker was a romantic through and through, a traditionalist in ecclesiastical matters who loved the symbols and mysteries of the Christian faith.

And he was a poet of great power, the composer of the defiant Cornish anthem 'The Song of the Western Men':

> And have they fixed the where and when?
> And shall Trelawny die?
> Here's twenty thousand Cornish men
> Will know the reason why!

Down on the cliff below the church stands a wooden hut that Hawker built as a retreat. Here you can rest and dream of the oddball parson who would sit here, a pipe between his teeth, and write his verses in a fug of opium fumes.

4

A is for Anger

… that healthy and yet thoroughly scary emotion. At least, we are told it is healthy. Let off steam at your workmates, exhorts the industrial psychologist. Go on, it's good to clear the air, and anyway that bunch of stupid failures deserves it. Scream and shout at your partner, advises the relationship counsellor; no holds barred if you really love each other, and the sex will be great when you make up. Howl and rant at farmers who obstruct footpaths, says… hold on – says who? Only a precipitate fool, I have just come to realise.

The path I was following was overgrown, for sure. In fact, the starve-acre Gloucestershire farm it crossed could not have looked more neglected. Everywhere were signs of hardship and hopelessness – thistly fields, limping sheep, collapsing sheds. If times are tough in the mainstream banks and high streets, they are tougher still out in the agricultural backwaters. But still… this farmer obviously hated walkers. Why else would he have let his hedge smother the gap where the stile should have been? And here he came, a grim-looking chap with a sour expression. Right, I'd give him an earful.

I delivered a self-righteous little homily. The farmer heard me out expressionlessly. He sighed gently, and the sides of his mouth twitched. Wordlessly, he pointed out the excellent waymarked stile that I hadn't noticed, twenty yards along the hedge. He turned and strolled away, shaking his head, and I slunk over the stile and off across the next field with my tail between my legs. I pictured him telling his wife that night, and I hoped it would bring a smile to two worried faces.

Oh, yes – A is for Ass too.

5

Covidiots?

A fine, amusing concept and a neat, inventive word – 'cov-idiot'. Someone who wilfully and selfishly breaks the rules of safety, or infringes those of good neighbourliness, during the Covid pandemic. Examples: one who buys and hoards every loo roll in the shop; a drunken oaf on a plane who refuses to wear a mask; a raver who deliberately sneezes all over the officer arresting him; or... or how about a group of people who have the brass neck to visit the countryside without knowing the rules?

Up behind the village on a gorgeous day, I spotted them – six youths, sitting in a tight circle at the edge of a wood, passing the pipe of peace. They were way off the footpath. They were trespassing, damn it! Couldn't they see the waymark arrows? They were indulging in at least two illegal activities at once! Their social distancing was all to pot! Literally! Covidiots!

My wife, Jane, talked me down. They're city kids, harming no one. Who's to say they have gardens or green spaces where they live? They might have been huddled in some unsavoury backstreet den, instead of out here in this green and pleasant land. At least some of what they're inhaling is good fresh air. As for sticking to the footpath – what does that even mean to them? Is the countryside only supposed to be available to those who can read a map and recognise a waymark?

It was a good point, I had to agree, when I held the mirror

up to myself. How long had it taken me to learn how to make my way around in the countryside, to be confident I was following a footpath and not trespassing on private ground? A good long time – years, in fact, during which I made a whole string of embarrassing blunders. I got myself into trouble with farmers and householders, walking disused railway tracks in the blithe belief that no one owned them. Can't you see the signs? Well, they are there. Those sheep are all in lamb – see? Now you've scared them. Excuse me, this happens to be my garden. No, you can't walk through that little bit there. Back the way you came, son. With my boot in your arse if you don't jump to it. *Now!*

In the pandemic year of 2020, more people than ever before visited the countryside and went walking there. Lots of them had never done that sort of thing before. Yes, some of them caused a nuisance. Some gates were left open; some cattle got out into lanes and people's gardens. There was a small amount of littering, of inadvertent trespassing. But how do you learn the rules if you don't try the activity? A bit of a chicken-and-egg question, that. And a bit of dog-and-manger on my part, if I'm honest.

Enough with the covidioms, and the labelling of covidiots too. I'm glad those youngsters chose to visit. I hope they come back, and their friends and families, to take pleasure in the fields and the open air, and to learn the significance of that little yellow arrow on the gatepost.

6

Walking in snow

It had been a long old slog out of the glen and up into the flanks of the Cairngorms. Snow lay coldly gleaming across the hills, the pure white of its unruffled sheet now spectacularly flushed with pink as the sun sank towards the Monadhliath Mountains in a giant blood-red ball, spreading fire along the western rim of the world. We had gone in up to our knees time and again, acquiring lumpy gaiters of snow that weighed us down. But now came the reward, as we stood blowing like whales at the crest of Cairn Gorm itself, looking around at the pristine snowfields and back down the long climb where the dints of our footfalls lay stamped like mammoth prints.

I had done this walk in summer, too, with stones clinking under my boots and green heather whispering around my trouser legs. That had been a fine and satisfying day on the hill. But a climb in snow adds magic, that elusive X factor. There is something about the deep, gritty crunch of snow packing tight under the boot, something about the slip and slither, the sense of not being quite sure what the next footstep and the one after that will bring. Any moment may bring farce – a tumble or a skid. Looking down from Cairn Gorm, I could trace a dozen smash marks and scars around our tracks, witnesses to the bumps and dumps inseparable from a good walk in the snow.

Allied to this knockabout aspect, walking in snow is brilliant exercise. You puff and pant, you sweat and struggle to the top of the hill, exercising twice the muscles and using up twice the calories you'd burn on the same walk in balmy weather. As for what you see around you, the birds in the bare trees, the movement of wintry skies, the burning tang of frost in the nostrils – it all brings home to you the simple glory of being fully alive. Tracking red deer by their hoof prints through the snow of the upper Findhorn Valley until I came across the creatures themselves was an experience I'll never forget – especially the moment when my companion handed me his telescope with a quiet 'There they are', and I peered through to be transfixed by the sight of fifty or more of the magnificent creatures pacing in stately fashion across a mountainside of dazzling unbroken snow.

I wonder how much of this primitive pleasure in snow walking has to do with pure childhood reminiscence. Were winters really as snowy as I remember them in the 1950s and 60s? It wasn't as if my little corner of back-country Gloucestershire was particularly prone to heavy falls of snow, though the nearby Cotswolds used to catch their share of drifts. As a child, one wasn't so much interested in walking through snow as in playing in the stuff – snowballing, tobogganing, snowman-building, rolling the dog in it, rolling oneself in it, eating it, peeing in it, shaking it off the trees onto the heads of one's sisters.

All that sort of thing was big fun to a six-year-old. But what stuck and lasted into adulthood were the smaller-scale characteristics of snow – the soft creak of it under gumboot soles; the curious burnt smell of it; the feathery touch on neck and eyelashes; the way it slanted a lace curtain across the landscape as it fell, or suddenly attacked like a swarm of icy bees out of a yellow sky. These little details still come absolutely fresh and unexpected at each snowfall. 'Oh, of course, yes – *that's* what it's like; now I remember.'

Snow in a dramatic mountain landscape such as the Cairngorms is a breathtaking spectacle and gives rise to some truly astounding moments in a walker's life. Maybe the most intense was spending a night in a self-dug snowhole way up in the wild Cairngorm heartland, hearing the wind howl outside while snug and secure in a glistening chamber whose walls reflected the gentle light of candles.

Yet for all the intoxicating buzz of such experiences, for me the most irresistible lure of all is the call of snow on ploughed fields and black skeletal trees. Maybe it's a residual memory of Mole and Ratty plodding homeward in *The Wind in the Willows*: 'The rapid nightfall of mid-December had quite beset the little village as they approached it on soft feet over a first thin fall of powdery snow.' What romance, what aching nostalgia! In childhood, hearing my mother read that, I would cuddle closer to the fire and be thankful I wasn't out in the cold with Mole. Now I find I can't get enough of the nip of frost, the tinkle of breaking ice in a hoof-pock, the scrunch of boots in a drift and the cold fingertips of flakes on cheeks and ears as I step out through falling snow.

7

Snowholing

Four snowholers are up in the snowy Cairngorm cleft of Coire Cas, taking a crash course in winter skills from mountain expert Andrew Bateman. It's almost literally a crash course, since part of it involves launching ourselves, suitably hard-hatted, down a steep snow slope with only an ice axe between us and oblivion. We do this feet first and face first, on our fronts and on our backs.

'Wa-hey!' cries burly Shaun, hurling himself head-foremost down the mountain and executing a perfect ice-axe arrest.

There's a serious backdrop to the tomfoolery, of course: stumble once at the head of a Cairngorm snowfield and, if you don't know exactly what to do, you can slide down 2,000 feet faster than an express train, but without the benefit of buffers when you hit the bottom. By the same token, we learn how to cut steps in snow and how to walk in stiff boots and in crampons, those fiendishly spiked instruments of torture. Encouragement and leg-pulling are the order of the day – and of the evening, too, tightening our sense of group membership over pints of Stag bitter in the Boat Hotel.

By noon the following day, we are all on the move up the snowy Fiacaill Ridge, our packs heavy with snow shovels and saws, ice axes, gas cylinders, crampons, sleeping bags. I gasp and puff a bit at first, but by the time we are up and over into

Coire Domhain's white hollow I have got the climbing tempo more or less to rights.

The high Cairngorm plateau is an inhospitable place. Snow lies thick, the wind whips across and visibility is down to a hundred yards at times. It's cold. But Andrew navigates us unerringly, using his patented system of pacing and timing, until by mid-afternoon we have reached the selected snow-hole site in the high cleft above frozen and remote Loch Avon.

Everyone is cold and tired by now, and we inwardly groan at the prospect of having to cut our own accommodation out of a solid snow bank. But the work warms us up as we saw great blocks of snow, shovel debris, sweat and curse, dig and giggle. Luckily, we break through into a set of former snow-holes, which gives us more rooms at no extra effort. What we end up with is a split-level wonky-roofed series of intercon-nected chambers. It feels like home, and heaven, by the time we've crawled into our sleeping bags and sampled the inde-fatigable Andrew's sausage-and-God-knows-what cuisine.

We are all dog-tired. Candles light the scene. Jokes, tall tales and jibes go the rounds, and so do the bottles of sleep-ing elixir – Baileys for the Durham lads; whisky for Andrew, Adam and me. It's not a comfortable night by any means, but the hard exercise and the whisky combine to poleaxe me until a ghostly blue dawn filters in through the doorway. Breakfast is a plastic bag full of muesli and dried milk, moistened with a generous helping of boiled snow. Struggling into half-frozen yet sopping wet outer gear and cold, damp boots is an ordeal none of us finds pleasant. But, once clad, we find that our body heat dries and warms the clothes and footwear remark-ably quickly.

When we emerge from our Arctic hobbit hole, we find a cold, windy day thick with hill fog. We abandon thoughts of bagging the second highest peak in the British Isles, the 4,295-foot Ben Macdui, and in another remarkable feat of navigation Andrew leads us out of the wind and murk, through the snowfields and over the icy rocks, down into the real world once more.

8

Natural remedy

If you're going to learn a new cold weather trick, the Finnish port of Kemi in midwinter isn't a bad place to do it. Kemi lies as far north up the Baltic Sea as you can get, almost inside the Arctic Circle. With the temperature at a refreshing minus ten degrees Celsius and the Baltic ice a metre thick, I waddled out across Kemi's frozen harbour like the Michelin man, heading for what the tourist brochure called a Lapp safari.

A red-hot Skidoo awaited me a hundred yards from shore. I'd never even handled a motorbike before, but on this bumpy and stinking steed I was due to ride out behind my guide Antii, like a nervous Mongol warrior in the wake of Genghis Khan, across the white wastes of the Baltic.

'Press big button to go, little one to stop,' said Antii. 'Any problem, raise hand. OK, let's go.' And he roared away, diminishing to a speck in less than no time. I pressed big button to go, and immediately lost all vision. My hot, anxious breath had frozen on my spectacles, cementing them to my snow goggles. I raised hand. A slithering U-turn, and Antii was back alongside me, laughing heartily.

'Ha, ha! You frozen eyes! Ha, ha! Give to me!' I placed the amalgam of goggles and spectacles into his furry mitt, expecting him to produce a handy aerosol of de-icer. Instead, he threw back his head, hawked like a skunk-smoker and spat a mighty green gob of phlegm all over the conjoined lenses. They slid apart.

'Now clean in snow!' barked Antii. I complied. 'Now we go out wild!' And we did.

I've used Antii's remedy for frozen lenses a few times since, and I have to say it's a natural. Free at the point of delivery, too. And undeniably green.

9

Dry stone wall

An early morning of Arctic air out on the coast of Northumberland, with the north wind making glass of the puddles and cutting like a knife through coat and scarf. There's no shelter for a fool rash enough to have got out of bed for a walk before sunrise; no sun, either, to warm his bones. Ahead rises the knoll beyond Low Newton-by-the-Sea, crested with a dry stone wall, and I make for its protection at a good trot.

Hunched on my hunkers in the loom of the wall, I run my heavy gloved hand over the white, grey and yellow lichens that form a patchwork across the rough stones. The dragging sound of the glove is suddenly cut by an explosive noise above me, halfway between a high-pitched bark and a sneeze. I glance up and freeze – but not with cold. A lithe figure as long as my hand stands on all fours among the capstones of the wall; then, as I watch, it rises on its hind legs and leans sideways to get a better look at the intruder. It's a stoat, pure white in its ermine coat, its round pinhead eyes fixed on my face.

It swears again, and cranes so far over that I'm frightened it'll fall on my head. What then? Will it be hungry enough to go for the jugular? How beautiful this creature is, and how deadly. It must have been hunting the wall for something hidden among the stones, some mouse or vole, perhaps hibernating, maybe cowering unseen an inch from my face with a fear far more abject and well justified than mine.

A flick like the closing of a camera shutter, and the stoat is gone, silently and instantly. I let out the breath I've been holding. Whatever else this day brings, it has already been touched by magic.

B is for Binoculars

… a bird-watcher's best friend, but also a walker's. Why didn't I think of them before? How many hours have I spent peering under my hand like a silly old sea dog, trying to identify the minuscule blob of a waymark across a misty moor, or judging from the shape of bovine dangly bits viewed at a great distance whether it's safe to proceed past a mild-mannered cow that might turn out to be a bull with a negative attitude? Now I just whip the bins to the faltering eyes, and Bob's your uncle. Waymarks spring out of hedges, lady cows turn into gentlemen (or vice versa) and stiles appear as if by magic in seemingly impenetrable hedges. They're great for looking at wild flowers and insects too, if you turn them the wrong way round.

Sexy or solid, though – that's the question. I've worked my way through three pairs of pretty wee ones, very high-tech, very high-spec and fatally easy to leave behind. One stayed on the top of the Long Mynd after a picnic; another especially light pair fell out of my jacket pocket on a Cheviot trackway without a sound or sensation; and the third… I still don't know what happened to the third.

Now I go for the galumphing end of the spectrum, the faithful life partner rather than the flashy tart. My dad's old wartime naval Carl Zeisses are brilliant, although they do tend to bang the knees as I walk. The Optolyth Alpins I've

just bought from a friend are the proper job, too. 'Ultraleicht',
it says on the end plate. They're not… but who cares? At least
they're by my side when I want them, not sitting five miles
back on a rock, waiting to be picked up by any passing Tom,
Dick or Harry.

11

Salt marsh

Half past seven o'clock on a still, cold January morning, with ice crusting the drainage fleet that is cocooned by motionless reeds behind the sea wall. The still water of the ditch is flushed with the faintest of satin pinks, reflecting a streak of the unrisen sun out beyond the mouth of the River Blackwater. I stifle another in a series of yawns and scrunch my way across the last few yards of the cockleshell beach. An hour ago, I was still in my warm bed, and for a moment I wonder what on earth I think I'm doing out here at this hour on the bleakest shore in Essex. Then a yielding carpet of sea purslane is underfoot, the astringent smell of a mudbank newly exposed on the falling tide stings my nostrils, and a faint and slowly gathering gabble and roar comes to my ears from somewhere out at sea.

A fox has passed over the saltings sometime during the night; I can see its fresh paw prints, more delicate than a dog's, crossing a mud patch in line astern. A puff of downy iridescent feathers in a clump of wind-dried sea lavender shows where a duck fell victim to a wildfowler at last evening's flight – I heard the pop-popping of the guns on the still air as I strolled on Maldon's quays at dusk. Now I raise my eyes from the marsh and mud as the gabblers come sweeping out of the dawn, 200 strong and silhouetted against a pink-and-gold sky over the flat grey North Sea – a great crowd of dark-bellied brent geese hurrying up the estuary to their feeding grounds among beds of eelgrass, as energetic and raucous as a pack of hounds – the very spirit of these Essex salt marshes in a cold January dawn.

12

Ships' graveyard

At first sight, I could hardly believe my eyes. The banks of the River Severn, as it broadened and widened from Purton towards the sea ten miles away, were muddy and grass-grown. But what was this square of cracked old timbers sticking out of the oozy river wall? It looked like the after quarters of a vessel, with sternpost and steering tiller all complete. Could there really be a whole ship down there, all but swallowed up in the grey estuarine mud? I lifted my eyes to glance along the river, and there they were – dozens of superannuated riverboats, coal barges and coasters, all rammed to the hilt into the bank.

I wandered through this Gloucestershire graveyard of ships, walking out along the slanting decks, peering through hatches into interiors filled with mud. It was clear why the boats had been used in this fashion: the ebb of the outgoing river, even this far inland, was swirling powerfully against the outer bend, sucking away tiny crumbles of mud wherever it could get hold of them. The shoulder-to-shoulder ranks of old vessels had become part of the flood defences, shoring and stiffening the bank against the greedy Severn tides.

The boats lay lifeless, like corpses half-exposed in some medieval graveyard. And just as in a graveyard, each vessel had her history briefly engraved on a plaque nearby, courtesy of the Friends of Purton. They clustered the margins of the

Severn in death as in life – *Orby*, *Abbey*, *Huntley* and *Harriett*, their timbers shivered, their sides split, transoms and hawse-holes still bravely held aloft, a poignant gathering.

Down beyond the ships, banks of purple mud and tan-coloured sand were shouldering clear of the falling tide. Three or four white-fronted geese were huddled there, visitors from Greenland come south for the winter. Oystercatchers piped their piercing calls, and a lone wigeon went whistling down-river across the streaky grey sky.

It's not unusual to find more exotic birds on these shores in winter, thanks to the siting just upriver of Peter Scott's world-famous Wildfowl and Wetlands Trust at Slimbridge. I remember visiting Slimbridge as a boy, just after it had opened. There was one tall tower hide, a few ponds and a small network of paths where Scott, strolling and observing quietly, would courteously greet visitors himself. Nowadays, Slimbridge is world-famous as a haven where ducks, geese and waders from all quarters of the northern hemisphere gather to spend the winter, often ranging downriver along the Severn.

Estuaries are magical places, but tricky – questionable ground on the boundary between land and sea, fresh and salt, half in and half out of the world. Those whose work takes them up and down the great estuaries are well aware of the inherent dangers of such powerful tideways. The lower Severn, in particular, on whose margins I grew up, was always a tricky place to navigate with its shoals and reefs, its eddies and rocky ridges and the extravagantly snaking course it pursues towards the sea. When the Gloucester & Sharpness Canal was opened in the 1820s, it cut out a tedious and difficult stretch of the river. But the dangers remained.

Beyond the ships' graveyard, I left the riverbank and fol-lowed the parallel route of the canal. Soon the towpath passed between a pair of castle-like abutments. They were built to support a mighty railway bridge that spanned the Severn until the night of 25 October 1960. Then, in a thick autumn fog and pitch darkness, two tankers – one loaded with oil, the other with petrol – collided with one of the bridge piers and exploded, sheeting the river in flame, killing five of the eight crewmen and wrecking the bridge.

Plenty of people around Sharpness retain vivid memories of that awful night. Sharpness is a rare survivor, a river port still handling cement, fertiliser and scrap metal far up the tidal Severn. I stopped to watch the cranes swinging bags of fertiliser out of the hold of *Shetland Trader*, then crossed the canal and made for the field path to Brookend and the log fire in the Lammastide Inn.

13

Animal tracking

'Now, I would think,' murmured Duncan Macdonald, nose to the faint paw prints dinting the snow on the banks of the River Findhorn, 'that's a brown hare. See how the front paws are quite far apart in their stride, while the back ones are close together?' Duncan circled a gloved finger round the footfalls. 'Quite a big fellow, I'd say – too big to be a mountain hare. There's half a metre, maybe, between the leading and the trailing paws, so he was – well, *cantering*, that would be the right word. Now, I wonder what spooked him?'

Going out tracking in the snowy Monadhliath Mountains of the central Scottish Highlands with Duncan, you can't help but think of Sherlock Holmes. Where the untutored visitor to these wild hills might spot no more than the occasional red deer, Duncan can read the runes scratched in snow, mud, heather sprig and pine bark by the birds and animals for whom these harsh surroundings are home. A countryside ranger with the Highland Council, Duncan lends his tracking talents and general wildlife expertise to the Speyside Wildlife tour company from time to time. I was lucky he'd found the time to come out with me today, in the coldest and snowiest winter the Highlands had seen for a decade, to explore the hillside and valleys of Coignafearn, a wildlife-friendly estate far up the strath of the River Findhorn.

The Findhorn snaked black and swift through the flat

meadows that floored the valley. Ice crusted the margins of the river and trailed from mid-water boulders in lacy sheets of wonderful intricacy. Beyond this rose the round shoulders of the mountains, blanketed white with snow and scabbed by dark rock outcrops hung with shark's-tooth icicles. Snow clouds were gathering up there in the western sky, an uneasy swirl of heavy grey vapour tinged with yellow. 'There'll be more big falls this winter,' prophesied Duncan, 'and huge floods down here in spring when it all melts.'

We followed the hare tracks along the river bank, noting where they had been crossed by the twin slots of a red deer's hooves, and then by the round cat-like prints of another brown hare. Duncan studied the tracks, inferring from their depth and rate of thaw how the two hares had circled and assessed each other, then gone on their separate ways. Meanwhile, low down along the river and out of sight of the hares, an otter had crept stealthily along under the overhang of the bank, leaving its webbed track with a faint groove where its rudder had dragged in the snow. Other, smaller prints might have been those of mink or of stoats in their winter coats of black-tipped ermine. 'Too blurred by the melt yesterday to be sure,' said Duncan.

Now the tracker's eyes, sweeping the white landscape, picked up a small continuous drift of movement along the mountainside half a mile off. 'Deer, a lot of 'em,' was his laconic call to attention. A great herd of red deer, perhaps eighty strong and led by a stag with splendidly branched antlers, was flowing across the snow slope with a graceful economy of motion. 'Odd,' murmured Duncan to himself, eye to telescope. 'Usually the stags and hinds won't associate in winter, but there's a real mix of the sexes in there. Too much snow on the ground to be picky about territory, perhaps?'

Fox and weasel, ermine stoat and feral goat, pine marten, red squirrel and red deer, otter and mountain hare: these are just some of the animals that find their winter food and shelter in the Monadhliath Mountains. Golden eagle, peregrine, raven and buzzard quarter the sky. There are wild salmon in the rivers and wildcats in the rocks. 'People go all over the world to see wildlife,' said Duncan as we turned up into a side glen, 'but Scotland has so much. Take the red deer: you come here in October and these hills will be just roaring with stags. Unforgettable – it'll live with you for the rest of your life.'

It looked as though the worsening weather had grounded the golden eagles of Coignafearn. A burst of snow buntings, some forty of them, went shooting overhead with tiny needly squeaks.

A fierce wind came whistling suddenly, driving scuds of snow before it. We took shelter in a pine plantation where deer had whittled the lower branches to antler-like points in their greed for the nutritious bark. Duncan picked up fragments of chewed pine cone. 'Decorticated by red squirrels – that's the technical term for this close nibbling. Great word for Scrabble, eh?'

14

Blue prince of the mountains

'The mountain hare, *Lepus timidus*, is possessed of a shaggy pelt, dark brown in hue, which in the depths of winter turns white for the purpose of harmonising with the fallen snow across which its owner speeds.' I quote from the school text-book – *Our Wild Friends of Mountain and Moor* or some such title, a tome ancient even when I got hold of it – that first inspired me with a passionate desire to go to the mountains in midwinter and see one of these lordly yet modest creatures. I knew brown hares, *Lepus europaeus*, from the meadows at home. What seduced me was the image of the upland beast, *timidus* yet vigorous, swift and furry, racing across a mountainside as pure white as itself, so that one moment you glimpsed it and the next you didn't.

No one had told me that mountain hares in their winter coats are actually blue. I couldn't believe it when I first looked through Duncan Macdonald's telescope. On a freezing February day in the Grampians, the two of us had been following a set of distinctive prints in powdery snow newly fallen across the Monadhliath Mountains: two neat round paw marks with four toes, close together, and two more in line behind. Sometimes the hind prints changed shape and took the form of two parallel grooves, where our quarry had squatted down on his long leg bones to nibble heather roots – we could actually see the tiny scrapings of teeth and hairy cheeks in the snow. Now here he was, framed beautifully in the round lens of the scope as he lay in the shelter of a stone a couple of hundred yards up the hillside: a most magnificent mountain hare, the first I'd ever properly laid eyes on in full winter coat. And that coat was subtly, but definitely, blue.

This mountain prince we had caught in our telescope was nothing like the pen portrait drawn by the author of *Our Wild Friends of Mountain and Moor*. Far from speeding timidly across the snow, he was lying on it openly in an attitude of complete relaxation. Once you had your eye in, he stood out from his surroundings as a prince should do. His nose was encased in a sort of comforter of thick cream-coloured fur. His ears, shorter than a brown hare's and laid back against his head, were a handsome dark grey. And his pelt, shaggy enough at this stage of the year, glowed with the sort of blue light you see in the depths of a snow crevasse.

Seemingly unaware of us – or at any rate unconcerned, every now and then licking his cleft lips as he glanced around him with eyes as black as blaeberries – he was a spellbinding sight. I was so absorbed in staring at him that it took me several minutes to spot his companions: two more hares within a few yards, each intent on its own digestive affairs, occasionally stretching or giving a yawn of cat-like delicacy.

Mountain hares seem to be holding their own in the Scottish Highlands at present, though accurate statistics are hard to come by. They are a different species from the brown hare, smaller and hardier with a thicker coat, thriving on moorland food that their lowland cousins would do poorly on – mostly heather, with some blueberries, juniper, thyme and whatever else they can pick up – and in winter able to keep going on stems of heather, gorse and other plants at need. They face problems, though, in places where heather has been overgrazed, or where forests have been planted across open moorlands.

Heather moors and stony mountains are their natural habitat. Tramping Scottish hills in summer, I have occasionally glimpsed their treacle-brown shapes slipping over the skyline, invariably in a momentary, tail-of-the-eye sighting. In hard winter weather, they descend to where there is a bit of shelter, a scatter of rocks, or the back of a hollow, out of the wind and the worst of the snow; it's there, on ground speckled with dark stones or streaked with windblown heather sprigs, that their not-so-white camouflage helps hide them from the eyes of foxes and humans.

To see a mountain hare in the snowy mountains you need luck, patience and the capacity to keep still and quiet. Your chances will be greatly improved if you put yourself, as I did, in the hands of a specialist such as Duncan. You'll certainly have to be prepared to venture high up in the Scottish hills, or out on the moors. It's all worth it when the moment arrives, and the blue-tinged prince of the mountains passes before you in all his winter glory.

15

C is for Curmudgeon Man

Curmudgeon Man: I hear his crusty footfall coming nearer all the time. Share my water bottle? Well, why the bloody hell didn't you bring your own? Do you good to go without – teach you a lesson, won't it? *Trainers?* Don't talk to me about trainers. When I started, it was all hobnails round here. Yes, yes, pretty view – now where's the path? Tired? Don't know the meaning of the word. Look, if you've got nowt worth saying, then say nowt...

Hmm. Not too attractive, that mirror held up to nature. Where does he come from, this bad old bear in his self-excavated lair? And why does he grab hold of so many walkers round about a certain birthday with a big o on the end? It's not as if we *aim* to fall victim to Curmudgeon Man. I love company out walking – at least, I think I do. The banter, the joshing, the arm along the road, figuratively if not physically. The questioning and challenges, the exhortations to look at this southern marsh orchid and listen to that whitethroat. All good, beyond question. My own expeditions would be far poorer without them. But, as Alfred Wainwright observed, silence can also be golden out on the hills.

I accompanied Curmudgeon Man on a walk in Northamptonshire not too long ago, and it wasn't a pretty sight or sound as he rebuffed his charming companion and her thrush-like repetition of comments and questions. 'Shut up, why don't you?' he growled. 'Yak-yak-yak!' I could cheerfully have kicked him. At last, they drew away and I had green lane, bramble and evening hush to myself. *Rude so-and-so*, I thought. *Some people, really! Quite honestly, if you've got nowt nice to say...*

Yes, have to watch that.

16

Forest floor

A dank and foggy dawn in the Forest of Dean; utter stillness at the heart of Russell's Inclosure. A car sighs far away on the back road to nowhere. The blood singing in the ears is the loudest sound at the heart of the wood, the coiling of mist tendrils between the leafless oak branches the only movement. Among the half tones and insubstantial shapes, it seems as though nothing will ever move again from the grip of winter. A single drop of rainwater from last night's downpour swells at the end of a tight black sycamore bud, fed by an invisible trickle down the incline of the parent twig, until weight and mass overcome surface tension and it bellies down through the cold air to plop into the old ironworks pond three feet below. No ripple wrinkles the mat of green weed and slimy twigs that has collected there over the winter; the raindrop is absorbed into the pond without fuss.

A solitary blackbird gives a tentative '*chak?*', a modest tapping of the baton foreshadowing the full-blown sunrise chorus that is still half an hour off. But the light is already beginning to steal in among the mossy trunks. Curls of mist are tinged with the faintest wash of pearl, reflecting the wan light down to the forest floor, where it lies trapped in a wide pool. So it appears, until the light broadens a little more and the pearly flood that laps the trees lies revealed: a carpet of pure white wood anemones, stirred by the first breeze of the day. Among the piled leaves of last autumn, fungal twigs and split old chestnut shells, they shine like a beacon, a promise of the oncoming spring.

17

Digby in glory

There's a corner of my garden in Somerset, just by the steps that lead up to the farm track, where Digby, the grey stone gnome with the knowing grin, mounts guard. From late spring to autumn, my six-inch sentinel keeps station overshadowed by hazel leaves and half submerged in moss, with only the tip of his Noddy hat showing through the foliage. From November to January, with soggy black leaves around his boots and the moss withered and brown, he stands out unprotected in the teeth of gales, rain, sleet and snow.

Then comes Digby's brief moment of glory. For a few weeks, his grubby greyness is transformed as he surfs knee-deep in a beautiful drift of snowdrops. And, looking out of the sitting room window at the trembling white bells of the flowers, I get my initial serotonin hit of the year, the first real sign that – no matter how the wind howls off the hills and the stripped trees in the field thrash madly against the clouds – winter is not going to last for ever.

That life-affirming first hint of spring was a sweet torture to the naturalist Richard Jefferies, confined to bed in the late 1880s with the lung disease that would soon kill him. Unable to savour at first hand the natural world about which he wrote so ecstatically, he could only look out through his window

– 'the bars of my prison' – and watch the unfolding spring like a passionate spectator at a play:

The bloom of the gorse is shut like a book; but it is there – a few hours of warmth and the covers will fall open. On the pollard willows the long wands are yellow-ruddy in the passing gleam of sunshine, the first colour of spring appears in their bark ... I see the apple bloom coming and the blue veronica in the grass. A thousand thousand buds and leaves and flowers and blades of grass, things to note day by day, increasing so rapidly that no pencil can put them down and no book hold them ... All these without me – how can they manage without me?[1]

18

New Forest in mist

It was one of those cold, muted Hampshire days in early spring, and the New Forest looked as if it were still deciding whether it was ready to admit the season of new life just yet. Silver birch leaves were quivering at breaking point all across Fritham Plain, rabbits were scuttering between green heather and gold sand scrapes, and a whitethroat was hesitantly trying out its scratchy little courting song from a gorse bush spattered bravely with yellow blooms. Yet there was no warmth in the pale ghost of a sun trying in vain to peer through the mist that hung over the forest.

A morning for brisk walking, then. After a couple of weeks cooped up in the house, Jane and I were glad to step out along the gravelled track that ran away from the forest hamlet of Fritham across the open expanse of heath where ragged-coated ponies were cropping the gorse. Clumps of ancient hollies stood out above the heather and bracken, their smooth branches twined with ivy, their trunks girdled with fresh green shoots of butcher's broom. There was a rich tang of wet earth and of sappy wood, the smell of a springtime about to unpack itself from the ground and the trees.

It was the Normans who brought us the notion of a forest as a hunting enclave. Deer have always needed trees for shelter and open ground for grazing, so forests were never intended to be great unbroken slabs of trees – they developed as mosaics

of woodland, water, rough grazing and wetland, with farmland and forest settlements creeping in over the centuries.
That's the way the New Forest is today, a rare and wonderful
expanse of varied country through which a walker can wander
pretty much at will.

From the open heath, the path dipped through the skirts
of Sloden Inclosure and Holly Hatch Inclosure, blocks of old
forestry sheltering yew groves and immense gnarled oaks as
swollen and spindle-limbed as any Arthur Rackham fairy tree.

'Look!' Jane exclaimed, gripping my arm to call a halt. Two
fallow does, one heavy with a fawn, were watching us from the
trees. Deer and humans stared at one another till the animals
tossed up their heads with an air of ineffable contempt and
trotted away.

Out from the trees curled the path, making back towards
Fritham across the wide heather wastes of Ocknell Plain.
Tiny mallard ducklings were scooting across Cadman's Pool
in a jostling line, and down in the boggy valley beside South
Bentley Inclosure a pair of snipe went zagging away as we
plodded noisily towards their feeding place through yellow
mud.

The mist never let up all day; in fact, it was thickening
once more when we got back to Fritham and shook off our
mud-laden boots at the door of the Royal Oak. But we'd seen
enough of the stirrings of spring on our New Forest walk to
add a spice of delight to our lunch of bread, cheese and Ring-
wood bitter.

19

The randy natterjack

The celebrated lovers I had come all the way north to encounter were certainly no shakes in the beauty stakes. The gentleman was squat, stubby, bandy-legged, furtive, pop-eyed and warty. So was his lady. Let's face it, these were the kind of looks that only a mother could love. Their choice of rendezvous, a stretch of coast beside the Cumbrian sea by night, was romantic enough, but the actual trysting spot turned out to be a shallow pool of rainwater, full of other couples hard at it. As for what the chaps were murmuring by way of sweet nothings, I could hear their rattling grunts and cheese-grater belches from the main road before I had even entered Lover's Lane. It was music to my ears, though, this spring night serenade by the natterjack toads of Eskmeals Dunes.

Natterjack toads are Britain's rarest amphibians. The habitat these nocturnal creatures require is so specialised, and nowadays so uncommon, that their UK population is for ever teetering on the brink of disaster. What they need is warm sandy soil near the sea, loose enough for digging the burrows in which they spend the days safe from herons, foxes, hedgehogs, cats and all the other predators eager for their blood. Their legs are too short to allow them to hop or leap, so they need territory that is only sparsely covered with short vegetation, easy to run through when hunting beetles. Natterjacks don't swim well (they drown if they get stuck in deep water);

they therefore require shallow pools to breed in. Not just any shallow pools, though. Natterjacks can't stand competition from common toads or frogs, so their breeding pools must be unattractive to rival species and inhospitable to dragonflies and water beetles, whose larvae have a great appetite for natterjack eggs and tadpoles. Ideal natterjack pools have little vegetation and are of a temporary nature, drying up after the toadlets have left.

It's really only marshy and sandy coasts that offer such specific living and breeding conditions. Yet during the twentieth century, something approaching 80 per cent of all such habitat in the UK was built over, turned into farmland or disturbed by leisure users. Nowadays, around forty sites play host to natterjack toads. They range from Hampshire to Dumfriesshire, and are almost all based around lonely stretches of carefully preserved sand dunes and salt marsh. Around half of Britain's natterjacks live on the Cumbrian coast, one of the least spoiled and disturbed in the country. Even so, the conservation workers who look after natterjack interests at Eskmeals and the neighbouring Drigg Dunes nature reserve – a range of vast sand dunes built up on shingle spits around the mouth of the Ravenglass estuary – face an ongoing battle to keep their fragile little charges safe, well and on the increase. If the spring is too wet, the breeding pools become too deep and the burrows flood. If there's too little rain, the pools dry up before the tadpoles hatch, and the whole year's brood can die. It's a ticklish business.

Out among the dunes by night, keeping quiet and still, it was extraordinary how much I could see and hear. Once you get up close enough to a natterjack to admire its glossy sheen in the beam of your torch, the glint of the green-gold eyes and the distinctive yellow stripe that runs from the tip of its nose to the broad of its back, you suddenly understand about beauty being in the eye of the beholder. When you note the dexterity with which the toads catch their ground beetle prey, and realise that their shifty, scuttling run is perfectly adapted to get a short-limbed, low-lying animal across open terrain with the minimum of fuss and danger, you witness 'fitness for purpose' in action. Natterjacks, it turns out, are beautiful, fascinating and enviably well-adjusted creatures.

Everything paled into insignificance, however, beside the sheer volume of their vocal intercourse. I have never heard a row like it. Dozens, if not hundreds, of randy male frogs within one small area were calling out through the darkness to potential partners. In natterjack mating circles, as in similar rituals of our own species, he that blows the loudest trumpet gets to spread his seed the soonest. Lying in the Eskmeals Dunes amid the grating, groaning and grunting of the natterjacks was a bit like staying in a cheap motel room with too-thin walls. The night hid my blushes, I'm glad to say.

20

Whatever happened to Lover's Lane?

At the top of Gravel Hill, just where it made the turn to reveal the view that John Constable should have painted, there used to be a Lover's Lane. Actually, 'Lover' is a bit of a euphemism. It was the kind of lane you didn't really like to take the children down. There was a grisly inevitability about what you were going to find there – ancient black-and-white girlie mags featuring unlucky young ladies who'd lost their clothing while wandering in the brambles, used prophylactics dangling ostentatiously from hazel twigs like some ghastly gamekeeper's gibbet, and plastic bags smeared with sniffing glue in the undergrowth.

Fair enough, village youths had to get their kicks one way or another in 1980s rural Suffolk, but it did make me a bit nostalgic for the imaginary Lover's Lanes of Merrie England, for Clara Peggotty strolling arm-in-arm with Barkis, or young Willum plucking a nosegay for his coy Susan. However, that sort of sentimental claptrap aside, what's noticeable nowadays is how few of those porny and druggy artefacts one finds decorating the murkier corners of our countryside. Wheyfaced teenagers have it all on screen, in house and on tap 24/7. No longer are they obliged to slouch off and get well out of sight of home in order to 'indulge their imaginations'. What a shame – the very act of puffing up the hill to reach the stash in the flowery banks of Lover's Lane must at least have put some country roses in the cheeks of that previous generation, if not exactly a bashful blush.

21

D is for Drovers

… the hard men who once travelled the green roads of our land. Everywhere you follow the ancient tracks, through holloways in the South Country downs or out along cobbled paths across the northern moors, you find signs of a vigorous commerce now vanished, a centuries-old traffic of hooves and boots: a wayside water trough under Kinder Scout, a tethering ring in an Angus stone wall, a clump of pine trees to signify a grazing place for sheep along the Peddars Way, a heap of grass-smothered bricks at a crossing of tracks on the Hampshire downs where a wayside inn for the drovers once stood.

They were tough-looking customers, these drovers, with their homespun coats and breeches, great felt hats and ragged beards. They soaped the soles of their stockings against blisters, wore brown paper next to their skin and reckoned to cover twenty miles a day at the steady 2 mph that was all the flocks and herds they drove could manage. They tarred the feet of geese, put pigs in leather galoshes and nailed iron shoes to the hooves of cattle, all to get the beasts unharmed along hundreds of stony miles. They carried responsibility as naturally as their cattle switches, bringing the valuable animals safely to the fattening meadows and to market, banking or bearing back thousands of pounds, distributing messages and parcels along the way.

Every time I walk the old roads, especially on a freezing

winter day or in a lashing rainstorm, I think of these hardy and dependable men, and wonder what they would think of me – cosseted in Gore-Tex and high technology, mincing round the puddles, worrying about angsty stuff in that stupid twenty-first-century way. An uneasy reflection, and a salutary one.

22

Keep it simple, stupid

My father was a determined walker. Through cloud and rain, mist and murk he strode, brushing all uncertainties brusquely aside. Apart from an old tin compass for walking in particularly challenging hills, the only piece of direction-finding equipment he possessed was the cloth-backed Ordnance Survey map, one inch to the mile, showing footpaths as strings of minuscule, hardly discernible red dots. That was it for him and for any young fellow, such as myself, rash enough to accompany him.

If – soaked to the skin, lost in fell mist, with the map a sodden sheet and mud to the fetlocks – I could have teleported us both forward forty years, what would Dad have made of the luxurious technology with which I lounge about the countryside these days? The Ordnance Survey 1:25,000 map that shows me not just the path in big bold green blobs, but every single field boundary along that path? And the Satmap GPS device that all but abolishes the need to take a proper paper OS map with me in the first place?

After a session of harrumphing, I think the old man would have loved it. Big bold maps? Bring 'em on. Maybe not the fiddliness of the Satmap, but undoubtedly its reassurances about where the hell we are. What he would have found questionable is the sight of walkers laden with enough high-tech equipment to conquer Kangchenjunga tap-tapping with walking poles along dead-level lanes, their attention fixed to a tiny screen, checking and rechecking the route like nervous lovers awaiting that critical text message.

We've come far in terms of safety since my father first braved the hills back in the 1930s. But those fabulous inventions, GPS and the World Wide Web, might have robbed us of something, too – the fortitude and hardihood, the self-reliance that Dad's generation of walkers possessed. Something to think on.

23

Death of the map

Last year, I went travelling with my new partner. She was petite, stylish and easy on the eye. She seemed so well informed too. Every time I made a mistake, she was able to put me on the right track. In fact, I just couldn't stop looking at her or consulting her. But the scales soon fell from my eyes. She was always running out of energy, for one thing; for another, she kept leading me up someone else's garden path. On a filthy night in a backwoods bit of Dorset, she got my car wedged between two hedges in a steep muddy lane leading to a piggery, having assured me it was a shortcut to Toller Porcorum. Enough was enough. Next day she was back on the shelf.

Ten-wheeler lorries being jammed up bridleways, coach-loads of pensioners bumping across stubble fields, the man who drove up the stairs and into the gents... what humiliating and dangerous tricks have satellite navigation systems *not* played on us, the over-trusting and frankly lazy travelling public? How on Google Earth have we allowed ourselves to favour such anaemic purveyors of half-truths and quarter-facts over the OS maps and atlases, plump with facts and knowledge, redolent of our rich heritage of national culture and history, that have so brilliantly sustained and informed our going out and our coming in for more than 200 years?

It was Mary Spence, president of the British Cartographic

Society, who released this particular cat amongst the satnav pigeons when she addressed the annual conference of the Institute of British Geographers in London. She told the conference:

> Corporate cartographers are demolishing thousands of years of history – not to mention Britain's remarkable geography – at a stroke by not including them on maps which millions of us now use every day. We're in real danger of losing what makes maps so unique, giving us a feel for a place even if we've never been there.[2]

Spence took as an example the Google map of the Winterbourne Stoke area of Wiltshire, which fails to advise travellers that they are in the vicinity of a rather special heap of old building materials: Stonehenge.

There are two pitfalls here, one more serious than the other (though not for its victims). The propensity for satnav systems to send us up a gum tree or over a river cliff is partly about computer-based techies creating maps without ever leaving the comfort of their nice warm screens to check out, in the real world, what they're advising us to do in the virtual one – but it's also our own silly fault for not paying attention and using a bit of common sense. I wouldn't have got those Dorset hedgerow scratches down my side panels if I'd heeded the still, small voice that whispered, 'OK, this is mud and not tarmac, and that is the sweet essence of Large Whites coming in at the window, so why don't you just back up and cut your losses before…' – *scree-eee!* – 'oh, well, never mind.'

Far more threatening to our national sense of self – and, much more importantly, to our personal edification and pleasure – is the notion of driving or bicycling through a landscape represented solely by blue, green, orange and white spider lines that knit together only blank grey spaces. (I say nothing of walking because you wouldn't get further than the first stile.) Lay the Google and OS Explorer maps of the Stonehenge area side by side. On Google: roads, a river, a ghostly hint of buildings, a flat land. That's it. On the Explorer: all round the mighty henge itself ridged and billowing downland, ancient trackways, processional paths, long barrows and tumuli where our distant lordly ancestors lie buried, the mysterious banking of the track, copses and spinneys bounded by unexplained earthworks, the River Avon coiling past Ham Hatches and Moor Hatches.

Hatches? What for? Why these vast earthworks? Which ruler sleeps under King Barrow? Who raced the 5,000-year-old straights of the Cursus? I can go to Google – the fantastically useful, unbelievably knowledgeable Google search engine, I mean, not the pallid Google pseudo-maps – and find out all I'll ever want to know. But I'd never have suspected the presence of this dense palimpsest of history – my own, my native history – if the OS map hadn't told me in its dry, economical, factual, absorbing, catalytic way of its existence.

Do we need all this stuff to get from Amesbury to Winterbourne Stoke? No, we don't. Should we delight in it, and feel grateful to be part of it, and smack our imaginative lips over it, and be inspired to come back and explore it with a flower book and an archaeology book on a sunny day pretty soon? Absolutely. That's our national heritage – delivered a little elliptically, but with a poetic fitness for purpose, by our priceless national treasure the OS.

24

Gellius Philippus: who he?

As I passed the barn at Willowford Farm, my glance was caught by a scramble of words cut into the surface of one of the stones. Nearly 2,000 years of wild northern wind and weather had smoothed the inscription almost flat but, peering closely, I could more or less make out the meaning. 'The Fifth Cohort of the Century of Gellius Philippus,' it announced in roughly lettered Latin.

It was not exactly a surprise to find such a relic up here in the shadow of Hadrian's Wall. I was following the newly opened Hadrian's Wall Path National Trail along the borders of Northumberland for a few days in early spring, looping off every so often – as I was doing at that moment – to follow one of the admirable circular side walks set up by local authorities for those who want a taste of the Wall without having to commit themselves to the full eighty-four-mile trek. Since setting off from Newcastle-upon-Tyne, I had spotted stones from Hadrian's Wall, cut in their distinctive square shape, set into field walls, barns, churches and houses all along the way.

In the 1,600 years since the Romans finally abandoned the great boundary marker they built between themselves and the barbarians of the north, Hadrian's Wall has been thoroughly quarried by local builders for its handy, ready-shaped stones. The wonder is that there was enough of the original building material left to allow the restorers of modern times to do such a good reconstruction job on the Wall itself.

It's curious how the sight of someone else's scratchings, daubings or doodlings gives us a fellow feeling for them across the centuries and the cultural divides. This summer, in southern Sweden, I came across the Kungagraven ('king's grave'), a mighty hill of stones at whose heart lay the burial chamber of some Bronze Age ruler. Its slabs were incised with figures of undulating dancers disguised as seals. Though their exact meaning was fogged by time, the grace and expressiveness of those sinuous forms came clearly across the 3,000-year gap.

Up in the Orkney isles on another occasion, crouching by torchlight in the depths of the huge Stone Age burial mound of Maeshowe, I was enchanted to hear the guide interpret the runes cut into the stones 1,000 years ago by Viking treasure hunters. There was a boastful 'We've pinched the loot, so don't bother looking', a vainglorious 'These runes were done by the Champion Graffiti Scratcher' and a plaintive 'I really fancy Ingibiorh – she's gorgeous!' Give or take a couple of words, those scribbles in stone could have been scrawled across any twenty-first-century garage door.

The round walk I was following from Gilsland proved a beauty. A really spectacular section of Hadrian's Wall ran down the bank from Willowford Farm to the abutments of the Roman bridge over the River Irthing. I crossed by means of a handsome modern footbridge, and up on the ridge beyond found Birdoswald, with its preserved layout of a Roman wall fort. The path back to Gilsland was gorgeous with sulphur-yellow clumps of primroses and the shiny gold of celandines, and these little harbingers of spring got me thinking about the heavy mob of the Fifth Cohort.

Hadrian's Wall must have been one of the most unpleasant

postings a sun-kissed native Roman could hope to avoid, especially in the long northern winter. Bitter winds, blizzards, poor and scanty food, interminable nights and the threat of attack by Pictish warriors or hungry wolves were added to the endemic military miseries of boredom, barracks life and bullshit.

In point of fact, most of the soldiers who built and garrisoned the wall were northern mercenaries. And for all I know, Gellius Philippus may have been the kindest centurion in the Roman army. But when did imagination baulk at realities? As I strolled down to Gilsland through the woods, I pictured the Fifth Cohort squaddies who scratched that message: swarthy southerners cursing their bully of an officer, shivering in the wintry Northumbrian winds, heartily wishing themselves anywhere but here.

Did the primroses and celandines bring those rough men, as they brought me today, a tiny slip of comfort in the sweet promise of spring? I'd like to think so.

25

Neatsfoot oil

The elderly farmer was leaning over a wall at Hallow Bank, inspecting his newborn spring lambs.

'Neatsfoot oil,' he said, ruminatively. 'That's what we used to put on the lambs. We'd have them in the shed on a cold night, all packed in tight, picking up one another's scent. Next morning, the mothers couldn't smell which was theirs, so they'd reject 'em.' The old man laughed. 'A good dab of neatsfoot oil, and all the lambs would smell of that, and the ewes wouldn't care which 'uns they got!'

Neatsfoot oil, eh? It sounded like something Fred Astaire might have dipped his patent leathers in before cutting a rug with Ginger Rogers. I knew I'd heard that word before, or something like it. Falstaff came to mind.

When I got home I looked it up. Not 'neat' as in 'natty', but from Old English '*nëat*', an ox or cow. As for Falstaff, it was part of his rant at Price Hal: 'You starveling, you eel-skin, you dried neat's-tongue, you bull's-pizzle, you stock-fish!'

What's more, I discovered when I dug around in the cyber-attic, they still make neatsfoot oil. It's great at softening boot leather, apparently. If you've got an ancient pair of dried-out old clumpers you're thinking about chucking away, neatsfoot oil might be just the ticket for rehydrating them.

You can buy the stuff in bottles and cans and demijohns from saddlers and gunmakers. And not just in such arcane emporia, either. It might sound like a product of 'Olde Eng-lande', but I'm pleased to report that neatsfoot oil has now joined the modern age. You can buy it online these days – in bulk, too, if in addition to your grandpa's boots you happen to possess a shed-full of lambs and a lot of puzzled ewes to fool.

26

Penwith granite

When I travelled through Cornwall on the way to childhood seaside holidays, it was always the rolling grassy hills and tree-hung valleys, the fine sand beaches and the tall red cliffs between Bodmin Moor and Falmouth, that called to me. We never ventured further west than St Ives, so I didn't find out about the bleakly beautiful region of Penwith until I was old enough to wander about on my own. It took a long time, but eventually I found myself falling deeply and permanently in love with this strange land, Britain's westernmost outpost, where holy wells hide under the fuchsia hedges and stone circles litter the empty moors.

There is nothing soft or easy about the landscape of Penwith. But there is an absolutely compelling air about a place so naked and open to the elements, so silent and other-worldly and so wrapped in wild weather. On a fine day, Penwith light has a clarity that brings a sulphurous glare to the gorse blooms and a blood-red glow to the heather; on days of sea mist or of driving Atlantic spray, the land seems to brood. The sculptor Barbara Hepworth and her second husband, the painter Ben Nicholson, tapped into this strength of light and the pared-back simplicity of the weather-moulded forms they saw around them, when they came to join the artists' colony at St Ives in 1939. And Penwith artists continue to catch inspiration from the curve of a beach boulder or a shoulder of moor, the upthrust of an ancient standing stone or the hollow of a crevice in the cliffs.

Granite underpins everything here and sets a hard, unyielding tone. Penwith is the most westerly of several outcrops of a great block of granite, on which Cornwall lies bedded. Subterranean upheavals about 400 million years ago punched the hot molten rock up through the bed of an ancient sea. Sandstone was changed by the heat into the glassy white quartzite you see everywhere about the Cornish coast, while escaping gases cooled to produce a mass of mineral lodes. The Cornish mined them for thousands of years – copper, iron, zinc, lead and the tin that became a mainstay of the county's economy.

The molten rock itself cooled off into a vast lump of granite. This is extraordinary stuff – a rock so tough that its name is synonymous with endurance, yet one that the gentle fingers of frost and wind can shatter, slice and tumble. Hence the formation of those weird-looking tors, pinnacles of broken granite resembling castle battlements that command the moorland ridges and coastal headlands of Penwith.

Granite makes for poor soil with few nutrients. Farming must always have been a struggle in such a stony, windswept and salt-sprayed environment, but hunger and necessity were great spurs to our distant ancestors. Some 3,000 years ago, they created a Penwith landscape of tiny stone-walled fields that still survives today. Walls, gateposts, stiles, farmyard barns, farmhouses and village cottages are all of granite. Houses tend to be of simple square design, built plain and massive to stand up to the wind and rain hurtling in off the Atlantic. In the wet, they seem dark and dour. But sunshine brings out a diamond shimmer from the quartzite chips embedded in the granite.

In my mind, Cornwall was always so completely bound up

with fair holiday weather, with sunlight and warm sands and with sparkling blue seas gently lapping the rocks, that I took a long while to come to terms with hard-edged Penwith. For years, I turned my back on the region between St Ives and Land's End in favour of prettier villages and softer country. Strangely enough, it was foul weather that opened my eyes to the subtle allure of Penwith – a walk along the headlands from Zennor to Cape Cornwall on a mad March day, with half a spring gale blasting in from the north and the sea bursting magnificently on Three Stone Oar and the Kenidjacks. I felt the cliffs shudder at the impact of the Atlantic and was buffeted sideways by the storm. That taught me about the resilience of granite, the feeling of being out at the end of the land and the power of the wind in an all-but-treeless landscape.

Next day, the weather switched. The wind died, and a sea fret came curling over Penwith. Wandering inland, I found myself passing between the buried houses of Carn Euny, an ancient village already many hundreds of years old when the Romans came to Britain. Out on the moor beyond, the squat monoliths of Boscawen-ûn stone circle shaped themselves out of the mist. It was as if the silent past had crept up near enough to touch and feel, in an ancient landscape unchanged by tide or time.

27

E is for Elephant

… and in particular the mighty Maharajah, who decided to assert his right to roam in famous circumstances.

When Wombwell's Menagerie in Edinburgh closed down in 1872, its seven-year-old Asian elephant was bought by Belle Vue Zoological Gardens in Manchester. How to get him there was the problem. Maharajah threw a tantrum at Waverley station, smashing up the railway horsebox he was supposed to travel in.

'Very good,' quoth his keeper, Lorenzo 'the Lion Tamer' Lawrence. 'I'll jolly well walk him to Manchester.'

The odd couple set off on foot along the public roads, travelling twenty miles a day and stirring up interest in every town and village they passed through. That might actually have been the point of the exercise: it's now reckoned that the wagon-wrecking and subsequent ten-day slow march could have been a publicity stunt by Belle Vue. If so, it worked brilliantly. Crowds thronged to welcome Maharajah to Manchester, especially once the news of an episode at a toll gate got about. Reports said that the toll gatekeeper at Victoria Park on the outskirts of the city, eyeing the vast bulk of the elephant, had rather unwisely inflated the fee. While he argued the toss with Lawrence, Maharajah simply tore the toll gate off its hinges, threw it aside and sauntered through.

The tollgate incident passed into myth. In Manchester Art

Gallery hangs Heywood Hardy's fabulous 1875 painting of the affair, *The Disputed Toll*, with Maharajah towering over the gate, his trunk and tusks about to do their work while the smock-frocked toll gatekeeper argues with the Lion Tamer. Slightly more ignobly, Maharajah's great skeleton still stands on display in Manchester Museum. Looming large in death as in life, this formidable walker and exponent of the freedom of the Queen's highway has never ceased to be an icon and an inspiration.

28

Summons soup with the Laird of Gight

How beautiful it is to stroll the wooded Braes of Gight! How charming the babble of the River Ythan as it sparkles through its sinuous glen! Really, this must be one of the most romantic spots in all bonny Aberdeenshire, especially on a fair spring evening such as this, when the little birds... hush! What was that? A skirl of ghostly pipes from the picturesque old ruin at the corner of the meadow...! Is there a glimmer of light in the slit windows of the Great Hall? Let's tiptoe up and peek inside, shall we...? Och, saints preserve us! It's the De'il himself, Auld Nick with forked tail and cloven hooves, a-gnashing his teeth as he sits feasting with the terrible Laird o' Gight! Quick, Jennie – run for it!

Such is the reputation of the crumbling old Castle of Gight – pronounced 'gecht', like the death-rattle of a strangled man. And very appropriate, too; this tumbledown stronghold of the Gordon clan in the meadow by the River Ythan has seen more evil plans hatched and more bloody deeds done than any pirate ship or bandit hideout. The Gordons built the castle strong and stout with arrow slits and gun loops in a Tudor era of unrest and lawlessness in Scotland, and they ran the neighbourhood like a Mafia sept.

Worst and wildest of them all was one of the few of that branch of the family who contrived to die in his own bed. William Gordon, fifth Laird of Gight, may not actually have been in league with the Devil, but he took great delight in doing that naughty old gentleman's work for him. If a sword or a bullet or a brain-crushing bludgeon would help reinforce William's claims on his neighbours' property, the Laird of Gight did not hesitate to use them. During the 1580s, he got into one quarrel after another, murdering two men in hot temper, then killing his own brother-in-law. In 1591, he was part of a gang that burned the 'Bonny Earl of Murray' out of his castle at dead of night, hunted the unfortunate man down in his nightshirt by following the telltale light of his blazing nightcap tassel and battered him to death. Bluidy Gight himself struck the fatal blows. Excommunication and outlawry did not stop William Gordon's rampaging, killing and crop-trampling – and when the Privy Council sent a representative to Gight Castle with a long list of malfeasances for Gordon to answer, the laird's response was to mash the summons into a bowl of soup and force the terrified messenger to drink it.

Nowadays the Great Hall, where so much of this fantastic story was played out, lies cold and silent over the huge stone kitchen fireplace and half-buried cellar vaults – dungeons, the imagination promptly christens them. It's a strange moment when one leaves the haunted ruins for the peaceful shade and riverbank paths of Gight Wood nature reserve. But Auld Nick is not so easily shaken off.

Just beyond the castle, the River Ythan rushes through a rocky narrows known as Hagberry Pot. In 1644, a band of Covenanters – religious dissenters – came to burn Gight Castle. The seventh laird, George Gordon, got wind of the raid and hurried to throw the family jewels into Hagberry Pot to save them from the raiders. When the danger was over, the laird ordered a servant to dive for the treasure. The man surfaced empty handed, vowing that he'd met the Devil down there, and the Evil One had no intention of giving up the jewels. He was ordered to try again. After a long, long wait the diver reappeared – but, unluckily for him, in four separate pieces. The jewels…? Aye, Jennie, they're still down there. But I'm no' gettin them for ye – no way!

29

Turncoats of the Peak

After weeks of snow lying deep and crisp and even, of gloomy horizons and murky skies, here was a clear, sunny morning over the Peak District hills of north Derbyshire. The remaining snow was shrinking into cracks and crevices under the wind-sculpted edges, those miniature cliffs of gritstone so characteristic of the Dark Peak moors.

'Of course, we can't guarantee seeing the mountain hares,' said David Mallon, striding ahead along the glittering sandy path over the Derwent Moors. 'But they're usually somewhere up under Derwent Edge. Lucky the snow's going – they're really hard to spot against it. On a day like today, though...'

If you change your coat to snow white for winter camou-flage, as the mountain hare does, you can't just switch your wardrobe to summer brown the minute the snow melts away. White hare against white snow: little chance for the onlooker. But white animal against grey stones, brown heather or black rocks: different story. Our chances of spotting the little herbi-vores with their furry, ever-twitching noses and athletic back legs had suddenly increased tenfold. It does help, of course, to be looking for mountain hares in the company of an ecologist who probably knows more about them and their habits than anyone currently active on their behalf.

David put in plenty of time at the chalkface before packing in the unsatisfying career of a teacher, branching out as a freelance ecologist and building a reputation for expert knowledge on all manner of mammals, 'mostly out in the Caucasus and the Himalayas – high places and dry places, you could say. You have to see the whole picture in ecological terms. If there weren't any herbivores, there wouldn't be any of the poster boys of conservation, snow leopards and jaguars and so on. The aim is to look after the whole environment that we all share – and that's the case with the mountain hares here on these moors.'

Up under Derwent Edge, we followed a dry stone wall, looking up across a wide expanse of moor blotched and patched with grey and brown. 'These moors are all managed for grouse shooting,' explained David. 'The heather's burned in rotation, so there are always bare patches for scratching and nesting, young green shoots for food and old tough heather for shelter. That's what the grouse need, and it's exactly what suits the mountain hares too.'

In the mid-nineteenth century, there was a craze for bringing mountain hares south from Scotland and establishing colonies of them on English uplands. Only those in Derbyshire and on the Isle of Man still survive. If you want to get a sight of these beautiful creatures in mainland England or Wales, this is where you have to come, to the gritstone moors on either side of the Snake Pass road.

We scanned the rocks and heather banks of White Tor, looking for a telltale flash of white against the sombre background. 'The hares move down below the edge in spring to shelter from the wind and to get together for mating, so they should be there...' murmured David, eyes to binoculars. 'Umm – yes, there! See him? At five o'clock from the dark rock on the left.'

To me, the mountain hare was the tiniest of blobs, hardly

distinguishable from the pale lichens on the gritstone rocks. We forged uphill on a sheep track to top the rise – and as soon as we did, up jumped the hare, magnificently, thirty yards away, a bounding creature with a back of pale milk chocolate and a snow-white chest. 'Just turning his coat,' cried David. 'Keep your eye on him – he'll stop in a moment!' So he did, freezing motionless against a rock as if posing for a portrait. Now I could see the blotchy black of his ears, the cream-coloured fur band keeping his nose warm and the faintest of blue tinges to the white fur of his chest.

We saw three more hares during the morning – one a streak of caramel and vanilla that bounced over the skyline in five huge springs, another a flash of white vanishing behind a rock and the third a long, satisfying sighting up in the blasting wind beyond the ridge, a big hare that loped and stopped, loped and stopped, before diving out of sight down a crevice.

These beautiful creatures don't need to turn white, as David pointed out to me. The Peak District doesn't get the snowfalls of the Scottish Highlands, and the hare's only predator, the fox, is rigorously controlled by the grouse moor gamekeepers. Yet the mountain hares of Derbyshire go on turning coat, as their ancestors did for uncounted generations, a genetic imperative hot-wired into their sinuous, elusive selves – born survivors in their alien adoptive environment.

30

St Swithun's Way

As I walked through Winchester in company with 200 others on a windy April morning, the cathedral bells were ringing out a Palm Sunday peal across the city. The wind riffled the choirboys' ruffs, billowed the red-and-white robes of the clergy and snatched away the oompah of tubas and trumpets giving 'Ride on, ride on in majesty' all they'd got. It was a splendid procession, all flapping scarlet and winking brass – the perfect ramp on which to launch myself into a three-day Eastertide walk.

In the cathedral, the choirboys sang like blackbirds. After the service, as I stood beside the shrine of St Swithun, the dean approached.

'Where are you off to with that pack and walking stick of yours? On pilgrimage? Well, it's been a great pleasure to have you with us, and may the saints go with you.'

When medieval pilgrims set off on their great adventures, they needed not only the blessing of their local priests, but also written permission from their bishops. For a man, there were several outward observances, too, by which he might be known as a pilgrim: an untrimmed beard, a long grey gown and a black or grey hat adorned with red crosses, a scrip or bag with a pottle or bottle and, of course, a staff. I had the shaggy beard, a rucksack for a scrip with a Palm Sunday palm-frond cross stuck in it and an ash-wood walking stick for a staff. No wonder the dean had taken me for one of the Brotherhood.

Pilgrims are scarcely a novel phenomenon in Winchester, ancient capital of England and starting point for medieval Britain's favourite penitential trek – the pilgrimage to the tomb of St Thomas à Becket in Canterbury Cathedral. Recently there has been quite a revival in the tradition of pilgrimage within Britain – to Walsingham, to Winchester, to Canterbury and elsewhere. I was setting out with a copy of *The Canterbury Tales* in my backpack, at roughly the time of year that Geoffrey Chaucer's famous pilgrims made their journey to Canterbury, to explore the recently opened trail called St Swithun's Way. This three-day walk from Winchester to Farnham forms the final link in a Winchester–Canterbury path for religious pilgrims, long-distance walkers and anyone else with a taste for fresh air and some of the most beautiful landscapes in southern England.

Our modern-day freedom to travel wherever we choose from St Agnes to Unst – to put our finger on a public right of way on an OS map and say, 'I can go and walk that right now, if I want to' – would have seemed an unattainable fantasy to Chaucer's fellow countrymen. The feudal system restricted the everyday movements of all but the most privileged to the locality where they lived. Social and religious obligations kept their noses to the grindstones of work, home and church. It was only on pilgrimage that the vast majority of people could throw off these stifling bonds and live a little.

Though most pilgrims undertook their pilgrimages with serious religious motives – in thanksgiving for favours received, to secure salvation, in penance for sins, to beg help from a favourite saint – it was also a golden opportunity to kick back and have some fun. People looked on pilgrimage as we might on an adventure holiday: a chance to get around, see some fresh scenes, meet new people and do something a bit daring. The mere fact of a knight, a plowman, a wife of Bath and a miller travelling and conversing together would have been almost impossible under ordinary circumstances. Add in the dangers of the road, of robbers and rapists, of conmen leading you astray, of plague and violence and (for some of the pilgrims) of the thrilling possibility of dalliance while footloose in a strange district, and pilgrimage could seem a pretty racy venture.

The scariest thing I met along that beautiful pilgrimage path was a yappy little terrier baring his minuscule teeth, and he sheered off when I invited him to take notice of my stick. The raciest sight was two girls being carried, shrieking and splashing, by their boyfriends through the watercress beds near Alresford. But I did come across signs of my medieval predecessors: the pilgrim crosses that they scratched like holy graffiti into the door frames of the village churches in which they rested all along the way.

31

F is for Flora and Fauna

… my favourite outdoor twins. I've been going out with both of them for a long time now – yes, I know it seems a bit daring, but they're inseparable, and… well, you can't have one without the other, as the old song says. Two sides of the same coin.

They certainly don't give it all up on first acquaintance – no, they're old-fashioned that way. Both absolutely beautiful girls, very natural, and both with that instant wow factor, but you have to put in a lot of time with them to appreciate them properly.

It's funny, though, there are differences between them. You never hear a peep out of Flora. And she's a down-to-earth kind of girl, very rooted – whereas Fauna's either all over the place, up in the air and gabbling fit to beat the band, you know, or she keeps herself to herself, as quiet as… well, as a mouse, and runs a mile if you make the wrong move.

Now, when they first caught my eye, both Flora and Fauna used to be very reliable about turning up on time (give or take a week or two) and in the usual places too. So it was no sweat to see them. But recently they've been getting a bit flighty, a bit unpredictable. Flora's retreated to the hilltops, where she used to be a valley girl, while Fauna's either much too early or doesn't turn up at all. Springs have been especially funny. Flora's started popping up when you just don't expect her, and

Fauna's been making all sorts of… well, 'saucy' moves before I've even got my thermals off! This spring, though, they were both sulky and didn't deign to put in an appearance till I'd almost given up on them.

I hope they're not thinking of leaving me. I'd really, really miss them.

32

Bempton Cliffs

Bempton Cliffs on a chilly April dawn. What would any sane person be doing here, shivering at this unfeasible hour on the wind-blasted East Yorkshire coast, binoculars heavy round the neck? There isn't a sensible answer. Anyone with any sense would be tucked up in bed. At this time of day, there's no one else to share the cliffs with – apart from a quarter of a million seabirds. Ah, yes.

In the half-light of a cold sunrise, the North Sea waves are creaming, pink and gold, at the feet of immense chalk ramparts. As for the seabirds, they perform their endless, dizzying spiral dance in mid-air, a mesmerising movement fit to suck a dreamer out from the precarious cliff and down towards that heaving sea, milky blue with chalk fragments in solution. The fishy stink is colossal and the sound overwhelming, dominated by the ceaseless, echoing kittiwake chorus – '*Eee-WAKE! Eee-WAKE!*'

The frozen hands go round the binoculars and lift them to the eyes, and immediately a watcher knows exactly why they're here on these particular cliffs. It's the start of the breeding season, and the greatest seabird show in Britain is getting under way. Fulmars with their huge nostrils sit highest on grassy tuffets, with razorbills and guillemots below them on bare guano-whitened ledges. Gannets perch on shaggy nests of grass, seaweed and plastic scraps. Kittiwakes cling to hairline cracks in the cliff face. Herring gulls line the lowest ledges, not far above the sea.

These cliffs will be alive with chicks in a few weeks' time. For now, though, there are no eggs – just the quick movements of mating, the fishwife squabbling over possession of six inches of naked rock and the promise of the endless cycle repeating itself like the wheeling flight of the kittiwakes.

33

Salmon on the Spey

I must admit I blubbed like a baby when Salar died of fungal disease below the Fireplay Pool. That was the final scene in Henry Williamson's classic nature saga *Salar the Salmon* – as honest and accurate a picture of the end of a wild creature as you'd expect from the author of *Tarka the Otter*, but still a bit of a choker for a sensitive and romantic boy of nine.

I got over it, but the story kindled inside me the desire to see an Atlantic salmon in the wild – a fire that never went out. Williamson had set his tale around the rivers and estuaries of north Devon, and I made a couple of expeditions to the banks of the Torridge and Taw. But they yielded not even a glimpse of a silvery back among the ripples, let alone the ecstatic leaping into the air that Williamson had so seductively described.

'Go to Scotland, to the Moray Firth,' said a fishing friend. 'The River Spey in the springtime, that's your best bet. It's… well, magical. There's no other word.'

Salmo salar, the Atlantic salmon, hatches in the headwaters of dozens of rivers throughout these islands, the River Spey included. Back to the very stream in which it first saw light it will come to spawn, guided from the open Atlantic by instinct, several years and tens of thousands of sea miles later. It leaves its parent river as a smolt, only a few inches long; it returns as a magnificent creature, the king of fish, weighing anything up to thirty pounds or more, its flesh pink with prawn juices, its muscles full of power. Salmon may make their spawning run at any time of the year, but spring is the definitive season. Once back in their native water, it may take the fish as long as a year to travel upriver from the estuary to the redds or gravel-bedded shallows where the females lay their thousands of eggs and the males fertilise them in a milky cloud of milt.

The Atlantic salmon is undergoing tough times just now. Hazards have always been legion – cannibal trout eating the eggs, eels and lampreys in the rivers, seals and porpoise at the estuary mouths, orcas at sea. That's not to mention dangers such as pollution and man-made obstacles, nor the netsmen and anglers who lure unwary fish. Recently, though, numbers returning to their parent rivers from the Atlantic have declined dramatically. Perhaps they are being taken in the catch-all nets of modern deep-sea trawlers. Maybe their traditional food supplies are melting away. No one knows the causes for sure. Rivers such as the Severn have been especially hard hit. But the more northerly rivers, and the Spey in particular, have maintained their salmon numbers well. A daunder along Speyside certainly looked like my best chance of finally seeing a spring-run salmon.

The Cairngorms had been blanketed in thick snow during the winter, and now the warmer air of spring was releasing torrents of meltwater into dozens of tributary hill burns, all tumbling down to join the confusion of floodwater in the Spey itself. When I arrived in Grantown-on-Spey, the white flanks of the far mountains were streaked with dark patches, and there was a continuous rumble and roar from the peat-brown river as it surged north-eastwards in full spate.

Whistling James Scott Skinner's great reel 'The Spey in

Spate', with its wonderful leaps and runs, I wandered for three days down the Speyside Way long-distance footpath towards the sea. It was a memorable walk, but I never saw a salmon – not a free one, anyway. Fishermen were standing chest-high in the falling water, and a couple of times I watched as a curving bow of silver was lifted into a landing net. Even though they would perhaps only be weighed and measured and then released into the river to continue their spawning run, there seemed something diminished about these captive fish.

Down at Tugnet, the river widened over rocky shallows to meet the sea in Spey Bay. The noise of the spate waters was stunning: the crash of waves and rumble of river-rolled boulders. No other human was in sight. I stood mesmerised beside the old icehouse, staring out across the agitated water. Suddenly, there it was: a long back gleaming in the shallows; a V-shaped tail trailing a string of spray; and then the sight of a big salmon half-leaping and half-hurdling through the waves – Salar returned, as beautiful and powerful as I had ever dreamed.

34

G is for Green Man

My ten-year-old self was lying back on the turf of Bulbarrow Hill in the shade of a beech spinney, book in hand, all alone in deepest Dorset. And I'll never forget the cold pang of terror when I looked up from my book to see an evil little face, with goat-like eyes and the most cynical of smiles, staring out at me from among the tree trunks.

The hallucination (if that's what it was) certainly had a lot to do with the story I was reading, 'The Music on the Hill' by Saki, a Gothic fantasy in which a woman discovers and destroys an offering to Pan in the woods and is gored to death by a stag driven wild by mysterious piping from a copse. I was a fanciful boy (and how the child has proved father to the man!), with a capacity for wild, often dark flights of imagination – easy prey for Saki's baroque whimsies. I can remember scrambling up and running off, not daring to look back, in dread of eerie music and the hot breath of a stag on my neck.

Nowadays, when I'm out walking and the path takes me deep into tanglewood, I'm occasionally conscious of a something or a someone there, a presence neither benign nor malign but watchful and quietly amused. I think of it as a manifestation of whatever it was in the medieval psyche that gave rise to the Green Man, that enigmatic carved face sprouting leaves and fruit from its nostrils that we see in so many of our country churches.

I've never experienced anything again like my childhood terror of the wildwood. But even if it isn't the sort of thing a proper grown-up admits to, I'm quite pleased, if truth be told, that the Green Man hasn't vanished from those psychic thickets quite yet.

35

Up the down and down the beach

A grey and blustery South Wales day with a damp south-east wind charging over the seaward tip of the Gower peninsula, rippling the waters of Rhossili Bay into white horses and setting the roadside primroses furiously nodding. In Rhossili village, a man shook his head at me over his garden wall, pointing up at the hurrying clouds. 'Going up on the down? You'll be blown inside out, I would say.'

I had a fancy that this unseasonable slice of cold and wind would blow over in short order, with warm sunshine spreading like butter over the countryside as it had always done on previous springtime visits to Gower. And even if it didn't, there is something fantastically exhilarating about being high up and blown about. In any case (I rationalised to my willing spirit as my reluctant body got going), what setting could be better for a windy walk than Rhossili Down, a great three-headed whaleback of a hill with the three-mile curve of Rhossili Beach at its feet like a calendar photographer's dream of delight?

Halfway up the steep slope of the down's southern face, I stepped to the edge and gazed down. The beach ran north and south in a flawless arc, shaped by the sea more perfectly than any man-made piece of art. Not a soul on it, not a footprint at this early hour. At the southern end, steep cliffs fell away to the green double hump of Worm's Head, a promontory that darted its uplifted head two miles out into the sea, with such a striking resemblance to a swimming sea monster that the Vikings who came ashore in the bay some 1,200 years ago named it Wurm ('dragon').

At the northern tip of the beach, a gently domed green island floated just offshore, its causeway covered by the still-flowing tide. In the sixth century, St Cenydd (or St Kenneth) built a lonely cell there. He was the son of one of King Arthur's knights, born the wrong side of the blanket and cast adrift like Moses to live or die. Seagulls rescued him from the waves, and angels oversaw his upbringing on Worm's Head. Through binoculars I made out clouds of seabirds around the head of the dragon, their nesting and breeding station for countless millennia. The angels, if any, must have been riding invisible among those ominously racing clouds above the summit of Rhossili Down.

Up there, the wind shoved hard, but I was able to keep it on my starboard quarter and sail straight for the trig pillar at The Beacon, the highest point in the peninsula at 632 feet. The far prospect was restricted by cloud and murky horizons. But with the whole of Gower and a good portion of the coast to east and west stretched out in view, the wind seeth-ing in the heather of the down and a solitary lark outfacing the wind with an angelic outpouring of song, I was happy enough.

A little further along the crest of the down, I came to Sweyne's Howes. Swedish or Danish settlers formed these tombs, most of them circular in shape, with low rings of boulders chosen for the pebbles of white quartz that seeded them and made them glitter in sun or rain. One of the noble dead of Rhossili Down was the chieftain Sweyne – maybe the same warrior that gave his name to Swansea. He and his companions enjoy a magnificent view over land and sea from their resting place in the heather.

On through the remnants of a Second World War radar station – concrete foundations dissolving back into the turf – and steeply down the northern face of the hill to the dunes of Llangennith, meaning 'St Cenydd's church'. Beyond Llangennith Burrows lay the beach, on whose windy sands a pair of tiny terriers scampered and yapped ecstatically. They showed me their tiny white needles of teeth in a brace of black-lipped grins, then raced away along the surf line. I faced into the wind and headed back along the beach under the green wall of the down, looking forward through spectacles misted with sand and spray to where the dragon of Worm's Head was gnashing the sea into white tatters of foam with mighty jaws of rock.

Slutch

What hat sets Alfred Wainwright apart is the individualism, the force of character that comes across so clearly on every page. In his handwritten and hand-drawn guidebooks to walking the fells of north-west Britain, lack of space confines him to a few crunchy footnotes ('A wet and weary trudge'; 'Penance for sins'; 'You will question your own sanity') and comments such as his summing up of conditions around Featherbed Moss on the Pennine Way: 'There is a good Lancashire word that well describes the conglomerate ooze and mud and mire of Featherbed Moss. The word is SLUTCH. Say it slowly, with feeling, and you have the sound of a boot extricating itself from the filthy stuff.'

In other books, and particularly in his autobiographical *Memoirs of a Fellwanderer*, he indulges in observations salty and strong enough to enhance his curmudgeonly reputation: walkers should not talk on the fells; accidents only happen to clumsy or stupid people; those who always walk in company lack gumption or are plain daft. Such were Wainwright's forthright comments aimed at fellow Brothers and Sisters of the Boot. Far stronger were his wider opinions on such matters as suitable punishments for violent criminals and football hooligans.

You had to take Wainwright with a big pinch of salt – and a lot of pepper too. And when you did, you learned that behind the gritty brusqueness lay a sensitive dreamer who built up his defensive carapace to guard a very tender inner man. Wainwright was brought up poor in a tense working-class household in Blackburn, and he developed an iron determination to make it up the ladder. When he moved to the Lake District in 1941, it was like a move to heaven. Though his workaday world revolved around keeping fanatically neat ledgers in the offices of the Borough Treasurer (a post he himself went on to fill for nearly twenty years), Wainwright's leisure was entirely and absolutely devoted to his love affair with the fells – an all-consuming obsession that was partly responsible for the atrophying and break-up of his first marriage.

Every weekend and on every holiday, Wainwright walked the fells, travelling to and from them by bus (he couldn't drive); every evening, he drew them and wrote about them in a creative daze that excluded everything and everyone else. 'It was a passionate courtship,' he noted with pride. 'Between finishing one book and starting the next, I paused only to refill my pipe.'

The first of his Pictorial Guides, *The Eastern Fells*, came out in May 1955; the final volume of the seven, *The Western Fells*, in 1966. They made his name and, for a time, made him even crustier, more unapproachable and more determined to play hide-and-seek with an adoring public who now kept their eyes peeled for the elusive 'A. Walker', as he styled himself. But it *was* only a game. Wainwright made a second and much happier marriage in 1970. When TV fame arrived in the 1980s, the old bear with the sore head was found to have mellowed quite considerably.

The supreme achievement of this complex, difficult and essentially private man was to demystify the fells. His maps and notes give you confidence to get up there and explore, and his words of wisdom tell you that it's quite all right to do it your way: wear what's comfortable; go alone if you want to; the only advice you need is to watch where you put your feet. 'Fellwalking is not a dangerous sport,' he assures you. 'It's a pleasure. Fellwalking isn't dicing with death: it is a glorious enjoyment of life.' What a relief to read that, in the midst of so much nervous nannying in today's walking world!

'The fells are not monsters,' Wainwright writes in my favourite passage of all his work, 'but amiable giants. You can romp over them and pull the hairs on their chests and shout in their ears and treat them rough, and they don't mind a bit. They are not enemies to be wrestled with. They are friends. Go amongst them as you go amongst friends.'

37

H is for Heroes

… specifically Hillaby. They say you should never meet your heroes, and I never did catch up with John Hillaby. He was too busy walking.

The achievements of this tall, spare, ludicrously energetic Yorkshireman (1917–1996) are not so superhuman as to feel completely out of reach. They are just utterly compelling. Hillaby walked from Yorkshire to London (*Journey Home*). He walked 1,000 miles with a camel train through Kenya (*Journey to the Jade Sea*). He walked from the North Sea to the Mediterranean (*Journey Through Europe*). Best of all, Hillaby walked from Land's End to John O'Groats in the spring of 1966, a joyful journey that inspired his finest book, *Journey Through Britain*.

Some books just live alongside you, don't they? I read *Journey Through Britain* as a teenager, and I must have read it twenty or thirty times since then. The sense of delight Hillaby conveys in observing a colony of young lapwings above Lothersdale, in walking stark naked on the Long Mynd, in singing and getting plastered in a Bucknall pub with a trio of bus conductors; his erudition, his huge knowledge of plants and birds and geology in a pre-ecology age; his sheer pleasure in the ecstatic physicality of waking up at dawn 'feeling as brisk as a bird', giving himself a shower of ice-cold needles of dew from his tent flap, and walking thirty miles before nightfall…

I know I wouldn't have lasted ten minutes in such rocket-powered company, but it was, and is, fabulous to read about.

Hillaby inspired me to go out wandering, to use my eyes and ears, to write about walking and take an endless delight in it. He's all but forgotten now. I'm sure he'd have been embarrassed to know he was my hero. But I adored the man I never met, and I cherish those books.

38

Google Translate

Walking in the Lake District by H. H. Symonds was my father's favourite guidebook. Writing in 1933, Symonds made no allowances for his readers. If you didn't understand the classical-language tags with which he peppered his pages, then off with you into the outer darkness along with charabanc trippers and girls in striped stockings, two of Symonds's particular bugbears.

Glancing through Symonds today as I plan a walking trip to the Lakes, I'm suddenly struck by a desire to know what he was on about. Google Translate will solve the problem… won't it?

'Standing here [on Looking Stead], περισκεπτω ενι χωρω, you get your best view so far of the northern slate fells.' Let's have a butcher's. 'περισκεπτω ενι χωρω' – 'I make a living.' Really? OK, perhaps he was just hoping the book would sell well. Next! How about Bowfell in evening sunlight? 'ο θεος αει Υεωμετρει'. Indeed? Let's see… 'God is a hydrometer.' Well, Symonds was a clergyman, so he might have had some inside information on that.

Up Langstrath Beck, there are 'bathing pools for gods and goddesses', where Symonds loves to take an ice-cold dip. 'Hinc atque hinc glomerantur Oreades,' he thinks as he dries himself. 'On this side and on this side, are wound up and left,' translates Google. Hmm. Perhaps our man forgot to put his watch on after his plunge.

Symonds deeply disapproved of the look of Haweswater Reservoir, under construction at the time. 'A real disaster, an engineer's vulgarism ... αρωτον μεν υδωρ, ο δε χρυσος αιθομενον πυρ,' he splutters. 'With water, and golden ethereal fire,' is Google's actually quite poetic effort. But what's this? Symonds himself has supplied a tongue-in-cheek translation: 'Water may be necessary, but gold in the hands of a public authority means a ruddy conflagration.'

Now that's one aphorism that hasn't dated at all.

39

Greenham Common resurgent

A beautiful sunny day in West Berkshire: just the afternoon to go strolling on the common. Skylarks climbed high in the blue overhead, pouring out passionate song. Golden cowslips and pale pink milkmaids bobbed in the breeze. Cows grazed contentedly. Beneath their hooves, under the turf of the common, lay hidden the ghostly shape of the runway that once slashed its concrete scar across this heath. Beyond the fence squatted the truncated, toad-like shapes of silos that once held doomsday weapons. In the event of war at the end of the twentieth century, those missiles would have lifted off the runway in the bellies of USAF bombers, bound for a dropping point somewhere over Russia.

'I stumbled on Greenham Common while I was taking the dogs for a walk, sometime after we moved to the area in 1978,' mused Derek Emes, chair of Greenham and Crookham Conservation Volunteers, as we strolled the common together. A retired civil engineer who's worked all over the world, Derek has laboured tirelessly alongside a band of like-minded volunteers to restore the disused Greenham Common cruise missile base to its former state of ecological richness. 'The nuclear silos were just being built, but the whole place was in a dormant state; the fence had been allowed to deteriorate, and I found I could get in and out pretty much as I pleased. I thought: what a lovely place! Of course, once the cruise missiles were installed and the first women's protest group arrived from Wales, the "Women for Life on Earth", everything changed.'

Greenham Common is not like any other common in these islands. From the Second World War until 1997, it was an airbase run for the most part by the USAF; for eight of those years (1983–1991), it housed cruise missiles with a nuclear capability. No one who watched television news in the haunted years of the 1980s, with international tension sharp and the Iron Curtain giving no hint of melting away, could fail to remember the Women's Peace Camp that established itself outside the gates, nor the fence-scalings, incursions, sit-down protests, chants, televised struggles with stolid policemen and other ways that the women found to keep their anti-missile cause in the headlines.

'The peace women weren't especially unpopular hereabouts,' noted Derek. 'But they weren't exactly welcome, either. Greenham Common is really two neighbouring commons, Greenham and Crookham, and the women found out that some local commoners still enjoyed ancient rights of access to Crookham Common. So they befriended them and were able to get onto that section and carry on publicising their cause.'

Eventually, the peace protesters saw their mission fulfilled. By 1992, the USSR's policy of glasnost, open engagement with the West, had neutralised its perceived threat. The nuclear missiles of Greenham Common were removed and returned to the USA. Five years later, the airbase was closed, and the Ministry of Defence handed Greenham Common over to Newbury District Council and the Greenham Trust. Since then, the 1,200 acres of Greenham and Crookham Commons have been managed as one enormous nature reserve.

Two factors vied for my attention as I walked the common:

the natural world that was re-establishing itself with astonishing speed and the ominous remains of the airbase that
still lay in situ. Here were mires and sphagnum bogs, ponds
and streams, acid grassland, mown meadows where orchids
thrived – bee orchids with their bumblebee-bum patterns,
green-winged orchids, Autumn lady's tresses with tiny white
flowers. Hares, rabbits, weasels and foxes found refuge. Dartford warblers nested, and so did skylarks and woodlarks. The
common was bright with great blue drifts of viper's bugloss,
yellow of ragwort, purple-pink of rosebay willowherb and
the pink five-petalled stars of lime-loving common centaury.
These throve next to acid soil plants such as bell heather, in
patches where lime leaching out of the broken old runways
had enriched the surrounding heathland. Nearby, old airbase
buildings quietly crumbled. The cruise missile silos, green
flat-topped pyramids with dark entrances, squatted behind
a triple layer of fencing like the burial mounds of long-dead
warriors. And a fire-practice plane lay in its moat of water,
no longer blasted with flame in simulated emergency, silently
rusting away.

This wonderful variety of wildlife, the resurgence of the
common's ecological riches after half a century in the shadow
of military development, had not come about by chance.

'All sorts of ideas were put forward for the base when it
was closed,' said Derek. 'A housing estate, a new airport for
London, a car racing track. But, in the end, we got what we
were lobbying for. The Greenham Trust bought the entire site
for about £7 million and leased the Greenham and Crookham
commons to West Berkshire Council for £1. Our conservation volunteers meet on the third Sunday of each month, and
we go out on a task – scrub-bashing, perhaps, or clearing
away rubble, cleaning up the ponds, or maybe doing some

hedge-laying or putting in a footbridge. Little improvements, but persistent.'

The shadow of the past lies long on this wild place, lending it an extraordinary poignancy. And the Greenham and Crookham Conservation Volunteers can't afford to be complacent, insisted their chair. 'The commons themselves may be safe now, but we're always having to challenge applications for inappropriate development around the perimeter – intrusive lights, too-tall factories, increases in road noise and transport movements.' Derek swept his arm wide in a gesture that embraced wild flowers, ponds, woods and streamlets. 'It's just so beautiful when it's all out in full colour on a day like this. A miracle, really, to think what it was like only ten years ago. And we are completely determined to keep it safe for the future. That's what it's all about.'

40

Covid Spring: two walks

Three Hares Field

From the crooked elbow of Slippery Lane, you can look back over the village and the valley. It's a view that never palls in any season: the red-and-grey roofs, the chimneys and windows among their trees, and on across the flat country to far hills – Quantocks and a hint of Exmoor, pale blue against the sky in the far distance.

It's a fight for life in the verges of Slippery Lane. The flowers have left the season of yellow (primroses and celandines), and they are slipping out of their blue attire too (bluebells and violets). Now crimsons and whites are all the rage, tall red campion shooting up, two feet tall, racing for the light against the delicate white fretwork of cow parsley – 'gypsy lace', the schoolchildren used to call it, and maybe still do. Snakes of spineless bryony twine round anything they can find to support them in the hedges.

This time of Covid is a curious mix of curse and blessing. The plug has been pulled out of the socket. No engine roar; no tyre swish from the valley road. No cars climb Slippery Lane, poisoning walkers with their diesel farting. Birdsong seems twice as loud; the woods seethe with insect hum. No contrails in the abnormally blue sky. And a tantalising spring of unbelievably sunny days in a long straight line.

Halfway up the hill, we glance over a gate and are struck

stock-still by something we've never seen here before: three brown hares, great fat fellows, twitching their black-tipped ears in the lush unmown grass of Long Field. They face one another like cats, socially distancing, but only just.

A chiffchaff has been getting his declaration in order down in Valley Wood. '*Chiff-chiff! Chaff! Chiff-chaff-chaff! Chiff-chaff!*' Now he stows his gab, and there's just the fat hum of a bee in the campion and a rustle of grasses in Long Field – Three Hares Field, it will be from now on – where the hares crouch and lollop, nibbling stems and measuring each other up, indifferent to our little existence.

The Bird Spa

On the northern edge of the village, the short steep lane called Stony Sleight demands a bit of care. The surface is rubbly and irregular, with ribs of exposed reddish rock halfway up. You stumble and stub your boot toes as you climb; you skid and slither on the way down. But it's a short way down from the hills to the village, and it's a favourite singing spot for birds towards nightfall.

In these strange limbo days of lockdown, walking has taken on a curious sheen of intensity. One's eyes and ears seem double-focused on the details of grasses and leaves, the timbre of birdsong and the shapes of the hills. Corners of the woods and fields that I had always taken as read now demand that I stop, look and listen, rather than powering on by with the next skyline in mind. There's an acute pleasure in this slower and denser tempo, once you surrender to it.

I've known of the old stone-lined sheep dip near the top of Stony Sleight since I was a boy. I must have trudged past it a hundred times. But until a few days ago I'd never turned aside to open the gate, sit on the bank and simply watch.

There must be a spring in the bank or the sheep dip itself, because the level is pretty constant – a few inches of dull bronze water with a muddy margin and some stones and rocks. Leafy ash branches swing low above the pool, offering concealment. Flies and midges are always circling over the water. In short, it's a perfect place for birds to take their regular baths.

I've stopped to watch the evening ablutions of the birds several times this week. The first on the waterline is generally a blue tit. A coal tit with a black waistcoat has been a regular. Other bathers have included a great tit, a robin and a young and wary thrush. Last night at the sheep dip, there was a chiffchaff with a dashing piratical stripe through its eye, and a female blackcap with a pale chest and velvety brown cap. They all follow the same ritual – a hasty duck of the head to begin with, then full immersion, splashing the water all over themselves and sending up rainbow-tinted showers of droplets, washing off dust, dirt and miniature parasites before flying up into the hanging foliage to preen and smooth their feathers.

It might be anthropomorphic to suggest that these little songbirds revel in their sheep dip shower-baths, but that's exactly what it looks like.

41

I is for Islands

… specifically those gloopy, gluey, marsh-and-mud islands of
the Essex coast. Why does no one go walking in Essex? If
ever there were a candidate for that supreme tourist board
cliché, 'Britain's Best Kept Secret', it's the moody and mysterious coast that lies downriver of London. Flat, people
think, perhaps; boring, tacky, brassy, what's the point when
you've got the Chilterns? But that is exactly the point – everyone who walks near London is in the Chilterns or on the
North Downs, and Essex is beautifully empty and free for an
island-hopper who can think outside the Hebridean box to go
wandering with binoculars and a good thick scarf.

Essex and islands? Yes, indeed, a whole jigsaw scatter of
them, out at the far end of causeways or short bridges, each
with its own grandstand of a sea wall path, each exuding that
very particular island magic of not quite being part of the
humdrum world. Here's a roll-call of my favourites: Canvey
Island, lying tight against the north Thames shore, half
grazing marsh and bird reserve, half housing, a hothouse of
down'n'dirty R & B music; huge wedge-shaped Foulness in
the mouth of the Thames, sealed off by the military but open
once a month for curious explorers to venture across; Wallasea
Island in the crook of Foulness, where the sea walls have been
breached to make a brilliant new bird marsh.

Swinging north, the islands of the Blackwater estuary: hard

up against Maldon and its sea salt works, Northey Island, a National Trust Reserve, where Danes once slaughtered Saxons; Osea Island in the throat of the channel with its zigzag causeway over the mud; big oval Mersea Island where sailing boat halyards chink musically as you savour a dozen fresh oysters in the Company Shed restaurant.

Go east, young man and woman – you won't regret it.

42

Freemining in the Forest of Dean

Deep under the floor of the Forest of Dean, I was walking half-crouched down a dark road. In front of me, a tunnel sloped away at thirty degrees into blackness. Behind, a tiny oblong of sunlit greenery steadily diminished. The only sounds were two pairs of boots scuffing the Hopewell Colliery's clay floor, and the *pit-pat* of water dripping from the rock roof.

'The Forest is like a saucer, do you see?' said Robin Morgan, born-and-bred Forester, his hands shaping his meaning. A glint of daylight from the distant mine entrance caught his classic pitman's profile: helmet, electric lamp, bushy sideburns, strong features. 'The old Speech House pub, he's down at the lowest part, right in the middle. The coal comes up to the grass in a big circle all round, at the rim of the saucer. And that's where the pits are.'

There is no more idiosyncratic corner of Britain than the Forest of Dean. These 30,000 heavily wooded acres in southwest Gloucestershire look west into Wales from a broad arrowhead of land between Severn and Wye. But the Forest is really a land apart, and the Foresters a people who do not quite fit any mould, English or Welsh.

At the centre of the Forest stands the Speech House, built in the reign of King Charles II to house the ancient Verderers Court. It was the Verderers who administered forest law;

they still do, ceremonially, today. All around rise the trees – oak, beech, birch, firs, hollies – thirty-five square miles of dense woodland cover, round whose periphery the Forest villages lie scattered. And below the trees, villages and roads, deep in the sandstone and coal seams, run the Forest mines, a tangled branching network of disused drifts, tunnels and levels stretching for miles in all directions, unseen and largely unsuspected by visitors to the Forest of Dean.

Robin is a freeminer. To qualify for this special status, you must be born within the hundred of St Briavels – in other words, in the Forest of Dean. When you have worked in a pit for a year and a day, you can apply for a 'gale' of Crown land and mine it yourself as a freeminer.

Robin first went down a mine at the age of thirteen, sick and dizzy, lowered 100 feet in a forty-gallon tin drum by his father and brothers. He's been a coal miner for fifty years, most of that time working for himself as a freeminer. Now, in addition to his commercially operating Phoenix mine, he has opened the old Hopewell Colliery as a 'live' museum to show visitors and locals alike what freemining is really all about.

There are only a couple of commercially viable pits operating in the Forest of Dean. It's good coal, but foreign imports have ruined the price. Foresters have been predicting the end of freemining for decades now, but the thousand-year-old tradition just won't lie down.

'I wouldn't dream of doing any other work,' Robin said as we stood at the gleaming coalface. 'It's what you're bred to. When you get under the ground – well, you're entirely your own man. Any worries you have up top just fall away. It's the best job in the world. I'd like visitors to the Forest to get an idea of it – and young locals, too, so the tradition of it won't be lost.'

43

Dawn chorus

As I arrived in Aldbury, one of the most chocolate-box-perfect villages in the Chiltern Hills, the church clock was striking four in the morning. Not a dog barked, not a bird chirped among the dark houses. The magnificent beechwoods of the Ashridge estate, high on the chalk escarpment behind the village, lay silent and wreathed in mist. Then a solitary blackbird started singing in a garden. Others began adding their mellifluous, expressive voices in ones and twos. By the time I had climbed the flinty track and was up among the trees, it sounded as if the village far below were hosting a blackbird eisteddfod.

The mist was shredding away between the silvery beech trunks as I reached a clearing at the crest of the ridge. A fallen bough offered a rough seat. I sat and shivered, gazing out over the valley where daylight was beginning to broaden, although the sun was still a good hour below the skyline at my back. In the treetops, pigeons were cooing, their throaty burble overlain by the fluting of blackbirds and thrushes.

Suddenly, a flicker of movement caught my eye. A tiny brown bird alighted on a fallen branch across the clearing, drew itself up and began reeling off a twittering, high-speed scramble of a song. Two hours earlier, hauling myself out of bed in the dead of night to go walking in the dark, I had sincerely questioned my own sanity. But now, watching the jaunty little wren flirt his retroussé sprig of a tail not twenty feet away, I thanked my stars I had made the effort.

There is nothing remotely like the experience of hearing the dawn chorus in full strength and at close quarters, especially when you are sitting on a beech bough, the only walker in the whole wide wood, with a grandstand view opening slowly at your feet. It certainly rates as one of the major thrills of anyone's year; a national treasure that's celebrated under the title Dawn Chorus Day every year on the first Sunday of May.

There's a serious side to Dawn Chorus Day in the UK, because in these islands that fabulous daily orison of the birds is thinner and quieter than it was thirty years ago. The RSPB reckons some of our most familiar songbirds are under threat from intensive farming practices. They include such favourites as blackbirds, hedge sparrows, song thrushes and yellowhammers – even the seemingly ubiquitous and indestructible starling. Publicising this decline is vital to helping to reverse it, hence the RSPB urging anyone who likes walking and loves birdsong to get up early and stroll out among the fields and woods at sunrise on Dawn Chorus Day.

It was a memorable walk I had, alone among the Ashridge beeches in the first pale flush of dawn. When the sun did get itself up above the ridge, it shone on woods ringing and trickling with twenty different intermingling songs. As well as the blackbirds, the thrushes and that flirty wren, I heard chaffinches, warblers and a blackcap. I thought I made out the football rattle of a lesser whitethroat, but that might have been wishful thinking. I saw a muntjac deer, almost close enough to put my hand on. Breakfast back at the Greyhound in Aldbury tasted like heaven, flavoured as it was with several miles' tramping and all that gorgeous birdsong.

Richard Jefferies, the sublime Victorian rural writer, was a great walker and wanderer in his youth. Late in his short life, confined to bed during a terminal illness, he gained solace from the dawn chorus heard through the open window of his sickroom:

It is sweet on waking in the early morn to listen to the small bird singing in the tree. The bird upon the tree utters the meaning of the wind – a voice of the grass and wild flowers, words of the green leaf; they speak through that slender tone. Sweetness of dew and rifts of sunshine, the dark hawthorn touched with breadth of open bud, the odour of air, the colour of the daffodil – all that is delicious and beloved of spring-time are expressed in his song.[3]

Ladder of life

In valleys of springs of rivers
By Ony and Teme and Clun,
The country for easy livers,
The quietest under the sun.

So warbles Alfred Edward Housman, blithely. It's beautiful deep country west of Ludlow, where the rivers encircle the crumpled hills. Heading for an afternoon's walking on Offa's Dyke up around Churchtown and the River Unk, I stop at the Sun Inn in Clun to give the rain showers a chance to die off. Conversation in the taproom is as quiet and easy as Housman imagined, in rich rural tones half English, half Welsh.

'Yes,' says one man, 'I've spent all my life on the bottom rung of the ladder.' His friend nods, slowly. 'Well,' he murmurs, 'I've spent all my life climbing that ladder.' A ruminative inch is sucked off the top of the pint. 'But some bugger keeps a-cutting the bottom off, so I never do get any higher, you see.'

J is for Jollity

… you know, that thing we all associate with walking. Don't we? Don't we, lads and lasses, eh? Heard this 'un? The missus – she's so bow-legged, she can walk over Ingleborough on both sides at once. Eh? Eh? Boom-tish, eh? Come on, yer miserable bastards, let's have a smile! And a song while we're about it, eh? 'Climbing over rocky moun-tain / Skipping rivulet and foun-tain…'

As a scowling teenager – and boy, could I scowl for England – I was once part of a group dragooned over Dartmoor by a walk leader like that. Needless to say, neither smile, song nor utterance passed our lips. When our man fell in a bog, we laughed, briefly. But that was the only jot or tittle of jollity in forty-eight hours of pure embarrassment leavened with large helpings of hatred.

Now that I'm a big boy, and don't basically give a damn what anyone thinks of me, I like a pinch of jollity with my walks. Or better still, after them, with a pint in the hand and another in the bush. Best of all is the Boxing Day ritual observed by jolly fools at the Seymour Arms, down a lane at the end of nowhere not too far from where I live. A post– Christmas pudding hike up the hill for a tune and a dance on the Bronze Age chieftain's tomb at the top; a dance and a tune in the public bar (wooden benches, wooden tables, 1950s decorations, coal fire); a proper pint drawn from a barrel; the mummers in ribbons and preposterous hats; music-hall songs and genial nonsense.

What has that got to do with walking? Nothing. But the jollity wouldn't be anything without the walk that special day, and vice versa, with knobs on – big red ones, eh? Eh?

46

Dunes of delight

Dreaming my dreams of springtime at a frosted kitchen window in a West Country valley still in thrall to late winter, I thought of May in Northumberland and couldn't stop grinning. Yes! That magnificent stretch of coast at Alnmouth I'd walked years before in high summer with its lonely, windswept beaches, the red-roofed village on the headland and a rampart of flowery sand dunes with gaps leading down to the sea. How would it be in the cusp of spring with the terns plunging after fish and the dune-backs crimson with cranesbill?

I couldn't wait. To stave off the cravings, I phoned my previous walking companion Iain Robson, recreation and access officer for the Northumberland Coast Area of Outstanding Natural Beauty.

'Yes, the terns'll be there in May,' advised Iain, 'and look out for puffins, too. Flowers? Carpets of bloody cranesbill, you're right, and cowslips should still be out. Oh, it's a beautiful spot – I envy you!'

Getting out of the train at Alnmouth railway station a couple of months later, I found a glorious spring morning, cool and blowy enough – this was Northumberland, after all – but calling me irresistibly seawards, where giant white ice-cream clouds contended for mastery on a sky field of pale porcelain blue. Down in the red-walled lanes of Alnmouth, I sniffed the tang of North Sea salt on the wind – no figure of speech, but a definite ozone sting in the nostrils, blowing briskly up the Lovers' Walk path. Nothing more invigorating for a man who'd been bent all winter over a keyboard like a six-foot builder's ruler.

These days, a nice firm cycle track leads down through the grazing meadows south of Alnmouth, depositing you in a mile or so among the tall sand dunes of Buston Links. Here was floral heaven. How the dune plants loved these lime-rich mini-mountains of sand with their damp slacks and sheltering hollows. The bloody cranesbill lay spread as Iain had promised, sheets of it in episcopal purple, each papery petal fluttering in the sea breeze. Further along, I passed a dune slope rippling so vigorously with floral bells – delicate yellow cowslips bowing and shaking, pale blue harebells trembling – that one half expected to hear a whisper of ringing and jingling in the wind.

Walking south along the beach in the shelter of the dunes, I watched arctic terns fluttering above their selected patch of sea and plummeting into the water with a splash, to rise almost instantly and fly off. I couldn't spot the fish they were catching, but through binoculars I admired their sleek black caps and scarlet stilettos of beaks. Several hundred yards out to sea were the puffins, buzzing along just above the waves with rapid little wing beats, as tubby and fussy as commuters late for the train.

On Birling Links, golfers in tartan trews were thrashing around, trying to keep their balls in order. Hmmm, tricky today, Gregor! A brassie, a spoon or a cleek, d'ye think? Curse this wind! Perhaps a baffie, Rodney – or even a mashie-niblick? I didn't envy them their 'good walk spoiled' one little bit. It was a day for briskly striding out, for hands in pockets and hair flying into tangles.

I could cheerfully have walked on and on along the windy beach and the flowery dunes. But it was time to turn inland, up through the gap in the dunes and across the Norman bridge over the River Coquet into Warkworth. Above the little town towered the great castle, ancestral home of the Percys, at whose gate Shakespeare has the Earl of Northumberland receiving the news of the death of his son Harry Hotspur in *Henry IV, Part II*. In that gateway, I ate my marmite-and-tomato sandwich, impudence in the shadow of dignity.

47

Apple confetti

They puzzled me at first, those delicate flakes of pink and white that kept circling in my beer glass. As quickly as I fished them out with a fingertip, more of the little papery craft would appear, dropping as if by magic. Confetti? But where from? I noticed a couple of funny looks from the other customers in the Carpenters Arms and went to the lavatory to check that I wasn't walking around with half my lunch in my beard or my nether buttons undone. A glance in the mirror solved the mystery. My head and shoulders were powdered with apple blossom petals, collected unbeknownst to me throughout this breezy spring day that I had spent roaming the orchards of the north Kent Downs.

I had been feeling a little woozy before I even reached Eastling village and the Carpenters Arms. There was a headiness around the orchards, a soporific air made up of the hum of bees, the warmth of May, the chirping of finches, the rich smell of the chalky clay and the sweet, heavy scent of the blossom. With nearly twenty miles under my belt, I found myself staggering about like a drunken sailor on the path between Newnham and Doddington. Half an hour with my head on my pack among the bluebells of Sharsted Wood sorted me out. It was the sort of incapacity a walker half-expects on a balmy spring day in the sleepy downland country of north Kent.

Maybe it's the shelter lent to this landscape by the dip and roll of the North Downs that makes the breeze blow so softly and the air seem so dense and drowsy. Everything is small-scale and intimate – the hedged fields; the squared orchards; the woods of beech, hornbeam and oak. The villages through which I went tramping sit neatly along a tangle of lanes, the main rise of the downs climbing away to the south. It's an elastic landscape built on a wedge of chalk hundreds of feet thick, laid down a hundred million years ago, when all of north Kent lay flat on the bed of a warm tropical sea.

How many of our living landscapes do we owe to long-dead volcanic upheavals? The one that burst out of the seabed here some sixty-five million years ago distorted the Kentish chalk and the greensand that lay beneath it into a bulging vault. Aeons of erosion wore away the soft chalk topping into a collar around a dome of greensand and clay, the foundation of the thick woodlands of the Kentish Weald. The chalk collar, meanwhile, formed the smoothish, steepish flanks of the North and South Downs that buttress the Weald on either side.

Together with the shelter of the downs and hills, the slight breezes and the long warm summers of the region, the north Kentish earth provided the perfect environment for fruit-growing. Things kicked off properly in the reign of Henry VIII, whose fruiterer, Richard Harrys, successfully established cherry-growing hereabouts. Apples, plums and pears followed, covering the hills and the lowlands all the way north to the shores of the Thames. Kent became 'the orchard of England', so much so that trainloads of sightseers would come out from London in Victorian times for a day among the blossoms.

On solitary walks, I'm an inveterate hummer of tunes and whistler of ditties. Yet early in the day, stopping on the hillside above the village of Painters Forstal, I was literally struck dumb by the weirdness as much as the beauty of the scene: a flood of pure white apple blossom clothed the rolling fields as tightly as a second skin. Down in the orchards, I found the explanation – the apple trees, far from being the house-high structures I remembered from childhood, were now stunted little things, row on row of chest-high treelets specially grown from dwarfing rootstock to make their fruit easier to harvest.

Never mind the Lilliputian stature of the trees – the scent and sight of their blossom enriched the day. And, in the afternoon, I finally found some proper upstanding apple and plum trees in Stuart Doughty's orchard near Doddington. Stuart grows what he likes because he likes them, he told me as he fingered the blossom-laden branches and murmured the names of the old traditional strains like a green druid lost in an incantation: Lord Lambourne, Emneth Early, Coe's Golden Drop, Kidd's Orange Red.

Back in the Carpenters Arms, one of the drinkers paused by my table on his way out. He dabbed up a couple of petals of 'confetti' with a wetted fingertip and inspected them, and then me.

'Enjoy the wedding?' he grinned.

Explanations would have been too tedious, words too pallid. 'Yes,' I said, 'oh, yes – a beautiful day.'

SUMMER

48

The Garden of Sleep

Only a few sights have really stopped me in my tracks, but the big wheat field near Sidestrand on the cliffs of North Norfolk was one of them. There had been some kind of financial cutback; the farmer wasn't spraying everything in sight with pesticides, and it looked as if someone had smeared the yellowing corn with blood. The poppies were back, and they'd come mob-handed, in uncountable numbers – sheets of the big papery flowers, a scarlet tide unleashed from underground, where the seeds had lain dormant since modern farm chemicals first came in. It was astonishing, mind-blowing – a sight I will never forget.

What would Clement Scott have said if he could have revisited the North Norfolk coast, his beloved 'Poppyland', while the pesticides were raining down? We think of the First World War, and the poignant associations of millions of blood-red flowers in Flanders fields, as the catalyst for the affectionate nostalgia we all feel on catching sight of a field of poppies in full bloom. But it was the London journalist Scott who first lodged the scarlet cornfield weed in the public heart. Visiting the Norfolk coast on assignment from the *Daily Telegraph* in August 1883 to write about the summer season at Cromer, Scott went walking through the clifftop cornfields and fell madly in love with the place.

A blue sky without a cloud across it; a sea sparkling under a haze of heat; wild flowers in profusion around me, poppies predominating everywhere, the hedgerows full of blackberry blossom and fringed with meadowsweet; the bees busy at their work, the air filled with insect life, the song-birds startled from the standing corn as I pursued my solitary way.[4]

Blue sky, sparkling sea, blackberries and meadowsweet, the birds and the bees... what powerful triggers, what teasing icons of rustic innocence for Scott's London-based readers in the days before *Countryfile*. Once he'd found digs with the miller in the unspoilt village of Sidestrand and hinted at a possible romance with the miller's apple-cheeked daughter, the spell was complete. But it couldn't have worked without the poppies, symbols of ephemeral beauty, that Scott sprinkled so cunningly throughout his writings, nor without the name he came up with to characterise these cornfields and quiet villages of the North Norfolk coast – Poppyland.

How ironic that modern agricultural practices should have killed off not only the simple horse-paced life of those rural communities but also the poppies and other cornfield flowers that added so greatly to their charm. The cause and effect couldn't be clearer: you spray the weeds with targeted poisons, and they die. The trouble is that one man's pesky weed is another man's beautiful wild flower. During the 1990s, EU attempts to reduce the notorious 'grain mountains' made it compulsory for farmers to take 10 per cent of their land out of production each year. Farmers who refrained from spraying these set-aside fields with pesticides were rewarded by the return of many species of arable wild flowers that had been assumed dead and gone – and by the reappearance of butterflies, birds, hares, hedgehogs, frogs, newts and lots of other wildlife that thrives on these plants and their seeds.

In 2008, a trend of poor harvests across the EU saw the set-aside policy abolished. But some environmentally friendly farmers continued with it on a voluntary basis, leaving broad uncultivated strips or headlands around their fields to encourage wildlife. These measures helped the poppy return – not everywhere, and not without blips and hitches, but it was a steady comeback, thanks to the Rip Van Winkle–like ability of the plant's seeds to slumber in dormancy for decades, then spring forth once more.

A dozen species of *Papaver* grow in the UK, some rarer and more endangered than others. Some, like the little prickly poppy, still cling to the cornfields, where agrochemicals continue to threaten their existence. But others, such as the common poppy, the one we all recognise, have learned to adapt to life on the margins, thriving on headlands and in road verges – you can see a fabulous display in the central reservation of the Lewes road out of Brighton, for example. They are on the way back in our arable countryside too, especially at a time of economic belt-tightening when farmers are trying to cut costs. Take a walk through the barley and wheat fields east of Cromer, and you can still see what Scott meant when he composed his poem 'The Garden of Sleep':

On the grass of the cliff, at the edge of the steep,
God planted a garden – a garden of sleep!
'Neath the blue of the sky, in the green of the corn,
It is there that the regal red poppies are born!

They don't write them like that any more. But you can

see exactly where the man was coming from. The sight of a blood-red flood of poppies moves us as much now as it did back then, and it probably always will.

49

Covid Summer: off-grid in Dragondown Wood

Quarry Hill looms on the skyline to the south of the village. A steep climb up and we have the hilltop to ourselves, a humpback plateau of thin grass over limestone, where the last of the early purple orchids are bowing to the inevitable. The long moment is savoured in an absence of traffic roar from the all-but-deserted valley road. The Covid pandemic has garaged all the cars. We sit and stare round the compass: north over the village to the snaky curves of Slippery Lane; west over the massive dark red face of the old quarry; and on down into a place apart, the green vale of Dragondown.

The vale lies under Quarry Hill, and a dragon lies under the vale. So the old story says. Anything or anyone could be hiding in those dense old woods that cap the slope beyond. Massive thistles grow six feet tall there, their multiple heads packed tight, defended by collars of formidable spikes.

A wandering path climbs in among the trees, and as it dips we find ourselves ankle-deep in wild garlic, its flowers beginning to droop in the shade of the canopy. A little spring issues from a cleft among the garlic, trickling along channels between miniature walls of rounded stones placed there by hand. We debate who it could be that has the time and involvement to create such a water garden; we get our answer down in the heart of the wood, when we spot a cluster of canvas tents and round wooden houses deep among the trees.

No flimsy bender tents, no moth-eaten shelters here. These are proper dwellings, stoutly made and carefully maintained, with a cookhouse, a pond and amphitheatre seating. These folk are not campers but permanent residents of Dragondown Wood.

Birdsong pours through the trees; a green light dapples the path as it winds behind the settlement. On a summer's day like this, off-grid living looks easy. In a freezing wet February, it must be all about grit and stubbornness. Hats off to anyone who can genuinely live this way.

On the upland beyond, we meet a bunch of young White Park cattle with black noses and long curvilinear horns. They snuff our fingers and sneeze explosively. Good job the virus is only for human consumption; not one of the heifers has a hankie.

50

With Rupert Brooke through
Grantchester Meadows

In 1909 Rupert Brooke, the golden boy of Cambridge University, decided to take up lodgings in the village of Grantchester among the meadows of the River Cam a couple of miles south of the city.

> Stands the Church clock at ten to three?
> And is there honey still for tea?

Those are the most famous lines from Brooke's poem 'The Old Vicarage, Grantchester', written in 1912, while Brooke was on holiday in Berlin. Far from being the sentimental schmaltzfest it's often taken for, the poem actually pokes wicked fun at the complacency of Grantchester's highbrow villagers. The golden boy could be pretty waspish. But he achieved heroic status in the public imagination by dying young during the Great War and by writing that war's classic patriotic sonnet, 'The Soldier' ('If I should die, think only this of me…'). The British at war were filled with nostalgia for the sun-kissed Edwardian world, and they found irresistible echoes of it in the verses of Brooke.

Brooke adored his 'lovely and dim and rustic life' in Grantchester. He wrote to a friend, 'I love being there so much – more than any place I've ever lived in. I love the place and especially the solitude so much.' He left his name in the village, inscribed on the war memorial in the shadow of the church tower and that celebrated clock.

The signboard outside the Rupert Brooke pub in Grantchester carries a picture of a clock with hands stopped at... well, I'm sure you can guess. I set out from there on a gorgeous summer's day of muted colours, with the chaffinches singing their hearts out in the trees and a pale sun trying hard to burn away the morning mists off the River Cam. Down the road, I passed the Old Vicarage where Brooke lodged with the Neeve family in 1911 – it was the honey from Mr Neeve's bees that made its way into Rupert's poem – and, next door, The Orchard, where he took a room when he first arrived in Grantchester. Just beyond, Grantchester Mill House stood over its rushing mill race, a symbol of peace and of quiet solidity as powerful today as it was a century ago for the young man scribbling his verses in the Berlin café:

> Oh, is the water sweet and cool,
> Gentle and brown, above the pool?
> And laughs the immortal river still
> Under the mill, under the mill?

I leaned on the wall, staring at the eddies and whorls of the water as it bubbled under the mill. An old-fashioned bicycle with a basket slung from its handlebars stood under a weeping willow on the river bank, and nearby a young undergraduate lay on the grass eating an apple as she read through her lecture notes. The crisp crunch of teeth in apple flesh sounded clearly over the mill-pool.

Out in Grantchester Meadows, I followed the path beaten out by countless undergraduate feet beside the river. Brooke and his friends often came here to picnic, chase each other through the fields and go skinny-dipping in the slow brown waters of the Cam. On this lovely afternoon, the river bank was dotted with recumbent young men and women, snoozing and kissing, reading and talking nonsense in timeless undergraduate style. Every minute or so, someone would leap up and spring into the river with a tremendous splash, to the accompaniment of loud cheers. A grey and grave pair of senior figures strolled the path with measured dignity, heads courteously inclined, hands behind backs, the very picture of academic deliberation.

'Well, my dear,' I heard one of them say as they paced impressively by, 'she was wearing the most out*rageous* high heels I have *ever* seen!'

Nearing the city, the path passed through a series of grazing greens set with willows and seamed with glittering water channels. Dogs rolled ecstatically in the grass, as if they had been injected with a super-strong dose of delight. Bicyclists whirred by. And, as the first spires and crockets of the Cambridge colleges began to show themselves beyond the treetops, I caught sight of my first punt of the day – surely the calmest and most sleepy of all modes of water transport. The boy in the stern was poling with one hand and texting with the other – a rather remarkable feat – while his girl, gracefully arranged in the bows, gazed at him with the kind of look that springtime was invented for. Some things don't change, it seems.

51

Gannets of the Bass Rock

You wouldn't want a northern gannet as a next-door neighbour. The biggest seabird in the North Atlantic is a quarrelsome individual, with a beak as long and sharp as an ice axe that it doesn't hesitate to use on anyone invading its personal space. It's a messy nester too. And it emits a raucous squawk only slightly less attractive than its ever-present effluvium of rotting fish. But there's something about a gannet – or rather, a gannet colony 100,000 strong – that ends up captivating you, if you can stomach the stink and the screeching long enough to get to close quarters with these avian dive-bombers and wide-sea wanderers.

Boarding *Sula II* in North Berwick Harbour on a calm May morning, I still wasn't sure whether the fates were with us or not. The largest island colony of gannets on the east coast is long established on the Bass Rock, a huge volcanic plug that towers 350 feet from the waters of the Firth of Forth, some twenty-five miles east of Edinburgh. Plenty can go wrong with plans to land on the Bass – usually it's to do with too much sea swell at the slippery landing place. If you can't land, the boat makes a leisurely circuit off the Bass to allow you to admire the gannets as they spiral above you or plunge into the sea after fish. That's always a bit of a disappointment, however stunning the spectacle. But that day, reckoned the boatman, we'd be canny.

The Bass gannets return to the rock in January from their winter quarters off the north-west African coast. By early spring, they are paired up; by May, they are guarding a single egg on their grass-and-seaweed nests. The fluffy chicks soon hatch, but then take a full three months to fledge. Most don't survive into adulthood. Those that live and thrive follow their parents south in August and September. On this day in early summer, the parent birds would be anchored firmly to the nests, where I'd be able to appreciate them at very close quarters indeed.

The extraordinary sight of a dense cloud of gannets streaming leeward of the Bass is commonplace to locals, but it never fails to draw gasps from visitors. The birds circle and circle and circle, as if incapable of fatigue. How they avoid mid-air collisions is a miracle and a mystery. It's only when you get your eye in that you notice individuals peeling off from the main body to return to their clifftop nests, and others arriving to join the ever-turning cartwheel of birds above the rock.

From down at sea level, I hardly noticed the noise that these 100,000 birds were making. But once I had stepped gingerly ashore, passing the fort and the lighthouse, and was trudging up the zigzag path to the summit, a rhythmical sound like the surging of a giant kettle on the boil began to make itself heard. By the time I reached the viewing place near the summit of the Bass, it had swelled to a muttering roar. The smell of the colony, by contrast, hit me all at once: a fishy stench that initially made me gag but soon shrank into the background of my consciousness. There was plenty else to concentrate on.

Gannets are big – three feet long, with a wingspan nearly twice that – and they are beautiful, with china-white bodies and inner wings, long pointed black wingtips and buff-coloured heads from which protrude those sharp grey beaks. The eyes are a remarkable cold blue, as pale as ice. I watched, fascinated, as birds returning to their nests from fishing trips greeted their mates with a thrusting together of heads, rubbing of beaks and intertwining of necks.

As a human, you get used to being anathema to all wild creatures. They shrink away, they run and hide, they take off. Not so with the Bass Rock gannets. There is simply no room to shuffle sideways without inviting a stabbing from your neighbour's dagger of a bill. If you fly away, a black-backed gull will have your egg in ten seconds flat. So you stay put, eyeballing the stranger, alert for catastrophe but more intent on your own affairs. As for the human intruder – I felt an acute sense of privilege at looking in, from a distance of a couple of feet, on the everyday life of a wild creature. It was something to treasure as I made my way back down the path towards *Sula II*, carrying with me like a keepsake a faint but fishy after-whiff from the gannetry.

52

Covid Summer: the crayfish of Ironmaster's Vale

The woods are full of secrets, and it's taken lockdown to give me eyes to see them. If it hadn't been for these remarkable times and their constraints, I don't suppose I would ever have taken such a close look at the map, day after day, to spy out the tangled webs of purely local walks. What a delight it has been to focus in on a knoll, or cleft, or patchwork of fields, and realise that my own countryside is still a mystery and an enticement.

Ironmaster's Vale runs east–west, a very twisty and narrow stream hollow that's not quite a gorge and not a valley either. Sunk in here among the trees are the ruins of an iron-grinding industry – arches, walls, spillways, sluices, old rotten beams thick with ferns; limekilns and millstones, caves and quarries.

A footpath meanders through the vale, with side turnings leading off through the nettles and butterbur. The narrowest and least noticeable of these unofficial trails leads to a most remarkable quarry wall, a concave sweep of grey carboniferous limestone about 350 million years old canted at a steep angle, with a cap of buttery yellow oolitic limestone lying horizontally on top, where it was deposited about 180 million years ago. 'De La Beche's unconformity' is its rather angular name – a geologist's thrill, and a questioning mind's delight.

Two boys were dipping for crayfish in the stream. They had caught one apiece, the lobster-like creatures about five inches long scuttling round the bottom of their bucket. These white-clawed crayfish, natives of Britain, are threatened by an invasion of American signal crayfish, which are bigger and tougher. The newcomers also carry a plague to which our chaps have no resistance.

So crayfish have their worries, too.

53

The figurehead of our wild lands

Countryside ranger Duncan Macdonald and I were out exploring a side cleft of the Monadhliath Mountains, one of the most accessible but least-frequented mountain ranges in Scotland. Our chosen glen was within walking distance of the village of Newtonmore, but its exact location has to remain a secret. Golden eagles are active in its upper reaches, and – incredibly as it seems to most people – there are those who'd like to shoot them or steal their eggs.

The first thing we spotted was a roe deer with her fawn, a dark brown infant with a white scut that flagged the retreat of mother and offspring into the trees. High overhead, a group of red deer stags was feeding along the ridge, their branched antlers outlined against the sky. Still in their 'gentleman's club' at this stage of the summer, by autumn they'd be collecting harems of hinds and warning each other fiercely away.

In the broad green bottom of the strath, or lower valley, we passed through the mossy foundations of houses that had once formed a cattle-herding community here. The Highland glens are scattered with the poignant remains of such former settlements, many of them emptied during the notorious nineteenth-century Highland Clearances in which families were evicted and their farms and fields destroyed to make way for more profitable sheep. Search around in the heather and grass near burns or rivers in a grassy, flat-bottomed strath, said

Duncan, and you're almost certain to find the foundations of the square-built two-roomed houses shared by a family and its beasts. Higher up the glen, often in sheltered hollows but always near a water source, look for the ruins of shielings, or summer residences, roughly-built huts where people stayed while the cattle grazed the rich mountain grass.

The way led up the side glen, along a stony track on which people would drive their beasts in spring to graze them all summer in the high mountains. Wild flowers carpeted the hill slopes – lady's bedstraw, eyebright, pink bonnets of lousewort, fragrant bog myrtle. Buzzards wheeled overhead; meadow pipits flitted and cheeped. As we climbed, Duncan gave me a short course in the geology of this wild landscape.

The Monadhliath Mountains are based on ancient schist, a grey rock up to 700 million years old. Like all the mountains of Scotland, they were subjected to unimaginable pressures when the Ice Age glaciers rolled over them, up to a mile thick. The rocks were squeezed, pressed, ground and smoothed into the rounded shapes so characteristic of the Cairngorms and Monadhliaths. When the glaciers melted and retreated some 10,000 years ago, torrents of meltwater spread the ground-up rock in the form of moraines, or ridges. The mountain rivers have cut through these high banks, whose rubbly material is exposed by landslips. Frost is still working on the exposed faces of the mountains, shattering them in frequent falls of rocks.

As an example of an unspoilt glen, the valley we were climbing that day couldn't have been better. And although the day's wind and rain weren't conducive to seeing a golden eagle soar among the mountain crests, we did catch two tantalising glimpses of this true monarch of the glen – split-second sightings of great wings with feathered finger ends, tilting round the slope of the mountain.

Golden eagles mate for life. A pair can control a territory of up to forty square miles and might have a dozen nests within that area, generally on rock ledges. You'll see fledged youngsters flying from late summer onwards, with conspicuous white patches. It's vital to avoid disturbing the eagles or exposing them to shooters and egg collectors, so nesting sites tend to be kept secret. But a day of sunshine and showers is often productive of sightings in remote glens for walkers who keep their eyes open and binoculars ready.

The golden eagle's future, disconcertingly, is still in the balance. 'Scots have a deep-rooted natural affinity with this bird,' said Duncan. 'It's an archetype, the figurehead of our wild lands. Yet we go on persecuting it, displacing it, poisoning it. I find that extraordinary. We've got to start celebrating it! Education and celebration, that's the key.'

Of all the wildlife splendours of back-country Scotland, the sight of a golden eagle in flight sits right at the top of Duncan's list. 'It still raises the hair on the back of my neck,' he admitted as we went back down the glen. 'Still gives me the biggest thrill. There's still nothing does it for me like seeing a golden eagle in a totally wild landscape.'

The Ringing Stone of Tiree

'Now, here are the reports from coastal stations. Tiree: north, seven, increasing gale eight. Precipitation within sight. Nine-nine-seven, falling rapidly.'

On a June visit to Coll and Tiree, the twin islands at the outermost edge of the Inner Hebrides, there is always a chance that the Atlantic may brew up one of its spectacular summer sulks. Tiree men, so they say, walk ten degrees out of true through leaning against the wind. Now I was for it: there was going to be an almighty blow.

'Tir-i-odh' – 'the land of corn', scapula-shaped 'granary of the isles' – lies low and green at the trailing hem of the Hebrides. Looking down from the Twin Otter plane as it bucked and side-slipped under the rising wind, I saw dark blue turn to milky turquoise, a tropical brilliance of clear water shallowing over white shell sand. Then we thumped down on Tiree's airfield among sheets of ox-eye daisies and buttercups thrashing wildly in the gale.

Out on the north-eastern shank of the island, the long-standing walls of the houses, freshly whitewashed for the summer, stuck out far beyond their skimpy modern saddle-back roofs. Chimney smoke streamed away and was blown to rags. One cottage retained its traditional thick topping of thatch, netted against the weather and weighted down with a fringe of dangling bricks and stones.

Spray whipped in from the north, where white rollers were charging into Vaul Bay to explode across half-sunken rocks. A line of lapwings hung twenty feet above the sands, balanced and motionless, unable to move forward. Soon they peeled off and tumbled away inland. I stood on the cliffs for half an hour, buffeted and shoved by the spattering wind, enjoying these wild sights and sounds, before turning west to come to Dun Mor Vaul ('the big fort on the cliff').

Life must have been tough for the immigrant Celts who built this broch, or round defensive structure, against Norse marauders around the first century BC. Double-walled, with the original stone lintels and jambs still in place, it stands high and exposed. For the first 200 years of its existence, there was not even a fireplace in the building.

Tiree, so greenly fertile, was still a valuable prize many hundreds of years after the broch was abandoned. By the late eleventh century, the Normans had conquered most of mainland Britain, but out in these wild parts their writ did not run. King Magnus of Norway sent an expedition over, and the pastoral islanders fell like scythed corn. The poet Bjorn Cripplehand, who witnessed the slaughter, wrote of 'the glad wolf reddening tooth and claw in many a mortal wound in Tiree.'

People have always been able to support themselves, to make things grow, in Tiree. What makes this island so fertile is sand – lime-rich shell sand blown several feet thick across the underlying granite. The soil that built up on the sand drifts grew famous grain for generations. Nowadays, more profitable cattle and sheep graze a grassy type of sward known as machair.

Tyree's green covering of machair is brightly studded with flowers – orchids, buttercups, yarrow, celandines, clovers, yellow rattle, stonecrop – pink, white, yellow, blue, purple.

Machair is a soft jewelled carpet, a pure delight to walk on. It led me down through Creagan Mora to the Ringing Stone, a boulder as tall as a man, rounded by wind and spray, its shoulders pocked with saucer-shaped indentations.

I picked up a pebble and struck it into one of the depressions. The Ringing Stone gave out a shimmering, metallic note. Inside lies a crock of gold, they tell you – but if anyone is foolhardy enough to split the stone, Tiree will instantly sink beneath the sea.

55

K is for Kyrgyzstan

… and Katboschfontein, Khatyngnakh, Kyrksæterøra, and many other places I'll never actually walk. They beckon from the index of my 1990 *Times Atlas of the World*, a constant resource and secret delight. Some of these places have actually ceased to exist since that atlas was published – Yugoslavia, Zaire and Czechoslovakia, anyone? Those with what I think of as 'crunchy names' – lots of 'z', 'kh' and 'x' all squashed together in a vowel-free stew – are especially irresistible. You can't dabble in this kind of magic without the risk of being transported on a dream carpet to Lord-knows-where.

I have to sneak a look. Let's take one at random: Xixabangma Feng! Sounds like someone pogoing recklessly downstairs on an outsize tuning fork. Page 24, grid ref E 11. OK… my God, it looks like a giant's porridge bowl. What a lot of white wrinkly stuff. Mountains, yes, of course, the Himalayas. That thick purple worm is the border between Tibet and Nepal. And there's Xixabangma Feng! 8,012 m – that's about… 26,000 feet. Wow, I'd never get up there in a million years, but imagine walking up through those brown foothills, the smell of the yaks, and all that blue sky…

Oh, the power of dreams. And not the Honda sort, either. There is no walk like the walk in the old book, the walk across the one-inch Bartholomew's map in its blue cover that you buy for a quid at the jumble sale.

Is there at this moment a walker in a house in Thayawtha-dangyi Kyun poring over a battered old atlas? Hmmm, where in the wide world shall I take a fantasy walk today? Let the dice decide… Tower Hamlets! Oh, irresistible! Thatched cottages, a castle, a fair maiden on the ramparts, the very sound and smack of Merrie England…

56

A proper Lakeland how-d'ye-do

Grey shawls of rain were twisting in the treetops around Nether Wasdale as I set off between the Screes and the Strands – two fine inns that face each other like rival cats across a tiny green. Last night, Wasdale had wept and roared. Coming back late from the pub to my B & B lodging up at Burnthwaite Farm, I'd met the Mountain Rescue team trudging down from the midnight mists and rains with a stretcher-borne victim of the fell-top storms. But today, a lightening of the western sky showed where better weather was already sailing into the outlying villages of the Lake District from the Irish Sea.

Hedge sparrows chirped and chaffinches chirruped. I crossed the swollen and babbling River Irt and turned down the long stony lane to Easthwaite Farm. You couldn't hope to see a more typical Lakeland scene: the grey stone farm among shelter trees lying under the craggy brown fell of Whin Rigg. The green in-bye fields and lower fellsides rang with the cries of Herdwick sheep, amongst which bounced the farmer on his quad and the sheepdog on its scuttering paws. Further down the lane, I passed a shepherd with a traditional tall crook, striding up one of the ribbon-like stone walls towards his scattered flock.

I recrossed the Irt by the old humpbacked Lund Bridge – built for packhorses on their way down the valley – and walked up the racing stream to the point where it issued in a broad sinuation from the foot of Wastwater. Clouds were pressed down over the brow of Great Gable at the head of the lake, dark and deep under its great plunging screes. Wastwater is the moodiest and wildest – many would say the most magnificent – of all the lakes, and today's bruised sky and thin veils of rain brought out all its sombre and mysterious beauty.

A mile to be savoured along the west flank of Wastwater; then I was making inland along a boggy walled lane that spilt me out through a gateway onto a wide moor seething with wind. There was blue sky ahead in chinks now, and blocks of golden light sliding across the fox-red flanks of Buckbarrow under the fractured dark crags of its head.

A raven went cronking overhead, and Herdwick ewes baaed madly for their fat little lambs. I swung onto a rutted green track, winding between stone-walled pastures on my way down to Nether Wasdale. Just beyond the tight huddle of buildings at Mill Place Farm, I met a solid block of Herdwicks skeltering toward me down the lane with a snapping dog at their heels. The shepherd nodded, and I nodded back: a proper Lakeland how-d'ye-do.

57

Nightjars and moths of Arne Heath

A cloudy summer's evening on the eastern shores of Dorset's Isle of Purbeck. I'm out walking the pathways of Arne Heath in the excellent and knowledgeable company of RSPB warden Mark Singleton and his colleague Rob Farrington. Our long-time friend Patrick Goldsmith has brought along his son Sam, a mustard-keen young naturalist, in hopes of hearing – or even better, seeing – a nightjar, one of Britain's most elusive birds. Its ash-grey spotted plumage blending perfectly with the lowland heath it inhabits, and active only in the murky light of dusk, this bewhiskered summer visitor is rarely seen. To hear its churring – a phlegmy rattle of a call – is the best one can usually hope for.

Nightjars are best seen and heard on warm summer nights such as this. They arrive in Britain from Africa in late spring – the males around the second week of May to sort out their territory, then the females a couple of weeks later. The males show off to the females, displaying the white spots on their wings and clapping their wing tips together above their heads. The churring – a vibration of the vocal cords that can generate 1,900 notes a minute – seems to be uttered partly to repel other males, partly to attract females. Each male has a number of churring posts to sing from. Nightjars can produce up to three broods a year, feeding the young on a gel-like pellet of insects packed tightly together. As soon as the young are fledged, they depart for sub-Saharan Africa, leaving the parent birds to linger until mid-September.

Lowland heaths are pretty rare survivals themselves. Dorset has lost over 80 per cent of the heaths it once possessed. What is left forms a fascinating mosaic of microhabitats rich in specialised wildlife. Arne Heath is founded on beds of sand and gravel left behind by the retreating glaciers 10,000 years ago. The heath developed where men had cleared away the forest, and the grazing of animals and cutting of gorse for fuel extended it. Rainwater filters through the sand, taking most of the nutrients with it, so what plants there are – heather, fragrant bog myrtle, pink lousewort, the cross-shaped yellow flowers of tormentil – tend to thrive on tough living and acid conditions. But if Arne is a harsh environment for plants, it's a haven for many species of insects and animals – smooth snakes, lizards, Dartford warblers, moths, bats, insect-digesting sundews, nightjars themselves – that have adapted to these tricky conditions.

On our walk out to likely nightjar territory, we spot poplar hawk and buff-tip moths, strangely shaped and superbly camouflaged to resemble leaves and twigs. The poplar hawk-moth looks remarkably like a crisp, dried-out poplar leaf, grey-brown and with a strange back-to-front appearance thanks to its stance, with the smaller hindwings pushed forward where you'd expect to see the large forewings. The buff-tip moth couldn't look more like a fragment of snapped-off birch shoot if it tried, with its body as shiny grey as birch bark and its flat buff-coloured face exactly resembling the broken end of a twig.

We pass acidic ponds, beloved of dragonflies, swifts and the little dark falcons called hobbies. We hear the scratchy, intense song of the rare Dartford warbler, and glimpse the dark shapes of Sika deer. Suddenly, a rich and throaty whirring catches our attention. 'Nightjar!' everyone exclaims at once, swiftly followed by 'Ssshhh!' Hawk-eyed Rob soon spots the nightjar sitting on a pine branch. It churrs for several minutes, while we watch it through binoculars with bated breath. Then it takes off and flies almost straight over our heads, a big, rather hesitant shape less than thirty feet off the ground. Sam stands spellbound, as do we all.

'Beauty!' whispers Mark, as our quarry alights in a birch tree, disturbing another male into flight. 'That's up with the very best views I've had of a nightjar.'

Country folk used to believe that nightjars sucked milk from the udders of their goats. There is a witchy charm about these mysterious, seldom-seen birds of the dusk. To see and hear them on their native ground, the wide heathlands of Arne, is something never to be forgotten.

58

Splatchers

'Two large oval boards,' wrote Arthur Ransome in *Secret Water*, 'with rope grips in the middle of them for heel and toe, and stout leather straps for fasteners.'

Oh, the magic of those home-made mud skates and the squelchy poetry of their name, 'splatchers'. That tough young mudlark the Mastodon demonstrated his pair to the Swallows, sliding across the Essex mudbanks like billy-o, swinging each leg round in a wide circle so as not to trip himself up.

Easier to read about than to do, I discovered. Maybe Essex mud was different from the stinking stuff we had at home on the banks of the River Severn. I made myself a pair of splatchers on the Ransome plan and ventured out into the unknown. The Severn's tidal mud, stiff and grey at first, turned within a couple of strides into a gluey porridge underfoot. I swung my legs round like the Mastodon, the splatchers slid up my shins like a pair of cricket pads, and I sank in up to my knees. There was one hell of a struggle back to shore, and a lot of explaining to do once I had squelched home, mud all over.

When I recounted the tale to an Essex islander years later, he laughed himself silly.

'What? Flat boards? No, mate, he was having a bubble. Your splatcher's a V-shape, like a little boat on each foot. Try that, you'll be all right.'

Finally, I will. I'm planning a summer walk out to the

Blackwater estuary islands. They do have causeways over the mud, but I think I'll go off-piste in my V-shaped splatchers – that's after I get round to making them. If I'm gone too long, look for a tuft of white hair in the mud. That'll be me, literally six feet under.

59

Worldwide seed of a single English field

It's very hard to think of a single English field that's more thickly steeped in symbolic importance than Runnymede. Kings and queens, lords and ladies, legislators, poets and guardians of tradition: down the centuries they have come from the four corners of the world to this flat, watery meadow beside the Thames, a few miles upstream of London, to pay their respects, reassert their good intentions and contemplate the history-making events of one summer week 800 years ago.

The meeting in Runnymede meadow in 1215 between King John and his disaffected and angry barons was a tense and mistrustful affair. The negotiations that led to the sealing of Magna Carta, the Great Charter, on 19 June 1215 were inter-woven with treachery, cynicism and tactical manoeuvring. But they laid the foundations for the civil liberties we still enjoy today.

To appreciate the raison d'être of Runnymede as a place of neutral debate, you need to get up high and look down over its setting. The long wooded ridge of Cooper's Hill forms the southern skyline of Runnymede, with the old trackway of Cooper's Hill Lane rising up through the trees to reach the Air Forces Memorial on the crest, 300 feet above the Thames. The memorial, a splendid pavilion, commemorates the 20,000 young airmen and women of the Allied forces who found an unmarked grave during the Second World War. It's a haunting place, the columns of names of many nations seeming to roll out endlessly – Beddow, Behan, Belasco, Bell; Bardichev, Patchesa, Natta, De Bretigny; Chander, Cherala, Gnanamuthu.

'They died for freedom,' says the inscription beside the memorial door. 'They died for the principles of Magna Carta,' would be as apt. From this high point, you see London spread out eastward, Windsor Castle rising to the west and Runnymede situated right between the two. Down at the foot of Cooper's Hill, after a sticky descent through the London clay, you come to the Magna Carta Memorial. The monument itself is underwhelming, small and spindle-shanked. Just beyond stands the memorial to assassinated American president John F. Kennedy, a great block of Portland stone approached by fifty steps in a somewhat portentous style. No matter; both memorials are lent dignity and significance by the modest strip of ground they overlook.

When King John of England met his rebellious barons on the green sward of Runnymede in June 1215, he was in deep trouble. Strapped for cash after losing his French possessions ten years earlier, the king had tried to make up the deficit with punitive inheritance taxes, alienating his powerful barons. What they proposed was extraordinary in the context of the day – no taxation without representation; freedom to worship as one chose; a curtailment of the king's hitherto unquestioned right to command, and a guarantee that justice should never be delayed, denied or for sale.

John wriggled and squirmed; he agreed, then went straight to the pope to have Magna Carta annulled. But the charter's principles stuck and took root in the national constitution. From the sedgy soil of the meadow by the Thames grew a notion of fairness and democracy that flourished and spread all over the world – something wonderful to contemplate as you turn back along Runnymede towards Egham and your homeward train.

60

L is for Landlady

… specifically the one who ran the K— H— pub in the town of M— in T— in the county of D— in the year of Our Lord 197—, when Dad and I set out on our first long-distance walk together, a good slice of the best bit of the Pennine Way. OK, I admit that I chose it from the *Good Beer Guide*, probably on account of talk of a 'sharp, fruity, creamy ale, well-hopped, with a long finish', or some such palate porn. And I further confess, m'lud, that it was the cheapest deal going. Was it £15 B & B & D for the two of us? Something like that.

We arrived leg-weary, blistered, peat-smeared, hungry, thirsty. For our commodore (Cockney slang – Google ahoy!), we got a dinner of rubber chicken, a breakfast of rubber bacon and a twin 'room' in the attic which was half of a DIY division of one of those Victorian skivvy's bedrooms you couldn't swing a rat round. The nether regions of our half of the space bulged hardboardily out over a hairpin bend in the staircase, so that you literally had to bend into a hairpin yourself to manoeuvre into the apartment. The single thirty-watt bulb dangled shadeless from the ceiling of the other room, shedding a tenth of its sickly light into ours through a hole cut into the top corner of the wall, like the one the snake came through in 'The Adventure of the Speckled Band'. Through the aperture, all night, came the drain-clearing snoring of a mighty couple from Birmingham with whom we'd shared the rubber chicken and the solace of a very large and loud TV, and whose offer of a good rub-down with oils Dad had regretfully declined.

The sheets? Pink, winceyette, slithered onto the floor. The beer? Unspeakable. The moral? Research before you leap. And be thankful it's the twenty-first century next time you're booking your stopovers.

61

Brocton Camp

'Your little son at it,' scribbled Erskine Williams on the post-card he sent home from Brocton Camp. What he was 'at' he depicted in a skilfully drawn little cartoon of himself, a trainee infantryman in puttees and cap, jabbing with a bayonet at a stuffed sack swinging from a frame. 'This is a thrust at the heart of an imaginary Deutscher,' he continued. 'It's rare sport, but hard work.'

Looking online[5] at Erskine Williams's humorous, cheery little sketches of life at the enormous training camp in the wilds of Cannock Chase – scrubbing floors, peeling 'taters', leaping into and out of trenches, chucking practice bombs – you can only marvel at ordinary men's extraordinary resilience when jerked so abruptly out of everything they knew as normal life. Many of those who passed through Brocton Camp were New Zealanders, some no more than boys, rushed at the double through their preparation for death or disablement on the other side of the world from their families and friends.

Sobering thoughts to begin this illuminating walk across the open heath and through the pine and silver birch woods of Cannock Chase, a 'green lung' on the outskirts of the industrial sprawl at the heart of England that's known as the Black Country. Dog walkers, runners, kids on bikes, families out for a stroll – they all flock to Cannock Chase for a breath of fresh air and a brush with nature. But it's remarkably easy to get away from everyone here; a few steps away from the main paths and trackways will do the trick.

Not far from the start of the walk, you pass the memorial and grave of Freda, canine mascot of the New Zealand Rifle Brigade. The brambly cuttings and embankments of 'Tackeroo', the camp's own railway, make a reference point as you walk south over heathland where roe deer bounce away with a flash of white rumps. The base of the great camp water tower, hut foundations among the sedges, a fragment of the old coal store. Far away among the trees to the east, to be passed on the return leg of the walk, the grassy banks of the firing ranges where the trainees aimed and squeezed, aimed and squeezed at imaginary Germans. It doesn't take much imagination to picture the shivering, stoical lads – half a million of them during the course of those four long years of war – gritting their teeth; doubling to and fro; route marching; cursing and grumbling; and somehow extracting that dogged soldier's humour out of the worst situations.

And then you reach the Katyn Memorial and the war cemeteries beyond. A polished marble plinth, simple and dignified, bears a crowned eagle and stands as testimony to the 25,000 Polish army officers, policemen, lawyers, landowners and priests murdered by Stalin's secret police in 1940 and buried in mass graves, many of them in Russia's Katyn Forest. From this monument to man's dark side, you pass through more beautiful, pristine heathland to arrive at the Commonwealth War Cemetery. Rifleman E. P. Fleming of the New Zealand Rifle Brigade lies here among hundreds of fellow soldiers – he died on 7 November 1918, four days before the end of the war, aged only twenty. Just along the lane, the German Military Cemetery holds every German who died in these islands during both world wars, buried in companionable pairs. Alexander Stidding, Hans Berger, Josef Schmidt – mere names, their personalities and weaknesses and quirks of humour as unknowable now as those of Rifleman Fleming.

These twin cemeteries are beautiful in their quiet conformity. Their image stays printed in the mind as you walk on past the silent firing ranges and back across the haunted heath.

62

I got 99 problems and a tent ain't one

A giant square of drenched and flapping canvas, a thicket of poles clanking like yachts in a stormbound marina and a very great deal of blasphemy. That is my first, my last and my only personal impression of the activity known to its fans as 'camping', and to the sane world as 'Get on that f—ing phone and find us a B & B before I go *mad*!' After my experiences on the not-quite-tropical island of Lundy, I will never, ever carry a tent again.

I was primed for the disaster in teenagehood, when Dad took us camping in the Dordogne. Our allegedly two-roomed tent, bought second- or third-hand, came in two enormous canvas bags and two gigantic jute sacks. The hundred or so poles fitted together, but only if you could relate the instructions (in German) to the arcane, home-made colour coding. By dusk, the framework was shakily standing. Then it became apparent that the canvas covering, as large as a clipper's mainsail, had been shrunk by years of rainstorms. It was like trying to squeeze an ugly sister into a princess's ball gown. Eventually, lubricated by my mother's tears and everyone else's hysterical laughter, the canvas consented to be pegged down. By that time, we couldn't even look it in the face.

After all these years, I thought the Dordogne scars had healed. Then came Lundy. I couldn't resist. I thought it would be all right, just one night. Just one little tent, honestly, and I'll never do it again.

A truer word was never spoken. Lundy? Don't talk to me about Lundy, or incessant rain, or thistles under bare feet, or that missing tent pole, or torches that haven't the decency to replace their own batteries.

I know my limits. I got 99 problems and a tent ain't one.

63

Orford Ness: a funny old place

'The Ness – now that's a funny old place,' says the man in the ferry office on Orford Quay. 'When the MOD had it, they tried to keep the locals out, of course, but we had our little ways. You'd take a boat out there at night, fishing off the beach, and the hares running up and down the shingle would sound like a bloody old troop of elephants. Then you'd suddenly see a crowd of gulls in the lighthouse beam, all shining white like ghosts and flapping away... funny feelings, that place always gave me.'

A funny old place, Orford Ness – a ten-mile shingle spit hugged tight to the Suffolk coast between Aldeburgh and the hamlet of Shingle Street. The spit has been very slowly growing southwards for the best part of 1,000 years, choking off the sea trade of the port of Orford halfway along its length and forming one of the loneliest, strangest and most isolated places in Britain. It's home to wonderful flora and fauna, and also to a most bizarre collection of buildings that settled on the spit during the course of the twentieth century like a flock of giant misshapen birds. When the National Trust bought the majority of Orford Ness from the Ministry of Defence in 1993, it was as though Rapunzel had been freed from her dark tower, liberated at last from a mysterious, much-murmured-about isolation.

I'll never forget coming down the road to Orford Quay

for the first time and seeing the slender arm of the River Ore running quickly seaward and the long tan bar of the shingle spit beyond, crowned with a line of what looked like chunky Chinese pagodas under a cloud of shrieking black-backed gulls. Orford Ness was still in the hands of the Ministry of Defence back then, as inaccessible as the dark side of the moon. Of course, that cast a mist of romance around the stark, blocky shapes on the pebble bank – a mist that didn't lift until the National Trust bought the Ness and opened it up to the public.

Since then, I've gone walkabout several times on Orford Ness. The National Trust runs it as a nature reserve, limiting the number of visitors to a few thousand a year. That's because the giant shingle spit is vegetated with rare species, supports colonies of breeding seabirds and is home to some of the least common (and least obtrusive) invertebrates in these islands. It's a never-abating thrill to chug over the tidal Ore towards the slippery landing stage, my battered old National Trust guide in hand, planning which of the trails I'll take today. To the lagoons? Along the marshes and the river? Out into the great grey desert of the shingle?

I wander the trails through the shallow furrows of hundreds of shingle ridges thrown up by thousands of storms down the successive centuries. Here grow the bulbous white flowers of sea campion, the tufty pink buttons of thrift and yellow-horned poppy with its big petals ready to fall at a touch. The ridges are carpeted with delicate mosses and lichens (it's strictly forbidden to walk on these) and with tangles of pale purple sea pea, a rarity in Britain. Thousands of lesser black-backed gulls and herring gulls breed here in the summer, and a small number of the very rare little tern.

'*Out-out-out!*' scream the black-backed gulls, swooping

close over my head with their beaks agape. They are not too happy to see an intruder crunching into their windswept fastness. Not that many others walk here, disturbing the gulls' courtships. The National Trust calls Orford Ness 'the last coastal wilderness in southern England', and for once the hyperbole is justified. 'Wilderness' sums up the atmosphere of this harsh, bare, remote place.

Perspective out here is hard to pin down. Distances become telescoped. Walking on Orford Ness is probably the nearest you can come in England to walking in the desert. And the shapes that pierce the huge level horizon seem as outlandish as any mirage: a bleak black tower straight out of Mordor; a grim grey metallic box of a building as big as a city block; a candy-striped lighthouse; and, off to the south, the enigmatic pagodas, seeming to lurch sideways under the weight of the storm-flung pebbles on their roofs.

If you're lucky or well organised enough to join one of the guided tours that visits the pagodas, it's an eye-opener. These former laboratories with their rotting pipes, peeling paint and hanging cables have not been specially preserved. They are being left for the rain, wind, sun and sea salt to reduce gradually to nothing. In these chilly chambers, atomic missiles – without their fissile material, we are told – were bashed, baked, frozen, spun, dropped and shaken to test their durability. Just why the laboratories were equipped with blast roofs if no explosives were involved remains a mystery – one among many, sinister and compelling, to ponder as I make my way back under a canopy of gulls to the jetty and the impatiently beckoning ferryman.

64

South Wales Valleys: iron and coal

The Valleys curve like multiple fingers up from the South Wales coast. They are bedded on rich mineral deposits. Their landscape of deep twisting valleys and humped intervening ridges was still pastoral until the late eighteenth century, with a widely scattered population of perhaps 3,000. Within 100 years, there were half a million people crammed into terraced cottages along every crevice and ledge. They had flocked into the Valleys – Welsh, English, Scots, Irish and a sizeable contingent from starving rural Italy – to extract and work iron ore and coal in the service of the Industrial Revolution. They turned South Wales into the coal and iron capital of the world.

As for the work the people did for the coal owners, and for ironmasters such as the Baileys and Crawshays – and what the work did to them in return – I learned about that as I read Alexander Cordell's *Rape of the Fair Country*, set in and around the Blaenavon and Nantyglo ironworks of the 1820s and 1830s:

> The side of the mountain had dissolved into a single fire; a maze of individual furnaces that blended their flames into an orbit ... This was the Bailey empire where the iron bubbles into a thousand moulds. Sweat pours here, beer is taken by the gallon, men die in mutilation, children are old at ten. Eyes are put out here, sleeves are tied with string.[6]

Now the Blaenavon ironworks stand stark and cold, impressive in their ruin. Their 200-year-old cast houses and brick-arched furnaces are being meticulously restored, along with the tall water balance tower which raised wagons full of rough pig iron up to the tram road that ran to the distant forges. Blaenavon, along with Merthyr Tydfil and Nanty-glo just over the hills, kept the world supplied with iron all through the convulsive changes of the Industrial Revolution. Workers who had accommodation as decent as the tiny cottages I found on display at Stack Square, in the shadow of the Blaenavon balance tower, were lucky. Most were jammed into jerry-built terraces, two families to a room sometimes, with no sanitation or clean water supply.

Such privation and hard physical work forged close-knit, self-reliant communities. None were closer or prouder than the Valleys coal miners. When Blaenavon's Big Pit closed in 1980, the miners and engineers did not sit on their hands, sobbing: they turned adversity into good fortune by making a visitor attraction out of their colliery.

The ex-miners make great guides, blackly humorous and friendly. Our group guide, Colin, gives us the full treatment as we crouch and stumble along iron-braced galleries 300 feet below ground. We switch off our helmet lamps and stand in pitch-black silence to imagine the plight of the eight-year-old children employed until the 1840s to open the compartment doors for the coal trams. Their wages were two pence a week, minus a penny for candles. Colin shows us hewn coalfaces, the polished cut coal gleaming in the lamplight, and tells us of the half-blind pit ponies' joy when they were taken to the surface for their annual week-long holiday in the fresh air.

'How often do you renew these elevators?' inquires a

palpitating American lady, as we rise up the shaft packed like sardines in the crude metal pit cage.

'Brand new, this one, my lovely,' says Colin reassuringly, as she nervously eyes the rust streaks and corrosion scars.

65

A message to mucky mankind

When I was a strapped-for-cash undergraduate at Durham University back in the 1960s, the most dramatic and outlandish cheap day out I ever discovered was a bike ride with friends down to the east Durham coast. Arriving on the beaches below Blackhall or Easington collieries was like landing on another planet. Working collieries lined the cliffs in those days, spewing their waste directly into the sea and onto the beaches. Aerial cableways, their endless chains of buckets dolorously clanking, spilled black, grey and orange rock, sludge and small coal, transforming the beaches and cliffs into hellish moonscapes. Dark waves, thick with coal spoil and untreated sewage, fell sluggishly on black sands. There was a bizarre thrill in wandering through this man-made landscape of ruin and desolation.

The last of east Durham's clifftop coal pits closed in 1993. The pits left as their legacy a coastline so thoroughly blackened, scarred and poisoned that many believed it would never recover. But almost as soon as the tipping ceased, nature began to elbow her way back in. Given time and a level playing field, she's amazingly good at doing that – even better when man decides to give her a hand.

County Durham only has a dozen miles of coastline and, in a minor form of modern miracle, these cliffs and beaches have come back from the dead. The sea is already nibbling away at the 'minestone', or colliery waste, that blankets the beaches. As for the hand of man – the disused mine buildings have been cleared away, the 'denes', or steep little coast valleys, cleaned of rubbish, the scrub cut back. Sewage treatment plants have been installed to clean up the sea. And, best news of all for those who love to venture on foot, an excellent path now runs the whole length of the Durham coast.

Forty years after my student excursions, I came back to explore the newly titled Durham Heritage Coast. I scrambled down the cliff onto Blast Beach below the site of Dawdon Colliery and wandered there, flower book in hand. Given the nature of the ground I was walking on – a thick, grass-grown ledge of minestone that had built up over the years on this blighted east Durham beach – I thought it would probably be a case of 'find the orchid… if you can'. But not a bit of it. Never mind struggling to spot any orchids – it was all I could do to avoid stepping on the things. They grew there in hundreds: tall, healthy early purples, in dense clumps that were scattered from the seaward edge of the industrial scab to the feet of the cliffs that formed the backdrop to the beach.

Early purples weren't the only orchids to have recolonised these outposts. I spotted the paler spires of southern marsh orchids beginning to make an appearance. The clifftops were spattered with bee orchids, once considered a great rarity hereabouts, their lower lips patterned to represent the hindquarters of a particularly well-upholstered bumblebee. I spent a long time puzzling over another, smaller species. Pyramidals? Well… they might have been. It didn't really matter, because there were so many more wild flowers begging to be noticed – yellow rattle with its loose-lipped petals, clovers, long strings of purply-blue vetches and the emerging busby-headed spikes of betony. It was as if nature had decided to cock a snook at

Man the Polluter. Thought you'd got me down for the count, eh? Well, choke on *this*, baby!

If plants were people, they'd be running our lives, organising our focus groups and probably kicking our backsides into the bargain. Resilience, tenacity, energy, a capacity to seize every opportunity and exploit it – these are essential assets for any upwardly mobile exec. Wild flowers have such qualities in spades. Their single-minded attempt to rise from the dead and take over the world each spring and summer is a quite extraordinary display of strength and determination. It's easy enough to take it for granted when you see the woods recarpeted with bluebells, the mossy banks spattered yellow with celandines and the hedgerows once again hazy with green leaf-buds on the burst. That just looks like nature reclaiming her own. But when you see a paving stone on a city street snapped clean in two by a thrusting spear of dock leaves, or a suburban park noticeboard garlanded, choked and dragged down by bindweed tendrils – then there's a frisson of sheer awe at the power packed into those blind green cells on the prowl. You can almost hear them humming.

Roaming on along the east Durham coast path, I passed through the oak woods of Hawthorn Dene, where blackcaps and wrens were duelling it out in song, and came to the smoothed-over grasslands where the pithead buildings of Easington Colliery once stood. Easington Beach had been the filthiest of the lot: a blackened wasteland, where a skeletal conveyor gantry vomited mine waste into a filthy, greasy sea; a scabby shore, where sea-coalers had filled plastic bags with gleaned lumps of waste coal to sell door-to-door. But under today's pale summer sunshine, the beach lay reddish-tinged, clean and beautiful.

There were more early purple orchids here, hard back

against the cliffs. I remembered a visit I'd made a few years ago to a country park that had been created out of an urban rubbish dump, and the thrill of seeing drifts of these handsome plants flowering and thriving on what had once been a tip of poisonous fuel ash from a coal-fired power station. Here on Easington Beach, too, the wild flowers in all their seeming modesty and fragility were once more sending out their triumphal message to mucky mankind: we were here before you, we're still here, and we'll be here long after you're gone.

66

Howlin' Dog Jackson

Gonna tell you a story
'Bout Howlin' Dog Jackson
Who swum clean away,
An' he wouldn't come back, son.

Howlin' Dog Jackson is the funkiest hound dog I know. He sings with our band, if the sax happens to be wailing. He runs downstairs with his back legs crossed. And if he wishes to cut you dead, he deploys the thousand-yard stare of a bluesman who has just caught sight of an empty jug a long, long, lonesome way away.

In one respect, however, Howlin' Dog Jackson lets down the fine old traditions of the blues with a bang. He'd rather drink water than whisky – not just drink it, but wallow in it. Let him once get the merest sniff of pond, pool, lagoon or lake when you take him for walkies, and he's outta there like a cork from a bottle, haring off and out of sight on a mission to immerse.

When you finally catch up with him, he'll be out in the middle of the mere, swimming round and round and round and round… And when you summon him, he *will not get out*. Call, cajole, threaten, whistle, beg till you're blue in the face, Howlin' Dog Jackson is in natatorial heaven, and he ain't comin' out, not never, not no-how.

———

Ah, but now... now I know about the Barking Bakery Trio of Mini Woofins Dog Treat Iced Muffins. Seriously! 'Paw-lickingly dogglicious treats for your pooch,' says their website. The 'woofins' come in carob and vanilla flavours, they contain crude ash and crude fibres (mmm!), and they nestle in a 'cute, bone-themed, clear plastic travel pod'.

When it's next time for walkies, I'll pack me a pod of poochie pastries. He'll be out of that creek quicker than a grizzly with a 'gator on its tail. Howlin' Dog Jackson... you're toast!

67

Covid Summer: Russet Mere and Monk's Kitchen

Leaving the village early on a hot, windy morning, we skirted the west end of Quarry Hill. Ash dieback disease has got a firm grip of the young trees here and is reducing them to pale skeletons in the wood. On the far side, we crossed the dry yellow pastures of Dragondown, where the cattle plodded one after another towards the shade of oak trees now turned as dark as iron by this two-month drought.

In the quiet green valley of the Russet Mere stream beyond Dragondown, a private revolution is taking place. The old knockabout farmhouses, beautifully sited but long neglected, have been bought up and spruced to the nines. The former dairying pastures of hoof-poached slopes and tough grass have been transformed into wild flower meadows thick with buttercups, knapweed, clovers and silky grasses with lovely names – Yorkshire fog, cock's foot, crested dog's-tail. Aspens in stout tree guards, rustic park fencing and carefully signed paths all point to new influences – welcome ecologically, but oddly troubling too. At what point do the economics of everyday farming fall below feasibility, obliging the old farming families to give way to well-heeled conservers of the countryside?

Food for thought as we wandered the path through these delectable meadows and up to the strange gritty outcrop called Monk's Kitchen. From there, a really wonderful view down over the track of an old railway sneaking round the foot of Quarry Hill, and out across fields and woods to a prospect opening over the distant coast and the Quantock and Exmoor hills beyond.

The path to Holdfast Farm below had been impenetrably blocked with a crop of wheat. Damn you, farmer! We pushed our way along the field margin, ploughed and sown right up to the spiky hedge. Hmm, yes, old-style farming ahoy!

Up on the rise beyond, we stood looking down on our neighbour village with its tall grey church spire, roofs and trees – a classic English view in early summer. And another harbinger of change, not so welcome: the hum of cars on the road below, their numbers, noise and pollutant fumes slowly increasing once again after those miraculous lockdown days in a countryside purged of traffic noise and stink.

68

Secret riches

Driving north through Kilmartin Glen for the first time, I got no sense at all of the secret riches of this modest-looking valley on the west coast of Argyll. The green fields of the glen stretched out towards low hills on either hand; the sun sparkled on Kilmartin Burn and lit up white-painted houses and stands of trees – a pleasant, unremarkable scene. It wasn't until I'd visited Kilmartin Museum and its wonderful exhibition that enlightenment came. Walking the valley armed with some understanding, it was as if the layers of history peeled back, leaving the landscape revealed for what it was – one of the most important and resonant archaeological sites in Scotland, the ceremonial burial and coronation place of kings and nobles over several thousand years.

Highly polished stone axes, tiny barbed arrowheads of white flint, tools of flint and bone and delicately patterned clay bowls and cups: the weapons, jewellery and everyday artefacts owned by the prehistoric inhabitants of Kilmartin Glen – either made by them or bartered from other people – still lie waiting to be discovered all across the valley. Some have been picked up by sharp-eyed folk in the fields and woods; others have been excavated from Kilmartin's astonishing scatter of cairns, chambered tombs and stone circles. Looking at these things under modern lighting in Kilmartin Museum, I marvelled at their subtle beauty and the way that careful display lends dignity and mystery to ancient objects – necklaces of polished shale rings, stone globes indented with elliptical lines like modern tennis balls, a patterned bowl from Nether Largie South Cairn that might have been made in Bernard Leach's pottery in the 1950s.

Out in the valley, I walked the side roads and paths, following a southward line suggested by the guide map. It's hard to imagine the difficulties faced by people several thousand years ago, trying to erect even a simple stone circle with only wooden rollers and levers to help them, yet here in Kilmartin Glen a whole string of huge, elaborate stone tombs was built from some 5,000 years ago onwards, along with stone rows, stone circles and individual standing stones, many incised with cup-and-ring marks, ram's-horn spirals, the outlines of axe-heads and suns shooting out rays.

Nether Largie South Cairn, the oldest of the tombs and the source of the Leach-style bowl, lay as a grey hummock in its field. Great shaped kerbstones formed the walls of a stone tomb that rose from a sheet of pebbles, hundreds of thousands of them. Sturdy slabs shaped the lintels of a doorway and roofed the deep pit of the central chamber. In a sycamore grove a mile away lay Ri Cruin Cairn, a thousand years younger, the chamber faced by a courtyard and bolstered by a sea of moss-green pebbles, its walls incised with axe-head carvings. Between these two massive tombs lay a third: the box-shaped cist or casket at the centre of Temple Wood's circle of thirteen standing stones.

These ancient, enormous stone monuments stirred my imagination. But I found them essentially unfathomable. The hopes and dreams of their builders remained inscrutable. Kilmartin possesses another ancient site, though, whose message seemed more open to interpretation and empathy across the millennia. Three miles south of Ri Cruin, the rocky knoll of Dunadd rises at the eastern edge of the flat boggy ground of Moine Mhòr, the Great Moss. It was an easy climb to the summit with its sensational three-hundred-and-sixty-degree view over the glen and out through Loch Crinan to the distant hills of the Isle of Jura.

Dunadd was the coronation place of the rulers of Dalriada, a kingdom founded here by sixth-century Irish adventurers. The smooth rock of their ceremonial platform still carries deeply incised symbols of kingship: a bowl to symbolise the ritual washing of royal feet; a great bristle-backed boar to indicate the strength and persistence demanded of a king; and a big eastward-facing footprint into which the prospective monarch would set his own foot. I did likewise, and an irresistible image came to mind – boats full of onlookers in the marsh; cloaked courtiers and their shouts of acclamation; noblemen kneeling on the bare rock summit; and the rays of the rising sun lighting the face of the boy who would be king.

69

M is for Music

… or at least what passes for it when I go walking: a constant babble of ballads, songs and snatches that trails this wand'ring minstrel like a pack of dogs. Does anybody else have a string of tunes constantly playing in their head to the rhythm of their feet, I wonder? Tum-titty-tum-titty-tum-titty-tum, tiddly-deedly, tiddly-deedly. Hmmm, not too bad – a jig or a hornpipe, probably heard last night at a session in the pub, and now sticking like a burr to the furry inside of my mind as I come one-two-three, one-two-three down the steps into Cranham Woods. But 'the runaway train went up the hill and she blew, wooo-hooo' as I climb the bank to Painswick – what crappy old stone has *that* crawled out from under? 'I'm a rambler, I'm a rambler, from Manchester way' – fair enough for Bleaklow, as long as finger and ear don't uncoolly conjoin in public. But 'the end of my old cigar, hoorah, hoorah, hoorah'? What is my psyche doing getting clogged up with that, when it's supposed to be marinating in the glorious landscape of Cadair Idris?

Walking is such a liberator, mentally as much as physically. One is endlessly borne away on tides of fantasy and introspection – and I suppose this unceasing flow of music hall rogueries and nursery fragments is the equivalent of what the movie pianist would come up with to accompany silent films. In the privacy of what John Hillaby termed the 'skull cinema', all sorts of one-reelers play as we walk – triumph and tragedy; farce and frivolities; one scene spilling in an instant into another, with ourselves as hero, victim and villain all rolled into one. No wonder the soundtrack, anchored to the tempo of our footsteps but simultaneously floating as free as thought, is so chaotic – and so irresistible.

70

Fanfare for the soldier

The Royal Geographical Society has launched a Discovering Britain project, exploring dozens of landscapes through walks great and small.[7] On a gorgeous summer's afternoon, we set out from the Wiltshire village of Tilshead to follow one of these walks through the heart of Salisbury Plain.

Stepping off the road into the vast Ministry of Defence preserve of Salisbury Plain feels like slipping through the screens of time. Here are no motor roads, no housing developments, no signs of industry. These dense, flower-rich, unimproved chalk grasslands, Europe's most extensive tract, have never known modern ploughing or farm chemicals. They have remained in this pristine, prelapsarian state thanks to the activities of the MOD, which uses the plain for military training to the exclusion of all other activity. Altogether, the MOD owns or holds rights over about one million acres of the UK, just under 2 per cent of the total land mass. That huge amount of land is pretty much free from unrestrained housing or infrastructure development. And in the training and live firing sectors such as those on Salisbury Plain, where very little farming that you could call modern or intensive takes place, wildlife goes about its immemorial business with remarkably little disturbance.

A mile or so down the white-dusted chalk track, we passed the enormous Old Ditch long barrow, one of the longest in the UK, over 400 feet from end to end. These ancient monuments, too, have escaped the plough and the developer's JCB – though one or two have occasionally collided with a tank.

The richness of the chalk grassland flora had us exclaiming out loud. Vivid royal-blue viper's bugloss, round lacy powderpuffs of field scabious, buttery sprigs of yellow rattle, sainfoin's convex pink petals like stripy Shakespearean breeches. Butterflies kettered and zigzagged over the grasses: clouded yellows, small skippers, marbled whites, chalkhill blues. Over all lay the soporific hum of bees and hoverflies busy among the flowers.

There were one or two soldiers, of course – cheerful, courteous men who stopped their bouncing carriers to enquire whether we were having a nice day before roaring off into the 'German village'. This mock-up of a Bavarian township, built during the Cold War, is still in use for training soldiers in fighting techniques in built-up areas.

We left the eerie, hollow-eyed dummy houses behind and took the homeward track across the flowery grasslands among pink mallows and great purple knapweed blooms. There are hidden hazards for the unwary in this timeless paradise, though. One of us stepped onto an innocuous-looking mud patch, went in up to the hips, and had to be hauled squelchingly out. It wasn't me – that's all I have to say on the matter.

71

Three Peaks of Yorkshire: a long, sharp shock

The Three Peaks Walk is a single day's long, sharp shock. The statistics can be simply told: you walk a circuit of about twenty-four miles, climbing around 5,000 feet on the way, taking in the three peaks of Pen-y-ghent (2,273 feet), Whernside (2,419 feet) and Ingleborough (2,373 feet). The idea is to do it in under twelve hours, thereby entitling yourself to wear the badge and tie of the Three Peaks of Yorkshire Club and to display its small-but-coveted certificate.

At half past seven on a lowering grey morning, I met Alan Hulme, area manager of the Yorkshire Dales National Park's south-western region, outside the Pen-y-ghent Café in Horton-in-Ribblesdale. We scribbled our names and time of departure and pushed the paper under the café door by way of registration. Pen-y-ghent stood blanketed in low cloud. The mountain looked like a recumbent baboon, its flat muzzle and paws sloping to the south. Like Whernside and Ingleborough, its limestone bulk is capped by millstone grit – hard, sparkling stuff. We snaked our way up out of green pastures squared off with limestone walls, up into the mist among slippery dark gritstone clints.

'Last time I was up here,' said Alan, 'there was a group of blind walkers being led up these crags – "left foot here, four-inch step here"... I asked one of them if he was enjoying himself. "Oh yes," he said, "it's fantastic – just so wonderful to be up on a mountain." That made me feel rather humble.'

At the summit of Pen-y-ghent, we found the OS triangulation pillar swathed in mist. It was a long drop down out of the clouds. At the bottom, we left the National Park's reassuringly stone-pitched path and headed into the quaking quagmires of Black Dub Moss.

'*Go-back, go-baack,*' cackled the grouse in the heather.

'Stupid birds,' growled Alan, just before he went in up to his hips into the softest, blackest bit of all.

At Ribblehead, nine miles out, the mighty Ribblehead Viaduct of the Settle–Carlisle Railway marched its twenty-four arches across Batty Moss. In the shadow of the viaduct, Alan and I passed long green hummocks and trenches in the grass – remnants of the shops, huts and hospital of the army of railway navvies, at times 3,000 strong, that camped out here while the viaduct was being built. It took six years, during which the navvies rioted, randied, drank, fought, achieved incredible feats of hard work with shovel and barrow, and died in droves from disease and accidents. Blazoned in gold above the central arch is '1875', the year the viaduct was completed.

Climbing up the interminable bank at Whernside, we got a good view south to the sphinx-like profile of Ingleborough, the third of our three peaks. On the fellside, a farmer astride a quad was herding sheep. His dog dashed up briefly to lick our hands before rocketing off to its duties again.

The legs were beginning to feel it a bit by then, but the path over the soft bog had been surfaced with flagstones salvaged from mill floors, an inelegant but effective measure. Alan and I put our heads down and slogged up onto the ridge, reaching Whernside's trig pillar – fifteen miles out from Horton-in-Ribblesdale, and the highest spot in Yorkshire – in thick mist once more. Two down, one to go.

The descent from Whernside was fiendishly steep, but a gentle stroll through green sheep pastures followed. At Chapel-le-Dale, we found the Old Hill Inn closed and bolted. Just as well, we agreed later. We would never have got up Ingleborough if we had stopped then. Ingleborough provides a nasty jolt at the end of the Yorkshire Three Peaks for anti-clockwise walkers. From a distance, the mountain looks no more difficult than Pen-y-ghent, but approaching over Black Shiver Moss you realise that after walking twenty miles you are now expected to climb an almost sheer 500-foot scree face.

'Wouldn't want to be climbing that myself,' smirked a lanky youth going the other way. Thanks, friend. We scrambled up somehow, with many a pause for a puff and blow, then steered for the final trig point – in a heavy mist, naturally. All around were the hut circles and crumbled walls of Iron Age tribes who regularly took refuge up there. In one corner lay the broken remnants of a rest house built for climbers in 1830, which was demolished on the day it opened by over-refreshed revellers.

Down in Horton-in-Ribblesdale, Alan and I clocked in at the Pen-y-ghent Café: ten hours and fifty-seven minutes to complete the twenty-four miles. A really good day out, we agreed in the bar of the Crown Inn, as we sipped our celebratory pints and massaged our rapidly stiffening and peat-stained legs.

A day or two later came the sting in the tail of the tale. A message from the Pen-y-ghent Café informed me that my registration had not been noted on the appropriate form. I was therefore not entitled to badge, tie, certificate or club membership. Entreaties failed to move the stern proprietor. If I cared to come back and do the walk again, having registered *properly* this time, then perhaps...

What can you say? I didn't say it. I don't think I could face the walk again, even to prove a point. But every time I pass through Horton-in-Ribblesdale, I allow myself an ignoble, unworthy, petty little sulk.

There! That's better.

72

Bye, Arnold!

I don't know if Arnold was really his name, but he looked like an Arnold to me – a whippet-thin Sheffield man in a singlet and very short shorts, with a huge backpack. His legs were as hard and bunchy as well-seasoned oak. He was standing with a bottle of water on the village green at Arncliffe in Littondale, under a blue North Yorkshire midsummer sky. Mouth turned down at the corners, he looked the picture of prim disapproval as he watched a group of walkers enjoying their lunchtime beer outside the Falcon Inn.

Arnold had walked over from Wharfedale that morning, as I had – but in a rather different way. While I had done six miles or so at a slow, reflective pace, Arnold had put about twenty miles of bog and rock behind him. This man's pleasure, it came out as we got talking, was to cover at least thirty miles of harsh terrain a day at a steady four miles an hour, stopping only for sips of water. He looked as lean and fit as a man could possibly make himself, and as joyless as a wet Tuesday in a temperance town.

'That'll not do them any good,' Arnold muttered, shaking his head judgementally at the jolly drinkers. 'They'll be all bloated up with gas and alcohol, and they won't get any good from their walking. They won't get the *benefit*. No, you'll not catch me going into any public house when I'm walking.' He eyed the ivy-hung Falcon Inn so smugly I wanted to smack him. 'It's just sheer self-indulgence, that's what it is.'

Oh aye, Arnold. I waited for him to screw the top back on his water bottle, and watched him set off stiff-necked along the lane, averting his gaze as he passed the Falcon's front door. Then I went into the pub and ordered what I'd been looking forward to all this while – a pint of landlord Robin Miller's beautifully kept Younger's Scotch Bitter.

I had been picturing this moment ever since coming over the rise of Firth Fell and looking down into Littondale a couple of hours before. Not so much in anticipation of the beer itself – though you'd be pushed to find a tastier pint in the Yorkshire Dales – it was more for the pleasure of watching Robin, latest in a generational line of Millers to run the Falcon, fill his white china jug from the barrel, then raise it high and let the bitter fall with a frothy crash and splash into my glass. This ritual fills the beer full of bubbles and life, so that it resembles the peat-brown oxygenated water of the River Wharfe (though it tastes rather better).

But it's not just the barrel-to-jug-to-glass ceremony that's so seductive about the Falcon. This inn has everything I look for in a country pub: friendly owners; good, unfussy food cooked on the premises by Elspeth Miller; a hatchway with the royal coat of arms above it, where Robin presides; a taproom with sporting prints and comfortable old settles; and a garden that looks to the hills. Just as important, it has none of the disqual-ifications: piped music to drown conversation; pseudo-beams and pretend brasses; couldn't-care-less bar staff; menu board chalked with fifty variations on pretentious freezer food. It's a pure delight to pitch up at the Falcon with a few miles under your belt, knowing that you'll be welcome (but leave your muddy boots at the door, please) and that you can get a sandwich and a drink without breaking the bank. You can even stay the night in one of the inn's snug little bedrooms, if the ale or the miles get the better of you.

Welcoming pubs like the Falcon are soon sniffed out by walkers. The fact is that most of us appreciate and enjoy a decent pub at lunchtime when we are out on a day's ramble. Whether in winter with a log fire, warm lighting and hot food, or in summer with a cool drink and a salad under a shady tree in the garden, the pub offers an hour's sit-down and a change of tempo and atmosphere – not to mention an opportunity for a loo stop that's a little warmer and more private than the blind side of a hedge. For those who walk alone, as I often do, there's the chance of company, some chat and a bit of crack before facing out again.

So I'm sorry, Arnold – but I'm with the self-indulgent walkers. Don't let me hold you up, though. No, really. I'll just pop in here, OK? Might see you back in Wharfedale. Bye!

73

The badgers of Little Stoke Woods

If anyone can steer you within watching range of the elusive European badger, *Meles meles*, it is David Thurlow, Natural England's warden. David looks after the National Nature Reserves of Ebbor Gorge and Rodney Stoke in the Mendip Hills, and he knows every cranny and cave of this delectable slice of north Somerset. Morning, noon and late at night, he immerses himself in the habits and habitats of wild creatures – including those nocturnal beings such as bats, otters and badgers that most of us would love to see but are resigned to viewing only on film. Our problem is, quite simply, our status as humans – large, conspicuous, noisy, strange-smelling, diurnal and generally threatening and unwelcome to the animal kingdom.

I'd always longed to get a proper unhurried look at a badger, one of the UK's largest, most populous and yet least-observed native mammals – Old Brock himself, lord of the underworld, as big as a mastiff, with bone-crushing jaws and earth-moving paws, builder of vast subways under our fields and forests. Now it looked as though my small dream might come true.

At seven in the evening, we set off four strong from the Rodney Stoke Inn – Jane and I, David Thurlow and his volunteer warden colleague Rod Hoskins. In David's Land Rover we jolted up an old cart track to the top of the hill.

'In general,' Rod told us, 'you'd expect badgers to be coming out of their setts around eight o'clock in the evening, pretty much all year round. They'll clean themselves, have a stretch and a scratch and then go hunting for worms or beetles or whatever they can find. In the winter they're a bit dopey – though they don't hibernate, contrary to what most people think – but in summer, this time of year, the cubs'll be wanting to play.'

The first spot we tried was top of David's list, but the wind was all wrong for it that night. His back-up place, however – down the slope and across an unmown hayfield – proved absolutely perfect. The four of us crept through the grass and into the skirt of the wood about thirty feet downwind of the sett, disposed ourselves around a log as low to the ground as possible and settled down in silence to watch and wait.

After a few minutes, a gentle nudge and motion of the head from Rod drew my attention to the shadows under the trees just beyond the nearest tunnels. Something large and dark was moving rhythmically there. At first it was hard to see what was happening in the thickening twilight, but then the shape detached itself from the trees and moved into the open – a big badger cub a few months old, stretching and yawning after enjoying a luxurious scratch on a tree stump. A grey body two feet long with humped shoulders, a dramatically striped mask of black and white, a surprisingly long and thick tail. All of a sudden, the badger was flat on the ground with another cub on top of it – a sibling who had sprung out from ambush in a flying leap. They rolled over, snarling and grinning and kicking, play-fighting like the hyped-up teenagers they were. Then two more appeared, as if parachuted into the clearing, to join the melee. It was a strangely moving episode of play, so similar to what one had seen one's own children do, yet capable of being broken and dispersed by the slightest cough or rustle on the spectators' part.

A flicker of movement much closer to us, and two female badgers came cautiously out of a tunnel mouth some thirty feet off. They snuffled closer and closer, sweeping their snouts sideways across the earth in search of food, an older sow and a younger one, looking up every now and then to assess our alien shapes for any sign of threat. Unable to see us clearly or to smell us, they were wary, but more intent on their feeding than on us.

To have those vivid black-and-white faces and those ancient but seldom-seen presences almost close enough to touch was a magical experience. Jane and I would have stayed transfixed all night. But the badger party broke up after half an hour. The females wended their ways; the youngsters went crashing off in line astern to see what they could find to eat in the now-darkened wood. And we got up slowly and went out across the field, startling grazing roe deer as we made our way back to the Land Rover, stretching and scratching and grinning at one another like a troupe of awakening badgers.

74

Shingle

As a child, I loathed shingle. It really could spoil a seaside holiday. Shingle stubbed your toes and bruised the tender soles of your feet. Then it threw you down on your knees or your bum for yet more bruises. Shingle ambushed you with tar splotches and rusty nails. If you dropped your pocket money, it was instantly swallowed, never to be seen again. You couldn't sunbathe comfortably on shingle. What on earth was the point of it? I hated shingle.

Now that I'm a big boy, I've learned to deal with shingle. In fact, I've come to love it. I dig my fingers deep into sun-warmed shingle for the pleasure of penetrating its cool underlayers. I sift its rounded pebbles for fossilised sea urchins and bivalves, belemnites of flint and quartzite gems, letting the stones trickle and fall with a subtle musical chinking.

Wandering the stony paths through the vegetated shingle ridges of Orford Ness on a hot summer afternoon, I see blocks of colour and drifts of movement – the rare little sea pea flushing the mosses and lichens with purple; the sea campion as delicately white as the finest porcelain; the big papery petals of yellow-horned poppy set trembling by up-currents of air stone-baked to a quiver over the pebbles. The crunch of my shoes among the stones and the far-off screaming of black-backed gulls are the only sounds out here, where Suffolk and the North Sea melt together.

On a stormy winter day at Shingle Street, just down the

coast, there's a pleasure equally acute but of an entirely different order. Huddled in weatherproof gear and watching rollers thunder down on the shingle, I hear Benjamin Britten's sea harmonies and rhythms as they first came to him on this shore, the hypnotic suck and roar of the stones, the waves piling them high, the undertow dragging them back. And in springtime there's music, unstructured but acutely moving, from the birds that nest on the shingle – melodious little flutes from the ringed plovers, sharp whistles from the scarlet nutcracker bills of oystercatchers.

Vegetated shingle spits are places of great beauty – a beauty that's moody and subtle, but that grows like a drug on anyone who takes their walking shoes and a pair of open eyes to the pebbles. Here you'll find a flora that rises in complexity and density from a thin covering of cleavers and sea beet to a close carpet of sea pea, sea campion and stonecrop, then to the great showy plants of the shore such as the yellow-horned poppies, sea kale, bright blue viper's bugloss and the big spiked flowers of sea holly, pale blue and wonderfully dramatic.

These spits are also fragile places. The plants have to be adaptable enough to withstand freshwater drought, thin or negligible soil, shifting ground, temperatures ranging from baking to freezing, storm-force winds and salt-water drenchings. Not even desert plants have to put up with this much adversity. And that's without the baleful hand of man, always keen to dig the shingle up for aggregate, to build on it, to drive all over it, to reduce its natural efficiency as a mobile sea defence by trapping it rigid with concrete sea walls.

Shingle is harsh, strange and compelling, a stark environment that's an untrumpeted national treasure. Seek it out this summer, when you're tired of the smooth blandness of sand, and let its moody beauty grow on you.

75

N is for Notebook

454... 455... 456. And that's it, till the next time I go walking. There they sit on their own special shelves, 456 of them so far – the little red-spined, black-jacketed notebooks that have tracked my walking life over the past forty years. I know there are 456 of them, because I numbered them myself, in thick black felt tip on the spine. They're catalogued by content on my computer: 74, Henry Williamson's Exmoor; 143, barnacle geese at Caerlaverock; 264, Wattenmeer mud walk. What a resource; what a treasury of memories! Finding the very spot where Tarka fought the otter hounds, crouching by the moonlit Solway Firth as 3,000 geese flew overhead with a jet-engine roar, doing the cancan for sheer *joie de vivre* in long black stockings of Frisian Island mud.

I probably wouldn't keep notebooks if I didn't write for a living. All that mind food, all those people and places, would be so much compost in the memory garden. The little black books are useful when I want to check if scabious grows on Watership Down, or whether it's gritstone or limestone in Miller's Dale. But most of them I never open once they're full. I just like to have them there, that great weight of memories hanging on my study wall.

Anal annals? Well, you could say so. Should I lighten up and chuck some of the old ones away – Notebook 49, to take a random example? Probably should, yeah. Let's just check.

Sligo and Westport, my first walk through Ireland… what have I scribbled here? It's hard to read through the Guinness stains… 'Reeled home at dawn, rain hammering down – sore lips from harmonica – all back to Olcan's after the session – never laughed so much, can't remember what about…'

Pure gold. And all mine.

76

Red squirrels of the Sefton Coast

If I could have written the script for a day's walking on the Lancashire coast, it would have been exactly like this – a bowl of unbroken blue sky, a brisk north-westerly to drive me along, a warm sun giving the elbow to the rainy-day blues, and a far view across the sea of the distant hills of Lakeland and North Wales as a *sauce piquante* to the whole expedition.

There's nowhere like the Sefton Coast in the whole of the British Isles – twenty miles of unbroken broad sandy beach, reaching north in a great curve between the estuaries of Mersey and Ribble, backed by the longest and finest stretch of dunes in the country and a scatter of pinewoods full of red squirrels. Considering the presence, just inland, of the seaside towns of Crosby, Formby and Southport – affluent places where well-heeled Merseyside and Mancunian footballers build their supersized brick palaces – it's quite remarkable how beautiful, how wild and lonely, are these sandy miles of broad coast.

As companion for my sunny, breezy walk I had senior ranger John Gramauskas, a man who knows all about wild birds, coastal erosion and the love life of the natterjack toad. We started through the shaggy sand dunes of Ainsdale National Nature Reserve, in whose shallow warm ponds the rare natterjacks lay their strings of spawn in springtime. Down in the dune slacks, or valleys between the sandy peaks, we walked in a tightly enclosed world of ochre and muted greens, of wind-tossed quills of marram grass and thick mats of mosses, liverwort and lichens.

Out on the beach, everything changed in an instant. The horizon broadened from fifty yards to fifty miles; breaking waves roared softly on sandbars, and the wind scooted us along. Oystercatchers flickered black and white with their silvery piping cries, and black-backed gulls squabbled over titbits uncovered by the receding sea, with cries as harsh and quarrelsome as squabbling fishwives. Sand had been spread between one tide and the next across ancient ledges of dried mud, but enough of the dark slabs protruded for John to be able to show me the hoof prints of red deer and roe deer, the large rounded marks of wild oxen or aurochs and a neat string of human footprints making seaward – all these prints impressed in the mud shelf some two or three thousand years before the Romans came to Britain.

The giant beaches and long ranges of sand dunes amazed and overwhelmed the senses after a while. It was time to make inland from Formby Point among the Scots and Corsican pines of the National Trust's reserve, in search of red squirrels.

It's almost impossible not to succumb to the 'aaaah!' factor when talking about red squirrels. We love them, and we invest them with personality, more than any other of our indigenous wild animals, even though most of us will never see one in the wild. Something about them seems to whisper of little paws full of neat leaf parcels, of teeny-weeny twig rafts and of fluffy tails spread as sails. It's the Beatrix Potter factor.

Squirrel Nutkin, eh? What a tease! *The Tale of Squirrel Nutkin* was one of my children's favourite Beatrix Potters; one of mine, too, come to that. There is something quite irresistible about Nutkin's cockiness and his cheeky prancing in front of Old Brown, an extremely scary-looking owl who almost succeeds in ripping his tiny tormentor to shreds. Nutkin escapes, but he leaves his beautiful bushy tail behind in Old Brown's beak – a frisson of Gothic cruelty more characteristic of Potter's little books than one might think.

The lasting impression is of an animal that's charming, lively and intelligent. Yet Britain's native red squirrel, resident in these islands since the close of the last Ice Age, has been waging a losing battle against disease, loss of habitat and food sources, and relentless competition from its introduced American cousin, the grey squirrel, since well before *The Tale of Squirrel Nutkin* was first published more than a century ago. Greys are immune to the deadly parapoxvirus, scourge of squirrel communities, but can transmit it to the reds, whom it condemns to a slow and horrible death. Now, though, the species has at least a fighting chance of survival in the protected surroundings of red squirrel reserves set up in Dorset, Hampshire, Norfolk, Wales, Cumbria, Northumberland and Scotland – and among the pine trees of Formby Point, out on the westernmost bulge of the wild and sandy Sefton Coast.

Strolling through the plantations, one among hundreds of visitors, I watched the squirrels bouncing from bough to bough among the dark ranks of trees. The impression of energy and alertness they carried with them was bewitching. One particularly fine fellow sat bolt upright at the roots of a Corsican pine, eating a seed held delicately between his rather knobbly fingers. A shaft of late afternoon sunshine lit up his coat of dark red, his pointed ear tufts and the tail that curled up the small of his back like a fiery puff of smoke. Say what you like about squirrels (and foresters do, with many expletives, as they see their trees being stripped of bark), the native red of these islands is an exceptionally handsome chap.

Although red squirrels will eat hazelnuts, berries or even fungi at a pinch, it is conifer seeds they really rely on. Their other basic requirement is to be separated from the bigger and bolder greys. The Formby Point woods are protected from the encroachment of grey squirrels by the isolation of their easterly location. Carefully wardened and maintained by the National Trust, the woods provide the smaller and more vulnerable reds with the conifer seeds and the lack of competition they need.

Next morning, I got myself into the woods by six in the morning, in order to have the place to myself and to catch the red squirrels in the lonely hour after sunrise when they patrol the treetops and the forest floor for food. With their shiny blackberry eyes on eternal lookout, they didn't bother their pretty little heads about the intruder. They scampered down the rough-barked tree trunks; they scuttered among the conifer needles and dug vigorously in the dry litter. I kept as still as I could and was rewarded when a pair approached and sat chewing pine seeds only a couple of leaps from my boot tips. An hour of sheer unblemished magic.

Hampshire chalk stream

'How about that beauty, Dad?'

My son George, leaning on the rail, pointed down into the clear water of the River Test, where it ran under Stockbridge's wide main street. With a lazy waving of its tail and a graceful sinuation of its indigo-spotted body, a brown trout was maintaining station in the dimpling current of the river. 'And there's a rainbow just behind, over that long patch of weed – see him?'

The rainbow trout, twice the size of the brown, was striped in crimson and faintly iridescent in the glancing light of the June afternoon. It was hard to imagine creatures more perfectly adapted to their environment than the two trout in the limpid chalk stream, not ten feet from the pair of craning humans and the thunder of cars crossing the bridge, yet oblivious of all but their own trouty purposes.

It is the chalk streams of Hampshire – and especially the subtly shaped, many-channelled Test – that bring dry fly fishermen to tears of delight. Not that ordinary anglers like George and me can cast a Greenwell's Glory or a Houghton Ruby onto those hallowed waters for love or anything less than a great deal of money. Fishing beats along the Test are some of the most sought-after and pricey in the country. For ordinary mortals with shallow pockets such as us, it's enough to wander through the river meadows and under the trailing willows, watching the trout in all their spotted summer finery and easy grace of movement.

Not all the magic of one's most enchanted places can be distilled into facts and causes, thank goodness. But once you have seen the billowing chalk downs that flank the river, you can appreciate the succession of events through which the Test Valley acquired its lovely shallow arc and its superbly clear waters.

The Test is a short river. In one smooth south-westerly curve of less than forty miles, it carves its way through the downs from its source just west of Basingstoke to its mingling with the salt tides of Southampton Water. The easily moulded chalk of these hills was squeezed concertina-style into ridges and valleys by pressure from the south some seventy or eighty million years ago, when subterranean upheavals were hoisting the Alps and the Pyrenees on high and displacing the surrounding landscape for thousands of miles in all directions.

The permafrost of the Ice Ages sealed the chalk into an iron-hard surface, so that when the big thaw finally arrived the meltwater poured off the glazed sides, scooping out the characteristic dry valleys that still indent the ramparts of the Hampshire downs. But the frost-hardened surface couldn't resist the millennia of revolving thaws and freezes for ever. It shattered and crumbled, allowing the rain to penetrate the permeable chalk below. Gradually the water sank through to form a vast reservoir deep beneath the downs. As the hills became fuller and fuller of underground water, springs began to shoot out from their flanks, feeding the infant River Test with water filtered to great purity and clarity by its long descent through the cleansing chalk.

Just south of Stockbridge, George and I went strolling along the banks of the Test – its many and varying banks. The Test is a profligate wanderer in several channels, courses shaped and diverted by countless generations of Hampshire workers. A river of such fast-flowing, clear and shallow water is a valuable asset. Over the centuries, the parent stream has been channelled and split apart to turn mill wheels that ground corn and sawed wood, to spin turbines for generating electricity, to flood the riverside meadows for their rich crop of grass. All this ingenious exploitation of the river has left a mazy tangle of waterways, plaiting and separating and reconvening like quarrelling lovers.

The trout love the purity of the chalk-filtered water, its clarity that lets them see danger a long way off, the high oxygen content from its fast flow and the ready-made larder of mayfly and stonefly nymphs, freshwater shrimps and other invertebrates thriving in the great trailing mats of weed that wave so elegantly to every nuance of the current. The gravel beds of the upper river are where the fish come to spawn early in the year, before anglers like my son have begun to dream of the new season's triumphs and disappointments.

Down below thatched and half-timbered Houghton, towards dusk, we watched a couple of fortunate fellows in thigh-high waders as they began to cast delicately from their stances in the middle of the river. The green and gold of sloping cornfields rose gently to the roof of the downs. All around lay the contented hush of a June evening.

'I'd be quite happy to live in that river,' murmured George, watching the trout. I knew exactly what he meant.

78

Soaked on Scafell Pike

The becks roar and the rocks gleam as Neil Dowie and I set out from Seathwaite Farm – the wettest place in England, say all the guidebooks. It's going to be a real soaking smother of a day, with mist and rain driving through Borrowdale, hiding the Lake District fells from the knees up. Looking up on the approaches to Scafell Pike at where the mountains should be, I see only a damp blanket. Never mind – if you don't anticipate foul weather in the fells, you're a mug.

I have a great companion with me, anyway. Neil, landlord of the Royal Oak in the Borrowdale hamlet of Rosthwaite, has decided to take a day off and come along for the exercise. Neil is not only a fanatical walker and explorer of the fells, he is a leading light of the local mountain rescue team. If you're going to get lost in the hills on a stinker of a day, Neil's the man to do it with. He also runs one of the world's cosiest, least pretentious and most walker-friendly small hotels, so a warm fire, a full glass and a fine measure of tall tales are guaranteed on our return.

I stump along, head bowed, in full mountain gear – Neil wears shorts, scorns the rain and strides up from Seathwaite and over the humped back of Stockley Bridge like a man on a mission.

'Up by the Corridor, back by the Ridge,' he crisply decides. Before I know it, we have swung up the old green pony track into the mist and are passing the thunderous waterfall of Taylor Gill Force. From this point on, visibility is rarely better than fifty feet. Black rocks, rain-slick boulders and drifts of even thicker mist loom up and fall behind.

We come to a junction of tracks at Sty Head. By myself, I would be baffled in the mist, but Neil yomps on up without a care. We inch around the slippery head of Piers Gill.

'A Victorian walker fell in there and wasn't found for eighteen days. Stayed alive on a slab of fruit cake and a slake of water. Lucky guy,' notes Neil laconically.

The scratches and scrapes of a million boots blaze a trail from Lingmell Coll to the summit of Scafell Pike. Up there, I stand on the cairn, momentarily the highest man in England. The view? My ancient red-backed copy of Baddeley's guide names a vast range of Lake District fells in sight from the summit of Scafell Pike. 'Also the Solway Firth and Scotland,' gasps Baddeley, 'the plain of west Cumberland ... the Isle of Man ... Slieve Donard in County Down, 100 miles distant.' Not today, baby.

Up through the murk and the icy wind come shadowy figures – other madmen, and one madwoman. Total strangers, we embrace, slap backs and grin like fools. We have made it.

79

Lammas meadows

Apart from cold green river water closing over my head, the most vivid childhood memory I have of summertime dinghy sailing (and spilling) at Twyning in north Gloucestershire is looking across the River Avon to the flowery meadows. Floods of scarlet, white, sulphur yellow and purple were spread like a celestial carpet across Upham Meadow and Summer Leasow, or 'Twyning Great Hay Meadow', as we called the huge field of tall grasses and sheets of wild flowers that bordered the river. I didn't know back then about Lammas meadows, those rare survivals of medieval farming systems. All I knew was that the Great Hay Meadow looked beautiful.

Since the Second World War, the glorious spectacle of such meadows in full summer flower has all but disappeared from our countryside, thanks to the impatient demands of modern intensive farming. A few months ago, I returned to the Avon at Twyning, expecting to find the Great Hay Meadow floored with blank, uniformly green grass like every other field round about. But things, almost unbelievably, were just as they had always been. Flowers and feathery grasses in their millions spattered the sunlit meadow with bright points of colour. Butterflies flitted, flies and bees buzzed in the knee-high grass. The richness and variety of the big field was a testament to the continuation of nature-friendly farming, in the old way and at the old pace.

Twyning Great Hay Meadow will always be my own 'special field', but a few miles away across the Herefordshire border lies the biggest and best-documented example of a Lammas meadow in the whole country. Lugg Meadow, bordering the River Lugg just east of the city of Hereford, is an extraordinary survival – a 300-acre meadow that, according to the ancient records of Hereford Cathedral, has been grown and cut for hay by the same means and under the same system of ownership in an unbroken succession since early medieval times, and perhaps since well before the Norman Conquest. Such are the tremendous links that the Lammas meadows maintain with our dim and distant past.

These traditionally managed and ecologically invaluable meadows have always been cut for hay at Lammas-tide, around the beginning of August. The holiday from which they take their name was celebrated at that time of the year by the Anglo-Saxons of the Dark Ages as *hlaef-mass* ('loaf-feast'), a festival to welcome the start of the year's harvest. And for thousands of years Celts had been celebrating their own harvest feast of Lughnasadh, dedicated to their god Lugh, the Shining One, Lord of the Grain. So it wasn't too surprising when the Christians in their turn got in on the act, taking over the old celebration under the guise of the Harvest Festival. And Lammas is still celebrated in different ways around the country – the Lord Mayor of Exeter, for example, presides over the hoisting of a stuffed and decorated glove onto the roof of the Guildhall to signal the start of Lammas Fair, while the Ould Lammas Fair at Ballycastle on the County Antrim coast sees prodigious amounts of yellowman toffee and crispy dulse seaweed eaten while horses race through the streets and dubious travellers tell you someone else's fortune.

Lugg Meadow, like hay meadows in every community

across the country in times past, is left to grow its crop of herb- and flower-rich grasses from 2 February (the old church Feast of Candlemas) until Lammas-tide, on or around 1 August. By then the flowering plants – among them large white ox-eye daisies, yellow rattle, clouds of heady-scented meadowsweet and communities of orchids – will have dropped or dispersed their seed for next year's flowering. At Lammas, the meadow is cut for hay – some of the most nutritious hay in the world. Then farm animals move in to graze and dung the cut sward, until winter floods bring the river up and over its banks to inundate the meadow. The floods soon drain away through Lugg Meadow's natural gravel foundations, leaving behind a rich silt that fertilises the ground, ready for Candlemas and the closing of the meadow once more as the new cycle of spring growth gets under way.

Not only does a true Lammas meadow follow this tradi- tional yearly cycle, but its management is split between a group of commoners, who have the right to graze their animals there in the autumn and winter, and its actual owners, each of whom harvests from their own strip of land the hay that grows between Candlemas and Lammas. These strips are marked off individually by posts or stones known as merestones or dole stones; the strips were originally doled out among the owners by lottery to ensure a fair distribution of good and poor land. The dole stones were usually inscribed with the owner's ini- tials. Lugg Meadow has over 100, many of them marked 'CB 1833' to show the position of six strips of former charity land bought by local wine merchant Charles Bulmer in that year.

Lammas meadows are under ever-increasing threat from road building, from floodplain housing development and from intensive agricultural practices driven by the desire to maximise profits. Luckily, there are organisations and individuals who are looking out for the wellbeing of the old meadows. The Herefordshire Wildlife Trust and Plantlife International between them own and look after more than half the total acreage of Lugg Meadow, while Natural England does the same at North Meadow on the Thames near Cricklade, famous for its show of snake's-head fritillaries in spring. Meanwhile, we have cause to thank farming families such as the Abbeys of Roydon on the Essex–Hertfordshire border, who continue to manage the flowery swards of Hunsdon Mead traditionally, even though fat profits could be theirs if they ploughed and reseeded the meadow. On the responsible shoulders of people like these rests the fragile future of the Lammas meadows, Britain's beautiful and irreplaceable wildlife havens.

80

O is for Ooooohhhh

… or the capacity to stop and stare; to be astonished, enchanted and generally struck all of a heap. Just recently, I've begun to take my time over walks, for a very good reason: the more slowly and deliberately I walk, the less immune – or perhaps I mean impervious – I become to every damn thing around me. When a yellowhammer sat three feet away on a hawthorn sprig in Hertfordshire a couple of weeks ago, I found myself breathing, 'Oh, you beautiful thing!' and trying to make it stay put by sheer force of will. Same with the hare that came loping towards me down a track on Wallasea Island out in the flatlands of the Essex coast. When it suddenly became aware of me and sprang aside over the potato flowers, I felt a visceral need to halt it in mid-leap so that I could inspect every inch of its sleek, rain-pearled body.

It never used to be like this. Once upon a time, walking was all about putting the miles to bed and yomping on over the next hill. I don't think I ever stopped to look at a bird, a flower or a grass-head – to properly *look*, as in absorbing myself in its colour and structure, the mechanical details that made the wing fold or the pattern of streaks that gave such brilliant camouflage in a reedbed. It was as though I were walking in a selective blindfold – a head-down cyclist's view of the countryside, all about the path surface and the next turning.

What's brought about this change in perspective? I haven't

a clue. Maybe it's just the sentimentality of advancing years. Whatever the cause, I find the art of slow walking, if you want to call it that, brings me far more pleasure – infinitely more – than the old yomping-and-stomping ever did.

81

Living on an island

'Living on an island is not easy,' observed Brother Gildas, stroking his magnificent beard pensively, 'and living as a monk is not easy. One's always on the fringe of things. But with sixteen or seventeen of us here on Caldey at present, the monastery is in a pretty healthy state, I'd say.'

Visitors to Caldey Island, two miles south of Tenby, are naturally drawn to Brother Gildas, the hospitable and gently spoken guestmaster of the island's Reformed Cistercian Order of monks. He took time out for a good long chat with me, even though he had forgotten I was coming and had a thousand other calls on his time.

Caldey is not exactly underprovided with guests in the summer months, when the ferry boats bring day trippers across by the couple-of-dozen every few minutes. Somehow, though, they don't destroy the remarkable air of peace and contemplation that has soaked into the very air of Caldey.

'We do rely heavily on tourism,' said Brother Gildas, 'Especially since hard times in farming forced us to shut down our dairy operation. Every day the boats can't come is a day without income for us. But, of course, we monks are here to work and pray and lead the monastic life. It's always hard when you start as a youngster, especially in winter. My cell has never looked so cold and unfriendly as it did on my first night. But I've grown to love the wind, the rough weather, the winter isolation when we're cut off. The island itself is a great teacher.'

Caldey has had its monks, on and off, for the best part of 1,500 years. They quit the island during the latter half of the Dark Ages in the face of Danish fire-and-slaughter visits, and again after the monastery was suppressed in 1539. It was not until the early twentieth century that a monastic presence was re-established here. There have been desperate times since; more than once, the monks have had to send out appeals for new recruits to bring fresh blood into a dwindling and ageing community. But somehow they have kept going, even entering the tourist market to the extent of making and selling Abbot's Kitchen chocolate and a range of perfumes.

Caldey is the most visually appealing of the Pembrokeshire islands, with a couple of broad shady beaches, an impressive range of cliffs and a thickly wooded interior from which the candlesnuffer turrets and red-tiled roofs of the monastic buildings peep out. Once past the gift and perfume shop and the high buildings of the monastery itself, you can quickly give the crowds the slip.

After leaving Brother Gildas, I found the abandoned medieval priory with its pointed archways and gatehouse-cum-pigeon-loft. The Church of St Illtud stood under a crooked finger of a stone spire. Inside, propped on the cobbled floor, an ancient tombstone with Ogham script and Latin lettering leant against the wall.

Up by the lighthouse, I struck out west along the clifftop path through clouds of brown-and-blue butterflies. Seals were floating, chin-up and fast asleep, in green water under the dusky red sandstone cliffs of Red Berry Bay. Down in Sandtop Bay, a loving couple had the broad sweep of clean sand entirely to themselves. I idled the circuit of Caldey, taking a couple of hours over it, and then went to say goodbye to Brother Gildas.

'Sometimes, I do ask myself whether living and praying this way in such isolation makes a scrap of difference to the world,' he told me. 'But I only have to lay my ear to a tree in the woods and hear the rustle and whisper of its branches, connecting with other trees' branches, on and on to the very edges of the wood, to know that we do have a wider effect on the way the world is.'

82

Tidal landscape of Worm's Head

Those old Vikings knew a thing or two. They were savvy enough to navigate their way from frozen Scandinavia to the lush grasslands and warm seas of South Wales.

And if, through some space/time portal, they had managed to get their hands on the Ordnance Survey's Explorer Sheet 164, how they would have nodded their extravagantly mous-tachioed heads to see the modern mapmakers' birds-eye view of Worm's Head, the Gower peninsula promontory that those Vikings first named 'Wurm', or dragon. With a blow-hole for a nostril and a wave-cut arch for an eye, a neck shaggy with rock plates and a bearded chin aggressively out-thrust below a menacingly open mouth, the long-headed monster that forges seaward from the village of Rhossili looks ready to take on all comers.

The prospect that Siân Musgrave and I enjoyed from Rho-ssili's coastguard hut on a grey and blowy afternoon was of the dragon from on high – the Outer Head with its blowhole rearing 200 feet from the crash of the waves, the Inner Head rising steeply to flatten out into a sharply cut spine, and the tidal causeway trailing towards land among agitated tide rips to form the broad tail of the beast.

'That's where we're going, down there,' Siân said, point-ing to the jumbled rocks and glinting pools of the causeway. 'We've got a few hours before it's covered again, anyway.' She bent down to pat Digby, her fantastically excited black Labrador. 'Just can't wait, can you? Oh, he loves dashing in the water. You'll see!'

The National Trust administers most of the spectacular coast of the Gower Peninsula. If you're out exploring the natural glories of the countryside, it's certainly no hindrance to have the company of a National Trust head warden, especially one as knowledgeable and enthusiastic as Siân. The rock pools of the Gower Coast, fed by clean seas and not over-explored, are reckoned the finest in Wales, if not in the whole of Britain. Their profusion among the rocks of the Worm's Head causeway is really a matter of geology, Siân told me as we negotiated the treacherously angled surfaces.

'This south coast of Gower is basically carboniferous limestone folded on top of old red sandstone, which pokes through here and there to form Gower's highest peaks. Then everything's been given a great shove from below, so that it's almost standing on end, and the upright layers have been worn down by rain and frost to form these awkward blades of rock we've got here.'

Looking back from the middle of the causeway towards the mainland, I could see for myself the strata of the cliffs like a many-layered cake, hoisted near to vertical, bent over in some places into arches, snaking hither and yon in others. Underfoot were the rocks of the causeway, canted by volcanic upheavals, then ground to stumps by the tides of many million years, barnacled and lichened – a formidable, bleak and breathtaking landscape through whose various tidal zones we slid and stumbled.

The long narrow gullies between the upended limestone plates had been refilled with sea water by the last high tide. Now, following the falling sea, they were trickling one into the next in a complicated system of spillways. Digby the Labrador went mad, splashing and snuffling through the pools, scampering after ripples and plunging his muzzle into submarine gardens of seaweed. Siân and I followed more slowly, absorbed in this living landscape in miniature.

What we glimpsed depended on the zone – between the highest (the splash zone) and the lowest (the lower shore) – we found ourselves in. Rusty orange-and-black lichens and green gutweed gave way to delicate pink weed-like coral; to sheets of barnacles and clumps of branched brown carrageen moss; then to the filmy green 'leaves' of sea lettuce; to oarweed like a translucent barber's strop; and to edible dulse weed. I chewed a bit raw and found that it exactly resembled a mouthful of lightly salted plastic.

'You should steam it first!' admonished Siân.

Near the edge of the sea, the life of the pools suddenly enriched – a quantum leap in quality. Into our fingers and shrimping nets fell edible and fiddler crab, ragworm and shore crab, sea mice and tiny pug-faced fish. The hours flew. Digby played himself to a salt-matted standstill. At last, it came time to make our way back to land with the tide on the turn, as it had turned twice a day since aeons before the dragon prows of the Viking longships came out of the mist and made for the Gower shore.

83

Dream island

'The first time I saw this island,' said Graham Thompson, leading me off on a stroll around Skokholm, 'it was from Skomer. I looked across and saw the sun behind Skokholm, silhouetting it on a sea of silver, making it look mysterious and untouchable. I thought to myself, "That's the one for me."'

Romantics love Skokholm. Graham, long-serving warden of the island, is one. Most visitors to Skokholm (pronounced '*Skoe-km*') know what he means when he confesses, 'I'm absolutely besotted with the place – it has true magic.' This slip of pink sandstone, two miles south of Skomer across the treacherous tides of Broad Sound, is three times as small as its sister island. Skokholm accepts only fifteen visitors at any one time, a tiny fraction of the numbers that Skomer receives. It still retains much of the air of dreamy isolation that arch-romantic Ronald Lockley so loved when he came to fulfil a boyhood fantasy by living the simple and adventurous life on Skokholm in 1927. Lockley stayed thirteen years, survived countless escapades and hardships and left Skokholm having written a bestselling account of his life there, *Dream Island*.

I had read *Dream Island* several years earlier, and – like a good romantic myself – I had brought a battered paperback copy in my backpack to read during my stay on Skokholm. The hand of Lockley is still evident in the timbers and ceilings and floors he built in the island's then-dilapidated farmhouse, and in the figurehead and steering wheel he salvaged from the wrecked coal boat *Alice Williams*. Lockley was a practical romantic. He was also a scientific observer of nature, carrying out the first proper investigation into the private life of the Manx shearwater, the remarkable seabird whose current nesting population of 150,000 in Skokholm and Skomer is the world's biggest shearwater colony.

On our walk around Skokholm, Graham and I saw rare red-legged choughs tumbling acrobatically above the cliffs. We found scarlet pimpernels with blue flowers, and enormous white drifts of sea campion. We walked on turf riddled into a fragile tissue by the burrows of rabbits, puffins and shearwaters – 86,000 burrows, Graham estimated, in an island only half a mile long. And everywhere along the grass paths and the scrub lay the contorted corpses of Manx shearwaters, literally shaken inside out by their ferocious predators the black-backed gulls. Shearwaters swim wonderfully well. But on land they can only hobble clumsily – and often too slowly – to the shelter of their burrows.

The day may discover only dead shearwaters on Skokholm, but the night comes thrillingly alive with them. Long after supper, at eleven on a starry summer night, I was standing by the lighthouse at the western end of the island with shearwaters rushing past from every point of the compass.

The wind hissed over their wings. Sometimes they came so close as to brush my hair and clothes. As each shearwater approached its burrow, it sent out a wheezy, frantic call to its waiting chick: 'Poppa's-*here*! Poppa's-*here*!' Birds flicked through the lighthouse beams, momentarily turning to silver before skimming on into the dark.

My shaded torch beam picked out a shearwater huddled

on the turf near its burrow mouth. One last hoarse wheeze of 'Poppa's-*here*!', and the bird heaved itself into the hole and out of sight. Listening intently, I could hear the coos and squeaks from underground as parent and chick were reunited – a very strange and moving moment in the dark.

84

Welcome to GB!

The entrance to GB Cave was a little concrete hut, down in a
brambly dell. Vince Simmons and Roz Bateman were waiting
for me there. Roz and Vince, proper cavers, were dressed in
special waterproof suits; I had on my rattiest raingear. Roz
unlocked the entrance door, and I gazed down a squarish hole
into darkness. The lamp on my helmet picked out a metal
ladder and a narrowing tunnel of rock sloping down and out
of sight. Behind us, the hut door closed with a clang, shutting
out the crisp light of late summer.

As a son of Mendip, with its range of Somerset hills whose
limestone heart is a tangle of water-burrowed caverns and passages, I had always meant to go caving. Somehow, I'd always
put it off. But today was the day. What would it be like to do
what the proper cavers did – sprawl on my stomach in the
grip of a rock funnel with my face in a muddy puddle and
350 feet of Somerset pressing down on the back of my neck?

Reading *Mendip Underground*, a caver's guide written by
local experts Tony Jarratt and Dave Irwin, I couldn't decide
whether to feel encouraged or not. There was no mistaking
what some of the technical terms foreshadowed: a low grovel,
a muddy wallow, a wet flat-out crawl and a desperate squeeze
did not need translation. The names of various features of the
Mendip caving systems seemed mixed in portent. The Ruby
and Crystal Chambers, Princess Grotto and Harem Passage

sounded appealing. But what of Agony Crawl and Sludge Pit Hole? Rectum Wriggle, Back Passage, Slither Pit? As for Something Nasty in the Attic, Vengeance Passage and the terminally named Abandon Hope…

'Muddy and damp' were my first impressions – a monochrome A-shaped passage, khaki-coloured under its thin mud coat. Vince went ahead, now bending low as the roof dropped to three feet above the cave floor, now straightening up as succeeding chambers swelled out on each side and overhead. I could hear the scrape and shuffle of Roz bringing up the rear, a reassuring sound.

We came to a squeeze, a place where the passage roof dropped sharply and the sides narrowed in. My helmet lamp showed a short tunnel through the rock, roughly two square feet in diameter and maybe five feet long. The soles of Vince's boots gleamed momentarily in the opening, and then he was through with an athletic wriggle. I got down on my belly, shoved my right arm out ahead as instructed and wormed forward. Getting through seemed impossible. The rock around me felt as if it were in contact with every part of my body except my face – and that was laid ear-down in a puddle of mud.

'Turn edgeways,' came Roz's calm advice, 'and just pull yourself forward.' I did as she said and slowly slithered out on the far side, as greasy as a newborn baby.

Now came a couple of fifteen-foot descents down slippery-looking walls of rock. But things underground are usually not as bad as they look. With Vince's 'put your right boot in the crack here; there's a good handhold just there' guiding me from below, I found I could spider my way down the vertical rock faces at the cost of a barked knuckle or two. It wasn't until the following morning that muscles I never even knew

I possessed began to complain about being woken from their fifty-year slumber.

As we walked, crawled and crouched our way south, a couple of hundred feet below the grazing fields of Mendip, my lamp picked out gems of underground architecture: smooth curtains of cream-coloured flowstone coating the walls, tiny pale needles of stalactites dripping from the roof, helictite in bunches like coral or frosted cauliflower heads.

'Calcite,' said Roz. 'You never get tired of the different ways it forms. Always different, always beautiful.'

Caves, I learned, are not great big hollow chambers underground, though they certainly contain plenty of those. Caves are whole systems of passages, tunnels, holes, caverns, grottoes, cliffs and boulder slides. Crystals of calcite forming in weak joints in the rock are usually their starting point; the chemical action of water on limestone widens them; pebbles or fragments of harder rock, washed in during floods, scour them out over the millennia to sometimes enormous size.

'Prepare to be gobsmacked,' Vince's voice warned me from the darkness up ahead. We scraped round a corner. 'Welcome to GB!'

It was a breathtaking sight. GB's Main Chamber opened up in a vast cavern, nearly 100 feet from floor to roof. A rock bridge sprang out across a ravine. Long stalactites hung among wavy curtains of calcite and haphazardly sinuating worms of helictite. Nearer at hand were smooth round knobs of stalagmites, bobbling the chamber floor. 'Don't touch them,' Roz warned. 'We try not to spoil the decorations.'

85

Hard hats and humorous shags

The Farne Islands are the last seaward gasp of the Whin Sill, the ledge of basalt that also upholds Bamburgh and Lindisfarne castles. The Farnes are low, craggy, treeless and windswept, the haunt of 100,000 pairs of breeding seabirds. Dark Ages people invested the islands with black-headed demons riding on goats. St Cuthbert spent eight years in eremitic isolation on Inner Farne, dodging rocks hurled by evil spirits and resisting their most lascivious temptations, before being persuaded much against his will to take on the mantle of Bishop of Lindisfarne in AD 684. Countless lives have been lost on the wickedly concealed tidal rocks of the Wamses, the Harcars and the Wideopens, evocatively-named groups of islets that make up the Farne Islands archipelago.

There's undeniably a dark and mysterious air to these lonely volcanic ledges in the sea. But it hadn't communicated itself to the cheerful excursionists on board MV *Golden Gate* as she swung out of Seahouses Harbour with skipper George Shiel at the helm. Binoculars and telephoto lenses were ready at the gunwales. The Shiel clan have been running trips from Seahouses to the Farnes since time out of mind, and George and his chums Eric and Ed have forgotten more about the seabirds of the islands than most twitchers would learn in a lifetime.

As *Golden Gate* rocked to the swell of the ice-blue North Sea, we admired the guano-whitened cliffs of Staple Island, where chocolate-jacketed guillemots stood packed in their thousands on the ledges. Puffins went skimming briskly over the water on blurry wings, like portly little commuters rushing for a train.

'Busy lad, the puffin,' commented George. 'Hereabouts, we call him the Tommy-Noddy.'

We landed on Longstone to climb the red-and-white striped tower of the lighthouse from which Grace Darling and her father William, the Longstone lighthouse keeper, made their brave dash in a rowing boat on the stormy morning of 7 September 1838. The Darlings only managed to save nine of the fifty-two souls aboard the paddle steamer *Forfarshire*, wrecked on Big Harcar. But the rescue made the twenty-three-year-old lighthouse keeper's daughter a national heroine.

We heard the tense, romantic tale from George as he took us down to Inner Farne. There I landed, to savour a couple of hours on the island where St Cuthbert wrestled his demons.

'I think you might need this,' George said laconically, handing me a builder's yellow hard hat as a parting gesture. I soon saw why.

It was tempting to think that those pre-Christian Northumbrians who populated Inner Farne with evil spirits must have done their visiting during the breeding season. Certainly the Arctic terns, nesting as they were on every available square inch of the island, proved furiously resentful of interlopers. My hard hat was pecked and excreted upon by terns defending their scrapes of nests and olive-coloured eggs. Once out of their territory, I perched on the edge of the cliffs and settled down to admire the shags.

You don't often get the chance of an intimate glimpse into the private life of this rather dashing bird of the remote sea cliffs and islands, but on Inner Farne they contest breeding space with thousands of guillemots and kittiwakes, and they have to nest where they can. It was fascinating to sit with camera and binoculars some three feet from a completely unfazed shag, recording its minute-to-minute squabbling, flirting and homemaking.

Shags are not black. They are the subtlest of greens, I can report, and their eyes really do coruscate with a hard emerald sparkle. They boast throats of the most brilliant yellow and, judging by their dry cackles, they possess a sense of humour that Arctic terns lack. When at last I had to tear myself away from their company, it was with extreme reluctance. But time and tide and George Shiel wait for no man.

86

Betjeman eyes

I wrote to Sir John Betjeman once, shortly before his death, to ask his permission to reproduce a few lines from *Summoned By Bells*. Back by return of post came a polite note in a wavery old man's handwriting, saying he'd be flattered and delighted to be quoted. A courtesy, that was all. But to me it meant more than its writer can possibly have guessed.

It was childhood reading that bathed certain West Country landscapes in a never-to-be-dispelled romantic glow for me. Long before I ever set eyes on Exmoor, my father's battered paperbacks of Henry Williamson's tales – especially *Tarka The Otter* and a now-forgotten collection of stories called *The Old Stag* – conjured vivid images of red stags running through oakwoods and otters snowed up in frozen estuaries. As for Dartmoor – through many nights of bed-bound adventuring on the trail of spectral hounds in the company of Sherlock Holmes and Dr Watson, I knew it for a fearfully fascinating place of moody mists, dreadful sucking bogs and dark tors outlined against the rising moon. It's the mixture of detailed local knowledge and romantic afterglow that gives our well-loved literary landscapes such authenticity and fixes them so deeply in our collective affections.

The poems of Betjeman have never brought me much pleasure as an adult. But *Summoned By Bells*, a blank-verse outpouring of pure nostalgia for the poet's childhood, hit the spot the moment I first opened it as a teenager.

> On Wadebridge station what a breath of sea
> Scented the Camel valley! Cornish air,
> Soft Cornish rains, and silence after steam …
> As out of Derry's stable came the brake
> To drag us up those long, familiar hills,
> Past haunted woods and oil-lit farms and on
> To far Trebetherick by the sounding sea.

The area of north Cornwall he evoked so beautifully – the stretch of coast around Padstow, Rock and Polzeath – was in fact known to me, because we'd had a couple of family holidays there. But Betjeman's long poem brushed the place with a subtle, bittersweet magic as I followed him up the lane to collect the morning milk, across the empty sands of Daymer Bay before breakfast, over the estuary to Padstow in the little ferry.

These were the rosier reflections of the Betjeman eyes that I gazed through as I read *Summoned By Bells*. Murkier, angrier glints struck into my subconscious, too – John's loneliness, his stormy relationship with his parents, his self-pity, his maladroitness, his lusts for hearty, healthy, unattainable girls.

> Misunderstood and not like other boys,
> Deep, dark and pitiful I saw myself
> In my mind's mirror…

Images like this fleshed out the picture, gave it layers of impact and meaning that excited the as-yet-unwoken adult reader in me. And, of course, they titillated the sulky

Kevin-the-teenager side of me, too. Yeah, *right*, man! It's so *unfair*!

Setting off on a cloudy morning a couple of years ago to walk my Betjeman corner of Cornwall, I hadn't even gone a mile before I met a bouncing bevy of bathing beauties cantering down the path and giggling about boys they knew back in Highgate. How Betjeman a moment was that?

A little further along, under the round green hump of Bray Hill, I crossed the golf course where young John used to dam the stream, and where as a sullen youth he'd been forced to caddy for his father. Beyond the fairway, the crooked little spire of St Enodoc's Church rose behind a feathery tamarisk hedge. Betjeman lies buried in the churchyard, just to the right of the path, under a slate headstone whose elaborately curlicued engraving must cause him a heavenly chuckle or two from time to time.

Walking on from St Enodoc's along the clifftop path to Polzeath, hearing cries and laughter from the coves and the faint thud of waves on sand, it was as if every archetypal image of the seaside holiday – Betjeman's, mine and everyone else's – had coalesced around these couple of miles of Cornwall. It wasn't just the poet's rose-tinted spectacles I was looking through, but my own as well.

I saw myself as a little boy on holiday in Polzeath, riding the Padstow ferry, running on the sands and getting into scrapes, exactly as John and countless other holidaymaking boys and girls had done in their turn. They were still at it, here and now in the new millennium, splashing and shrieking in the surf. Somewhere among them there'd be the new young romantics, ecstatic at the delight of a Cornish holiday and gazing around them through Betjeman eyes.

P is for Poetry

... although I really ought to have filed it long ago under 'D is for Doggerel'. Why is doggerel always seen as the poor relation of poetry? Just because it goes 'tumpty-tumpty-tumpty-tum' and is nice and easy to memorise? Honestly, which of us would remember a word of the maiden speech of Kim Jong-Un to the people of North Korea on 15 April 2012 if it hadn't been rendered into doggerel in *The Paris Review*?

Here's a choice dictum from Kim's address:

> We will walk in this path
> Till our shoes all wear out,
> Then we'll grow new shoes,
> In our gardens, like sprouts.

Obviously the Supreme Leader is also a walker – a good omen for world peace.

Through Sloch na Marra to Rathlin Island

Swooping through Sloch na Marra, Valley of the Sea, I wondered more than once if our little ferryboat would manage to rise and breast the next green slope of the waves. Sloch na Marra is well named. The liveliest tide rip off the Atlantic coast of Northern Ireland, it twists and roars in angry furrows between the ferry port of Ballycastle and the L-shaped island of Rathlin some five miles offshore. At times on that blustery July morning, sinking into the trough of an especially steep wave, Rathlin disappeared from view, and I was left looking up at the racing blue-and-grey sky and the sardonically grinning faces of a bunch of island boys who were returning home from some wild night out in Ballycastle.

All things come to an end; a few minutes later, we went bumping out of the foothills of Sloch na Marra into calmer water. Rathlin Island began to shape itself out of the spray. The island resembles a bent arm, its upper half running from tall western cliffs towards a crooked elbow at the north-east corner, its forearm sloping south to Rue Point. The ferry swung round and made for the few white houses of the harbour village, tucked into the sheltered crook of Rathlin's elbow.

The island's cliffs seemed to grin a rugged welcome, a cheerful exposure of white calcareous teeth. Travelling round the coasts of Britain, one gets so accustomed to seeing chalk as a topping, the white icing on the geographical layer cake, that the curious topsy-turviness of Rathlin Island's construction comes as a shock. Here, the lower storey of the island is of pale chalky limestone, the upper layer a capping of dark basalt spread like molten chocolate by the tremendous volcanic convulsions that formed the Giant's Causeway and the spectacular cliffs of the Antrim coast.

Rathlin's cliffs are burrowed with caves where grey seals breed. In one of them, the islanders will tell you, the fugitive Robert the Bruce sat on a day of despair in 1306 and learned a lesson in perseverance from a patient spider. The cliffs are also seamed with ledges where seabirds nest, mate and rear their chicks by the hundred thousand each year. In the cold, clear water around the island flourish sea cucumbers, sponges and soft corals. Rathlin is a sea-surrounded paradise. It's quite extraordinary that the island is not swamped by tourists; on that brisk morning at the height of the holiday season, the jubilant youths and I had the ferry, the sea and the stupendous island views all to ourselves.

Landing on the little jetty, the lads went skeltering off about their own affairs, and I struck out west along a narrow-walled road between neat hayfields. Blood-red lanterns of fuchsia trembled on the hedges, and thick carpets of heath spotted-orchids bent this way and that to the gentle push of the south-west wind. I passed a marshy lake, where tufted ducks were sailing, and watched spellbound as a handsome full-grown hare went bounding away across the grass. Enough to make the heart sing, these signs of healthy natural balance sustained by the small-scale, old-fashioned agriculture of Rathlin, the tiny human population of seventy-odd and the physical isolation of the place.

From the crest of the island, I looked north-east to see the long peninsular silhouettes of the Mull of Oa and the Mull of Kintyre, fifteen miles across the sea in Scotland. For all its lonely situation, Rathlin Island was always a ripe strategic plum for invaders. In 1642, Duncan Campbell landed here to deal out slaughter and despair among the islanders. One of Rathlin's hills is still known as Crocknascriedlin, the Hill of Screaming. It was from there that the island women watched Campbell's soldiers butcher their men before they, too, were rounded up and thrown to their deaths on the rocks at Sloak na Calliagh, the Pit of the Hags. So the very place names of Rathlin continue to recount its story.

There was screaming enough today on Rathlin, growing ever louder and more raucous the nearer I came to the cliffs at the western end of the island. When I rounded the corner, I saw why. A quarter of a million seabirds were squabbling, wheeling and swooping around Kebble Cliffs – kittiwakes on black-tipped wings, guillemots and razorbills thronging the sea stacks, puffins at their burrow doors in the grass ledges of the cliffs. The stink and the noise, the everlasting circling and the dizzying height above the creaming waves made my head spin. A living landscape in perpetual, mind-boggling sound and motion that had me clinging to the rail of the viewing platform, breathless, gasping and transfixed.

The Walls of Derry

'… so the riot was in full progress just here, bricks and bottles flying, everyone yelling across the barricades. And then this figure appears – headband, you know, the real 1970s jogger – and he ran right through the whole thing, quite oblivious. And everybody stops – soldiers, police, rioters – everything quietens down; everyone's staring at this lone jogger.'

Standing at the entrance to the Bogside, Tom Carlin broke out in a chuckle. 'Everything freezes for a few seconds. The jogger gives a wave and runs on out of the picture – and it all starts up again. One of the craziest moments in the Troubles, and everyone seems to remember it.'

Tom and I were walking the walls of the city known to loyalists as Londonderry and to nationalists as Derry. It took five years (1613–18) to enclose the heart of the settlement in a strong belt of stone twenty feet tall and equally as wide, buckling the city into its high defensive position. The Maiden City, they still call it; these walls have never been breached. The nearest they came was during the epic siege of 1668–9, a story that every local schoolchild knows off by heart. Walking the walls, you see the whole thing unfold, a living history lesson.

England's despised King James II, as Tom put it, must have been a very arrogant kind of a man. He not only set siege to the Protestant-held city for fifteen weeks, but he spoiled his own chances when a Catholic victory looked imminent.

Governor Robert Lundy (still burned in effigy each year by local Protestants as a traitor) had agreed to surrender if the Jacobite troops pulled back three miles, but James decided to make a point by riding close to the walls by Bishop's Gate. 'That was when they let loose at him with a cannon from the church tower,' said Tom, 'and gave him the famous yell of "No Surrender!"'

At Bishop's Gate, we climbed down from the walls to see St Columb's Cathedral, built in 1633 in handsome style. In the entrance hall, mounted on a pedestal, was the great iron mortar bomb fired into the city with the Jacobites' surrender terms jammed into its fuse hole. 'The world's first airmail letter', Tom styles it. In the chapter house, a museum to the siege, we found the four great gate locks of the city along with their keys, which were daringly grabbed by the thirteen original – and now immortal – Apprentice Boys.

'Killed at the boom,' read the memorial to Captain Michael Browning, 'in the hour of victory while encouraging his men in the face of terrible danger.' It was Browning who brought relief to the city on 28 July 1689, ramming his ship *Mountjoy* through the wooden boom the Jacobites had built across the Foyle. He was shot dead in the attempt, but *Mountjoy*'s men were able to land the supplies she carried. They were desperately needed: a quarter of the 30,000 locked in behind the walls had died, and the rest were starving. Almost every dog, cat, horse and rat in the place had been eaten.

Down at the far end of the walls, we came to the Tower Museum. A potent symbol of hope stands here: the replica of an Irish round tower, built in the 1970s at the height of the Troubles by a Bogside man, Paddy Doherty.

'We called him "Paddy Bogside",' Tom Carlin told me, 'and we called the tower "Paddy's Folly", because he went ahead and built it when everything around it was being destroyed. But he always intended it to be a museum, a mark of regeneration for Derry. It gave us hope at a very bad time.'

90

Larks over Hubberholme

When the larks struck up over the Hubberholme meadows, I thought I must have died and gone to heaven. I was sitting outside the George Inn by the old packhorse bridge, dangling my bare feet in the peat-brown shallows of the River Wharfe, a pint of beer in my hand and fifteen miles of prime Wharfedale walking under my belt. The liquid beauty of that reeling, seamless birdsong in the summer evening air hit me with the sweetest of unexpected blows. It seemed to encapsulate everything I had walked for, all that my five senses had revelled in through the long day on the sun-warmed limestone terraces above the river.

I had hardly seen a soul as I followed open paths a couple of hundred feet up in the flanks of Wharfedale. I passed in and out of the yards of lonely farms in whose barns the hunted Methodist preachers of the eighteenth century had roared hundreds of souls across Jordan to salvation. Such red-blooded history, singing out of the pale stones! On the far side of the dale, soundless blobs of red and blue moved slowly – walkers following the Dales Way long-distance path. But no one came up the track I was wandering along, and when I turned uphill and put the crest of a ridge between myself and Wharfedale, I became king of a whole wide empty world.

Soft, pliable, productive limestone underpins much of Yorkshire's dale country. But there's true Yorkshire grit here too, as you might expect. On a hot August day, there's a scent in the air of a gritstone moor that's as heady as a hop kiln – the fruity tang of bog that's been thoroughly soaked all spring and is yielding its rich, rooty savour to the liberating warmth of summer on a dry breeze. The sweet smell of cut hayfields and a distant whiff of cow dung float up from the walled meadows of the in-bye land along the floor of the dale below. Every now and then the cold, metallic stab of beck water, strained through mosses and wet peat, slides a thin blade across the nostrils – across the tongue too, as you bend your head into a spring bubbling between rocks and drink till you gasp. Sparkling stones full of quartz chips skitter beneath the boots. Their parent rocks feel coarse and warm to the touch, like the skin of a beast. You walk in a constant fall of light and shadow, rain or the threat of rain, for ever chasing the sun across fellsides cut by the glaciers into hollows and smooth whalebacks.

After a day of walking through landscapes as subtle and sensuous as these, one comes down a long walled lane at evening to the overnight farmhouse or pub in the absolute belief that the Pennine hills, and the Yorkshire Dales in particular, knock every other kind of summer hiker's playground in the world into a cocked hat. Morning, especially if it's a good old Yorkshire spitter, generally brings a sense of reality in with the breakfast. These landscapes retain bite, as anyone can confirm who has been lost in one of the region's treacherous hill mists. The wise thing is to look on such experiences simply as drops of tabasco on the sweet oyster of Dales country walking.

91

Salt marsh and mudflat: Cobnor peninsula

It was going to be a beautiful late summer's evening. Looking from the Sussex shore into Hampshire, we saw the western sky ablaze with light behind a skein of cloud. The tide was too far out for swimming from the great sands around the mouth of Chichester Harbour, but the three of us – Jane, me and our eighteen-year-old daughter, Mary – had energy to burn. A dusk walk, then: something intriguing, somewhere we'd never explored. How about the flat and lonely Cobnor peninsula that hung like a skate's wing in the middle of Chichester Harbour's vast flats of marsh and mud? That seemed to promise a tasty combination of a tang of green countryside and a salty smack of the sea.

In the muted light of late afternoon, the chalk ploughlands of the downs walled in the northern skyline with pale silver. Nearer at hand, rich, warm, silty earth glowed in the freshly ploughed fields of the coast. Swallows were skimming there, fuelling up for their flight to Africa. From the peninsula's village of Chidham, we made for the shore along a beautifully mown and kept grass path whose hedges were heavy with blackberries in every shade of green, red and black – sharp to the point of sourness on the tongue, though, this early in the season.

Out on the seawall path, we looked across the low-tide mud and its green fringe of salt marsh to the squat grey spire of

Bosham's church above a cluster of waterfront houses – every chocolate-box artist's dream of delight. Mary strode away, hair streaming behind her like the mane of a wild horse. Jane ran down the sea bank into the marsh, exclaiming over the flowers growing among the sea-purslane tangle – the large blue many-rayed sunbursts of sea aster, drifts of the more delicate and darker-blue sea lavender, pink stars of centaury, purple flowers of common mallow. I trod the sea wall path among shin-high thickets of sea beet, as dark and tough as school cabbage, each big crinkly leaf seamed into wrinkles in order to retain and channel as much fresh rainwater as possible in such a salty environment.

A ramshackle wooden jetty linked the bank to a beached old boat at the Cobnor Activities Centre, where cracks wriggled like eels through darkly glinting banks of mud. Youngsters without much joy in their lives are helped here to gain a savour of independence and a sense of themselves. The voices of the volunteer assistants came floating across the marsh.

'Seen Dominic?'

'Oh, he'll be stuck nose-first in some mud bank somewhere! He'll be fine!'

Far out in the slack-tide stream of Bosham Channel, I could see a slime-smeared dinghy sawing back and forth, its youthful tillerman bumping here and jolting there. If that was Dominic, he was having the time of his young life.

Down at Cobnor Point, I caught up with Mary and Jane, and we walked on in company across a strand of cockle shells and small flints. The broad sweep of Chichester Harbour's more seaward reaches opened up briefly, then we turned the corner of the peninsula and were walking north-west into a narrowing perspective of glinting mud flats. Old wooden stakes showed where Victorian attempts to reclaim the tidal water for agriculture had come to a sticky end.

Nowadays, the thousand acres of Nutbourne Marshes form a nature reserve, where wildfowl spend the winter in their tens of thousands. It looked as if nature had her eye on the farmland of the peninsula, too. A new sea bank had been built, well inland of the old one. The sea had been creeping landward with ever-increasing force, undermining the flood defences and burrowing away at the foundations of the wonderfully gnarly and contorted old oaks that clung precariously with arthritic root fingers to the very lip of the land.

Up at Chidham Point, a fingerpost pointed us inland towards the village and the pleasures of its pearl of a pub – the Old House At Home. Before setting our backs to the marsh and our feet to the field path, however, there was time for a last gaze westward across the glistening mud flats and slowly filling creeks to where the sky was barred with stripes of cloud edged with brilliance, as if inlaid with gold wire by the caged sun sinking beyond them.

92

Bat-watching in Petworth Park

Bats get a bad press. People find them ugly, creepy, scary. They suck your blood and give you rabies and tangle themselves in your hair, right? Well, no, actually. Bats, seen in the calm light of reason and common sense, are rather beautiful, highly specialised and delightful creatures – and extremely useful at hoovering up midges and other thundering nuisances. Sussex is a county rich in bats – in fact, all seventeen of the UK's native species are resident, and fourteen of these have been found on the Petworth Estate in the western region of the county. That was where Jane and I headed, one drizzly evening towards the end of summer.

A damp, cloudy evening, steamy with moisture and the threat of rain, is just the kind of evening not to be bat-watching. But our evening rendezvous at the gates of Petworth Park had been fixed many moons ago. Crispin Scott, the National Trust's regional nature conservation adviser, was waiting with his young son Alf to take us for a walk on the wild side of the park, superbly landscaped in the mid-eighteenth century by Capability Brown.

'Bat detector,' Crispin said, handing over a stout black box knobbly with buttons. 'I'll show you how it works when we're out in the park. But let's have a look at the tunnels first.'

In the brick-lined tunnels that connect Petworth House with its servants' quarters, thousands of bats of seven different species hibernate the winter months away – Brandt's bats; grey and brown long-eared bats with huge ears; Daubenton's bats, which hunt insects over water; common pipistrelles; whiskered bats; and rare Bechstein's bats. But on this late summer evening, the eerie tunnels lay empty of bats.

Out in the park, the light was beginning to fade. The great house stood, shadowed by rain, in a man-made landscape of subtle curves and hollows. In front of us, a spinney of oak and sweet chestnut perched artfully on a scenic knoll.

'Clumps on lumps,' said Crispin. 'Very good for bats – the air's still, there are plenty of insects, and it's sheltered.'

Waiting among the trees for whatever the dusk might bring, Crispin brought us up to speed on the Petworth bats. No artificial fertilisers are used on the estate; this encourages insects, which in turn attract the bats. Each bat species has its own preferred habitats: barbastelles, for example, like lightly wooded places, Bechstein's bats prefer heavy tree cover, while Daubenton's need water over which to hunt insects. A common pipistrelle is only as long as one's thumb but can easily pack away 3,000 midges in one night. Noctules are bigger than the other bats – they can tackle a cockchafer.

Bats hunt and find their way by echolocation, emitting a stream of sounds too high-pitched for human ears and measuring the returning echoes as they bounce back off objects. The echolocation is so precise that the bat is able to identify an insect even if it's sitting motionless on a leaf, and can pick it neatly off as it zooms by. Each species transmits at a different frequency – soprano pipistrelles at around 55 kHz, common pipistrelles at 45 kHz, Daubenton's bats generally at 45–50 kHz, noctules down at 25 kHz. The bat detector device reduces the transmission to a sound we can pick up – a crackle or quick vibration, which accelerates sharply to the 'feeding buzz', a wet squelch exactly like blowing a raspberry, when the bat closes in on an insect.

We were scarcely expecting much action on this damp evening, but, as we waited in the 'clump on the lump', little black bullets suddenly started zipping round the glade.

'Soprano pipistrelles,' whispered Crispin. 'Tune your detectors to 55 kHz.' The pipistrelles streaked by in pairs, with the juveniles, learning to hunt, following their mothers in close formation like tiny fighter planes. Three or four bats soon became twenty or more, some of them flying within touching distance of us, crepitating and buzzing.

'I've never seen such a good display,' exclaimed Crispin, 'and these are the worst conditions of any bat expedition I've done!'

Down by the lake, there were noctules flying overhead, their echolocation translated by the bat detectors into a '*chop-chop-chop*' as of miniature helicopter blades. Daubenton's bats hunted insects over the water, crackling like burning stubble as they darted with a flash of pale belly through the beam of Crispin's torch. Natterer's bats, on the wing after small moths, made bristly noises. There were quiet ploppings and quackings from out on the dark water to remind us that other denizens of the lake were about their nightly occasions.

Walking back through the park, we saw the great house lost in the night. Of its scores of windows, two solitary squares shone as beacons of light and human presence. All around us, the feeding frenzy of the pipistrelles continued unabated. Then Jane gave a sudden exclamation. A bat had flown so close, it had actually knocked her glasses off.

93

A stroll on the Goodwin Sands

Three miles off Deal on the east Kent coast lie the Goodwin Sands, a ragged-edged block of sand ten miles from top to toe and about five across the waist. Twice a day, the sands break the sea surface. I had seen them from the coast path, rolling clear of a falling tide like the gleaming shoulder of some vast submarine beast. They looked inaccessible, more dreamlike than real. I was amazed to discover that I could actually land out there and take a walk across the dreaded Goodwin Sands.

'Yeah,' said the young steward as we sped out of Dover hoverport on board the hovercraft *The Princess Anne*, 'we all had a barbecue on the Sands last time. Got the charcoal going, cooked up the sausages and burgers… it was brilliant. We've brought our cricket gear this trip. Might have time for a game if we're lucky with the tides.'

The Princess Anne lifted her black skirts and raced, roaring and shuddering, out of Dover. She carried a motley bunch, 300 or 400 adventurers who were seizing the moment. Tides low enough to allow a hovercraft to land passengers in daylight on the Goodwin Sands are rarer than hen's teeth.

In the days before modern electronic navigational aids, the sand reef claimed thousands of ships and tens of thousands of lives. A fog or a foul night turned the Goodwins into a deathtrap. The boatmen of Deal, Dover and Ramsgate were famous for the daring rescues they carried out – but for every life they snatched from the jaws of the Goodwins, hundreds were lost.

Ships would strike on the sands with a thunderous crash; masts and rigging would tumble. Those lucky enough to survive the impact would be crushed to death between waves and sands or drowned as the rising tide swept them away. The glutinous sand of the reef would hold and suck down the remains of the wreck. Come daylight, investigating boatmen might find a complete ship stuck in the Sands, or perhaps only a funnel or a set of disembodied masts. Sometimes, the suction was so powerful that a vessel wrecked at night would literally vanish before morning.

The Princess Anne slowed and settled herself with a bump.

'Back on the craft by ten to eight, please,' boomed a tinny loudspeaker voice. The square bow door opened, and we flooded out on to the Goodwin Sands.

They lay low and wide in evening sunlight, a dun brown plate of sand stretching off to a line of breakers a mile away. The entire surface of the reef was pitted with 'swillies', round holes with a few inches of sea water gleaming at the bottom. The sand felt hard and cold under my bare feet. My instinct was to stride, then run – to race as far as I could across this virgin island out in the sea that would offer itself for an hour at best.

Black-backed gulls and a little company of seals watched us use up our time in more or less eccentric fashion. Two men set up a postbox and sold 'posted on the Goodwin Sands' cards, ready-stamped. A municipal park bench appeared as if brought by a djinn; a figure promptly stretched out on it and went to sleep. An elderly couple popped champagne and toasted each other. Kids shovelled souvenir sand and shells into plastic bags. Birdwatchers and seal fanciers stalked their prey.

'Majesty! Majesty!' trilled a Christian group, raising their arms ecstatically to the wide evening sky. A hovercraft attendant in a red skirt took guard with a cricket bat in front of a furled umbrella and smacked a tennis ball high into the air.

'Catch it, Shirley!' everyone yelled.

A cheery scene, like a Blackpool outing, but eerily infused with the precariousness of this extraordinary, once-a-year location. You must not outstay your welcome on the reef. As the tide comes in, water rises up through the sands and separates the grains. They become a soft, sliding morass, quivering like a jelly at every footfall, sucking down the feet of anyone who stands still. The outlines of the swillies blur and dissolve, whirlpooling and liquidising. Firm ground becomes sinking sands, over which the water soon closes.

It seemed hardly any time before the captain was up on the roof of *The Princess Anne*, calling 'everyone back on the craft, please' through a megaphone. An attendant was sent haring off between the swillies like a red-waistcoated sheepdog to round up stragglers. A last impassioned prayer from the Christians and a few ringing pagan yells from the beer drinkers sounded the knell of our brief moment of glory on the Goodwins.

On the way back to Dover, a nautical archaeologist told me of the extraordinary sight she'd once glimpsed on the Goodwin Sands – a wooden troopship wrecked in 1703, revealed for a few seconds far down in the side of a giant sandhole, complete with the swords, musketoons, leather hats and naked skulls of the misfortunate passengers. How full the world is of windows onto wonders, opening and closing before we can do more than glance momentarily through them.

94

Q is for Quagmire

The oddest and most ominous place I've ever walked, by a country mile, is what Elizabethan antiquarian William Lambarde described as that 'most dreadful gulfe and shippe swallower', the Goodwin Sands. But the boggiest, the suckingest and gloopiest, is the spring-sodden morass of Dunsop Head. This treacherous mire has swallowed both path and fence posts, and it lies in waiting for anyone unwise enough to fancy their chances of 'hopping across – come on, two minutes and we're over'.

Dunsop Head occupies a saddle of ground at the head of Whitendale, a remote valley in the Forest of Bowland where hen harriers are said to breed. These large pale birds of prey, partial to young grouse and therefore the target of gamekeepers' guns and poisons, are very rare indeed.

Jane and I longed to see a hen harrier. We set out from Dunsop Bridge and soon found ourselves squelching gingerly across the mire. Jane stretched for a mossy fence post. Beneath her hand, it slid into the bog like Excalibur in reverse. Her legs followed it, up to the hips. She floundered, and I, turning back to offer a helping hand, sank up to mid-shin. Jane stayed calm. She leaned back and raised one leg, then the other, out of the slutch. She crawled like a crab to firmer ground, sodden, beslubbered and steaming.

We scraped, kicked and wiped off the black muck, heads

bent low over the disgusting task. At last we finished. We looked up and glanced around. Three stalwart twitchers had been watching our travails from the path beyond. Each sported a grin of pure schadenfreude.

'See the hen harrier?' they called. 'No? Well, it flew right over your heads.'

95

Englyn on Snowdon

We were climbing Snowdon by the Watkin Path, sweating it up to the saddle of Bwlch y Ciliau, where a fine cold breeze hit us at the same moment as the stunning view over the lakes and mountains of the Snowdon Horseshoe. 1,000 feet below lay Llyn Llydaw, a deep inky blue lake, with the Pyg and Miner's tracks threading its shores on their way up to Snowdon. Crib Goch, the Red Comb; Glyder Fawr and Glyder Fach in the range beyond; sharp-peaked Y Lliwedd on our right hand – magnificent mountains, a view like a bracing slap in the face after the enclosed valley we'd been traversing.

Does King Arthur's great sword, Excalibur, lie in the waters of Llyn Llydaw? Does Arthur himself sleep under a cairn up there, or was he borne away in a dark barge by the fair ladies of the mountains after falling, pierced with an arrow, at Bwlch y Saethau, the Pass of the Arrows? We climbed to the pass and up the final precipitous, tricky scramble, speculating on Snowdon's legends with what little breath we could spare.

Up on the rocky summit, as we stood in the wind by the cairn-like trig point, the view was even more breathtaking: Cardigan Bay and a shadowy Isle of Man, the long Lleyn peninsula, Cadair Idris in the south, Anglesey and the Menai Strait to the north. Mountains, corries, crumpled rock walls and tiny lakes lay scattered at our feet.

George Borrow ascended Snowdon in the summer of 1854,

arm-in-arm with his stepdaughter Henrietta. As usual, the author of *Wild Wales* drew attention to himself by showing off, reciting from the summit an englyn 'consisting entirely of vowels with the exception of one consonant, namely the letter R':

O Ri y'Ryri yw'r oera, – o'r âr,
Ar oror wir arwa;
O'r awyr a yr Eira,
O'i ryw i roi rew a'r ia.

A hill most chill is Snowdon's hill,
And wintry is his brow;
From Snowdon's hill the breezes chill
Can freeze the very snow.

'Such was the harangue,' wrote Borrow, mightily pleased with himself, 'which I uttered on the top of Snowdon; to which Henrietta listened with attention; three or four English, who stood nigh, with grinning scorn, and a Welsh gentleman with considerable interest.'

AUTUMN

Jays in the ilex

The jays are back in the ilex tree, screaming like harridans as they contest ownership of the acorns. Jays are funny birds, proper popinjays in their jaunty plumage and saucy flickers of blue, yet hard to love because of their springtime harrying and infanticide among the songbirds. September is the month to see them at their bullyish best, six or eight at a time swarming over the ilex in a brief but intense orgy of gobbling, bouncing among the prickly dark leaves and filling their bellies with the hard little nuts.

Yesterday's storm has found out the weaknesses of the old tree. This morning, a broken branch lies in the dew-soaked grass under the ilex. Lifting the limb to drag it across the lawn to the woodshed, I notice a flicker of movement in a crevice between two of the crocodilian plates of bark. The scarlet shells of three ladybirds are visible. I must have dislodged them when I moved the bough. They crawl along the miniature canyon and out of sight. How many more ladybirds and other insects are already battened down for winter under the scaly bark? I set the branch gently back in the grass. They need it more than I do.

Big Meadow

No landscape I have ever known holds the sheer undiluted magic of the wetland meadows where I used to play as a child. Whatever their map names might have been, to my friend Andrew and me the vast old grazing field and its bordering strip of weedy waterway were simply the Big Meadow and the Old Canal. They lay, an endless source of dreams and delights, at the bottom of our lost-and-gone Gloucestershire village in the floodplain of the River Severn between Gloucester and Tewkesbury. We were down there every day of our lives, a pair of gumbooted scallywags. I can't pretend we were the greatest young conservationists; in fact, we terrorised the place with airguns and stones. But, running amok, leaping from gates, falling from willow branches into the canal, we absorbed by a kind of fabulous osmosis the natural glories of what I have since heard described as one of Britain's finest and richest wetlands.

Hares ran over the medieval furrows of those fields; water rats plopped into the ditches. Dragonflies darted. Ragged robin, milkmaids, orchids and brooklime spattered the damp meadows with colour. In spring, the rain-streaked Gloucestershire skies were full of zigzaggety snipe and the ragged-looking, clumsy fliers we knew as peewits, my favourites, with their indescribably plaintive and hair-raising calls. In summer, the canal would bake to a pungent stew of mud and weed. Each season held thousands of charms, but winter was the best of all. Winter brought the floods.

Our meadows were the alluvial floodplain of the River Severn, which snaked its way from Tewkesbury to Gloucester a couple of miles to the west. That lush green grass, those well-set wild flower seeds, the soft earth so attractive to curlew and lapwing with its abundance of worms and insects – all were nourished by the rich minerals of riverbed mud, generously and thickly spread in the early months of each year by Farmer Severn. High spring tides triggered this bounty, pushing many dozens of miles upriver from the Severn's estuary and forming the mini-tsunami known as the Severn Bore. When these incoming tidal surges met fresh water rushing down the river from cloudbursts or snowmelt in the Cotswolds or the Welsh mountains, the Severn would burst its banks at the weakest place in the flood defences – the meadows that lay just upstream from Gloucester.

You could never tell when it would flood, which morning would be the one when you'd round the corner of the lane on your tricycle to find water stretching to the horizon, hedges drowned, cows marooned and the Finlays and Thayers sweeping the brown tide out of their kitchens. In a week or so, the drowned grasslands would freeze into a surface like thin glass, a fantasy skating rink for scarfed and gloved adventurers. White-fronted geese, yellow-nosed swans and whistling squadrons of wigeon packed the sky, a watery yellow field inverted over the floods through which you splashed home at dusk.

The Severn floods were no recent phenomenon. They had been inundating the floodplain landscape for thousands of years, moulding it and smoothing it into a flat apron of fertile mud. Out of the plain rose the area's characteristic steep little hillocks, known as tumps, where Andrew and I would swoop through the air on home-made swings roped to the branches of cider apple trees. It was the floods that kept the meadows and wet woodland patches safe from building development, and it was the small farmers of the villages on higher ground who maintained the variety and wellbeing of the local wildlife with their old-fashioned husbandry, leaving the grass uncut until the flower seeds had set, trusting their cattle and Farmer Severn to enrich the ground rather than drenching it in chemical fertilisers.

It turned out that the Big Meadow and the Old Canal were not for ever and ever, as they had seemed to be. In came the agrichemicals of the 1970s, the drainage and hedge-ripping and riverbank tidying of the '80s. The rich treasure of the wetlands was all spent and squandered in the space of three decades.

Somebody must have come to their senses, though. I paid a visit to the Big Meadow last summer, my first for a few years, and I found that under the care of Gloucestershire Wildlife Trust the officially titled Coombe Hill Meadows Nature Reserve is flourishing once more as a properly maintained wetland. Birds, flowers and hares are back where they have always belonged.

I'm so thankful to have been a child in the 1950s, when one was expected to be out of doors and away over the fields all day, ranging widely and getting into a lot of mischief. And I'm delighted that the decades of late twentieth-century degradation under the chemical regime of intensive farming are over, and that the meadows once more lie beneath flights of lapwings. They've never ceased to figure in my dreams, the flicker and tumble of peewits and their creaking, melancholy cry for ever haunting the cloudy skies over the Big Meadow and the Old Canal.

98

Gassy Webcap, Bedstraw Smut and the dreaded Cramp Balls

Now then, kids, before you set off for your evening out in the autumn woods, I want you to pay close attention to Old Uncle Christopher and his *Lurid Lexicon of Freaky Fungi*.

First of all, stay right away from the Hairy Nuts Disco, OK? It's all senior citizens in there – Bearded Fieldcap and his cousin Whiskery Milkcap, and disgusting old Gassy Webcap, too. And that snooty pair Bald Knight and Upper Crust, the rotten snobs. Not to mention that Bastard Toadflax Rust – steer well clear of him!

A bite to eat? The Cryptic Bonnet's pretty good. But don't spoil your appetite with too many Scurfy Twiglets, and don't be tempted to try their Bitter Poisonpie with Witches' Butter. Twist your guts right up, that will.

If you fancy a bit of a dance, head for the Snaketongue Truffleclub, that's my advice. Just mention my name to Egghead Mottlegill on the door. He ain't pretty, but he's a pal. A couple of veggie cocktails on the house – a Potato Earthball and a Cabbage Parachute should set you up nicely. Maybe a Dewdrop Dapperling to get you groovin' on the dance floor.

And just keep your wits about you. My old mum used to scare me with a lot of nonsense about the Twisted Deceiver and the Contorted Strangler in his Dark Crazed Cap. Load of old tosh, I know. But do be sensible! Hotlips and Bedstraw

Smut, or a quick Powdery Piggyback with The Flirt – sounds tempting, eh? I know! I know! I was the same at your age. All I'm saying is – watch out for Dead Moll's Fingers, and that Hairy Earthtongue of hers. You don't want to wind up with Wet Rot or Weeping Toothcrust, do you? Let alone the dreaded Cramp Balls!

99

The Great Ash Massacre

There is a silent slaughter going on all across the land, and it's breaking my heart to see it. The ash trees, those graceful entities with the pinnate leaves, wind-whisperers and guardians of ancient wells, are dying, not in their hundreds or even their hundreds of thousands, but in their tens of millions. The aggressor is *Hymenoscyphus fraxineus*, or ash dieback, a fungus of Asian origin that entered Europe in the early 1990s and has been chewing its way westward at frightening speed. It got across to England in 2012 and has since spread inland and upcountry like a sea surge.

The minute spores of *Hymenoscyphus fraxineus* can ride on the winds for tens of miles to land on a new host tree. The spores penetrate the leaves and then the main trunk, and the fungus grows inside the tree, blocking the tissue that transports water around the tree's circulatory system from the roots. It's easy to spot an ash tree under attack from *Hymenoscyphus fraxineus* – the crown thins, twigs crack off and drop, leaves blacken and develop cancerous spots that soon widen. Sooner or later – frequently very soon, perhaps in a single season – the tree becomes prey to other fungi and diseases, sickens and weakens, rots and dies. Apart from very expensive and intrusive individual injections with fungicide, there's no known remedy for ash dieback.

I remember all too clearly the havoc wrought by *Ophiostoma novo-ulmi*, Dutch elm disease, in the 1960s and 1970s, when 90 per cent of all our elms died – twenty-five million trees across the country. Anyone who can recall that horrible epoch had better brace themselves, because six times as many ash trees are expected to die. The United Kingdom has up to 200 million ash trees, accounting for about one in ten of all our broadleaved trees. Of these, perhaps 5 per cent may be resistant to the fungus, and about 1 per cent may be able to pass on this resistance to offspring. But the fact of the matter is that we can expect to lose up to 80 per cent of our ash – a staggering 150 million trees or more – over the next decade or so, from woodlands and hedgerows, parks and gardens. Ash canopy has a wonderful propensity for letting light in through the well-separated lobes of the leaves, so the plants of the woodland floor that need such dappled sunlight to thrive will be greatly diminished. Hundreds of creatures – from insects and lichens to birds and dormice – live in, on and by the grace of ash trees, so our woodlands' interdependent ecosystems and their biodiversity will sustain a desperate blow. And the landscape will be transformed visually – it will be balder, poorer, less shaded, less green.

Nothing will truly replace the ash. Perhaps over decades a stock of resistant ash trees will develop, but that's for the long term. This is a disaster in the making and unfolding. There will be others; our interconnected global economy makes them inevitable.

So what can we do, apart from lament? We can pile up the dead wood into wet and dry heaps; we can leave the corpses of the woodland trees where they fall, to rot down for wildlife to exploit and inhabit. And we can replant, and plant anew, with good home-grown species from biosecure nurseries – aspen and sycamore, whitebeam, wych elm, wild pear and hawthorn, local trees grown locally. That's the small seed from which a more resilient British woodland may eventually emerge.

100

Covid Autumn: India in the Cotswolds

I'd just about heard the name of Sezincote, but no more than that. I thought it must be another of those gorgeous Elizabethan manors of golden stone that the Cotswolds are so rich in. Queen Bess probably stayed there; Charles II might have dodged pursuit up an oak tree in the park – that sort of thing. But what we found tucked in below the woods near Moreton-in-Marsh was quite a shock to behold.

A day of grumpy weather – nearly as grumpy as Jimmy Anderson. I kept my phone on constant refresh, trying to keep up with the missed catches, rain delays, Pakistani obduracy and other obstacles falling in the path of England's Greatest Bowler as he strained to capture his 600th Test wicket at Southampton.

Moreton-in-Marsh is a lovely town with a very wide sheep-straggle of a high street tortured by traffic; Bourton-on-the-Hill a beautiful little sloping village of honey-coloured houses made miserable by 4×4s, fat cars and inexcusably fast and noisy motorbikes pelting down its narrow roadway. Between these two we crossed long fields of harvested barley and wheat with cotton-reel bales of straw regularly spaced, as though giants had temporarily suspended some esoteric game and left all the pieces on the board. Rusty barns, far views across a rolling landscape of green and brown and church towers and gables of that remarkable golden stone peep out from trees far and near.

South of Bourton, we came on a slice of the Mughal empire set down in the Cotswolds – the extraordinary Sezincote House, built in 1805 for Charles Cockerell to the designs of his brother Samuel Pepys Cockerell, who incorporated Georgian, Muslim and Hindu architectural styles in a glorious, jolting mishmash of a building. We walked slowly along the fence at the foot of the slope leading up to the house, marvelling at the minarets, enormous curving orangery, cupolas and great green onion dome capping the whole thing off. George, Prince Regent, visited in 1807, and it's pretty clear where the inspiration for tarting up his Marine Pavilion in Brighton came from.

Other delights of the walk: huge old oaks with acorns sprouting galls like the tentacles of sea anemones, and a hedge full of large plump bullace, fat as damsons and bitter as sloes, which we picked into a bag. If the rumoured resurgence of this awful coronavirus pandemic comes to pass in the bleak midwinter, it will be a Covid Christmas, and a miserable one at that. Better hurry up and get those bullace fruits to form a bubble with gin and sugar. They'll be ready to come out of isolation in a Kilner jar just in time to lift our spirits.

101

R is for Rights

Oi, you! Yes, Farmer Palmer, I'm talking to you! Get off that bloody tractor of yours and come here and look at this. What can you see, eh? That's right, nothing. Neither can I. Well – what *should* I be looking at? You haven't got a clue? Huh. I'll tell you, then. A footpath, that's what. A straight line comprising the hypotenuse of this corner of your meadow, encompassing a public right of way for pedestrian access within the meaning of Section 12A of the Highways Act 1980. All right, sunshine? OK, so it's not a meadow. OK, a wheat field, then. Whatever.

So where's the path, eh? Go on, show me. What, that little mouse track? Not good enough, old mate. Don't you know your Highways Act 1980, c 66, Part XI, Section 135A? Eh? Well, let me enlighten you. You should've reinstated that public right of way to a minimum width of one metre within fourteen days of sowing your stupid crop that's blocking my path. One metre! What's that in old money? Don't get smart with me, my man, it's three foot three. And how wide's that apology for a path you've so generously left? Two foot seven. Don't bother to argue – I've checked it. See this tape measure? Never leave home without it.

Why don't I go round the side? I'll tell you why, mate – because I know my rights, that's why. Yes, I *know* it's only a couple of yards longer, but that's not the point. Yes, I *am* going to stand here arguing all day. What's that? You'll give me two seconds to get over that stile within the meaning of the Self-Righteous Prick's Act of Right-This-Minute? How dare you quote the law at me, you... ow! For God's sake! OK, OK! What's *wrong* with you people?

102

Climbing irons

On the little tump of a hill where I used to walk unsupervised as a child, a rope swing dangled from a giant old oak. I longed with all my soul to climb to the top of the tree, just to see what was up there. But I couldn't even reach the lowest branches. It gave those summer picnic walks a bittersweet tang, that unfulfilled dream of mine.

Among the oak trees of my imagination, however, I had the ability to climb like a monkey, as I skulked in my bedroom with *Tom Brown's Schooldays*, 'frowsting', as Tom Brown's creator, hearty old Thomas Hughes, would have called it – an absorption with the savage old tale every bit as obsessive as that of some spotty boy keening over Instagram today.

How I loved that book. Huzzah for the school and Old England! The jolly larks, the awful fate of sneaks and cowards. New boys tossed in a blanket and roasted in front of the hall fire. Beatings and bullyings, sausages and ale and a singsong for all. And above all else, the magic and mystery of 'climbing irons' – enigmatic items that enabled boys to shin up trees to fantastic heights without tumbling out again.

But what exactly *were* these climbing irons? Thomas Hughes didn't actually describe them. There were no illustrations in my copy of *Tom Brown's Schooldays*. No one could tell me – not my teacher, not my dad.

Some dreams never die. Someday I'll find a pair of

climbing irons, hidden away on a dusty shelf in some time-warped camping shop. I'll know them when I see them. And when I do – look out, forests of the world. I'll be walking you vertically, up and up, till I top out at some unimaginably wonderful view, with only the birds for company.

103

Heather moors

The bilberries were probably not quite ripe enough to pluck but, after a dozen miles of footslogging over Spaunton Moor, I wasn't feeling too fastidious. Judging by the plumpness of the pigeons that went clattering up out of the bushes and the coveys of grouse I'd seen whirring off over the heather, there were plenty of berries for all. I walked on, munching a purple handful, taking delight in their acid sharpness on the tongue. Only a pint of Black Sheep bitter could top it, and I was going to be savouring that as soon as I'd made my way down the bank to Lastingham and the Blacksmiths Arms.

Yorkshire boasts two National Parks – well, two-and-a-bit if you count the snippet of Peak District that just pushes in from Derbyshire across the southern border. The Yorkshire Dales National Park straddles the centre and west of the county. With its beautiful green valley bottoms and charming lime-stone villages it is, so to speak, the prettier and politer sister of the two. The North York Moors, by contrast, hunched in their defensive circle up in Yorkshire's north-east corner, seem at first acquaintance colder, harder and less easy on the eye.

My first encounter with this unforgiving but enthralling landscape gave me a taste of peaty purgatory I'll never forget. It might not have been the cleverest move in the world to attempt to cross the North York Moors by following the route of the Lyke Wake Walk, a notorious quagmire, immediately after a thirty-six-hour downpour in the middle of a particularly wet spring. Before I ventured out onto Rosedale Moor, I didn't know about the water-retentive qualities of thick black peat, its capacity for sucking down and detaining a walker's legs to the accompaniment of a foul stench and even fouler noise, like a gargantuan and malevolent sea anemone. But neither did I have any notion of the tonic tang of the moor air or the sheer exhilaration of being entirely alone in a circle of silent, cloud-shadowed upland.

There is something about the look and the feel of the North York Moors that pushes most folk down into the comfort and shelter of the valleys. These spectacularly wide and rolling hills between the Yorkshire coast and the great glacial valley of the Vale of York represent one of the largest continuous areas of heather moor in Britain, some 500 square miles of it. Heather moors in such vast swathes can seem sombre, even grim, in the low light of a typical moorland winter's day – hard old hills clamped under a rough black coat. When you've trudged their stumbly, stony paths in the rain and taken a few tosses in their treacherous green sphagnum mosses, you spit and sulk and tell yourself you loathe the moors. Yet on a fine autumn afternoon, with the sun bringing brilliant purple tints out of the late-flowering heather, the warm bog pools smelling as rich and fruity as plum cake and stonechats making their characteristic 'clicking flints' calls, this darkly brooding country can seem like an intimation of upland heaven.

It is 150 million-year-old gritstone, sparkly and crumbly, that – together with reddish sandstone and a capping of boulder clay – makes up most of the underlying rock of the North York Moors. On Bridestones Moor in the eastern quarter of the National Park, you can see the gritstone scoured by rain and wind-whipped specks of grit into bizarre shapes, like the heads of noble giants rising on slender necks from the heather in which their bodies lie sunken. When you add to wind, rain and frost the erosive power of crashing and cascading water tumbling off the moor for century after century, as the last of the Ice Age glaciers melted 10,000 years ago, it is small wonder that the rocks of the moor were gouged into deep channels by the meltwater continually thundering southwards towards the low ground of the Vale of York. Roads across the moors tend to follow these same shallow north–south glens even today.

A much more impressive witness to the power of water in this landscape is the mighty Hole of Horcum, not far from Bridestones Moor – an enormous hollow 400 feet deep and three-quarters of a mile wide. Geologists claim it was formed by glacial meltwater. Locals say that's rubbish. The hole was made by the Devil scooping up a clawful of the moor to fling at a witch, who had cheated him after agreeing to sell him her soul. Blinded with rage, he missed with his throw – and there is the high cone of Blakey Topping, clearly in view a couple of miles off, to show what became of the rocks of Horcum when they fell to earth. Geologists, dull fellows, what do they know?

104

The lord of Inivae

When autumn bites in the Hebrides, you can bet it bites hard. The north-west wind screams in from the Atlantic, bending heather and grass before it, sending the last of the birch leaves whirling off inland like flocks of frightened sparrows. The whitened sea thrashes up against cliffs and rock stacks with a boom and shudder. A grey shawl of cloud blurs out the familiar angular shapes of the hills. As a season for lying as still as possible in a crevice of the hills, exposed to all the elements can throw at you, it seems like a madman's choice. But this is when the red stags are rutting, so this is when you huddle on your waterproofs, fill the old hip flask, take your fortitude in both hands and get on out there to crouch under a rock and marvel at the greatest show on Mull.

Until you have seen and heard a red stag in the full throes of his mating-season mania, you haven't seen raw nature at work. The impulse that drives this magnificent creature to throw up his many-pointed head and bellow like an anguished grampus, to challenge all pretenders to his sexual throne, to fight – sometimes to the death – while maintaining his overlordship of a harem of females and to suffer torments of anxiety that see him cantering here and cantering there, losing weight and energy until he emerges at the far end of the mating tunnel worn out and wrecked – that is some urge. There might be as much as six weeks for each mature stag of five years or older to make sure that his genetic hoof print is impressed as widely as possible, and every stag is prepared to run himself literally ragged to achieve that. Although there can't help but be a little smack of the peeping Tom, a tingle of prurience, about being a spectator of such frantic love action among the deer, my own impulse to witness this A-list event of the animal kingdom was strong enough to see me enduring a force-seven gale on board the ferry *Isle of Mull* as she butted her way out of Oban 'with a bone in her teeth', as locals say of the white wave of bow-wash that foams away from the stem of a ship in a storm.

It was a brute of a crossing, let's be honest, even in the sheltered waters of the Sound of Mull. But once across on the island, things changed magically, as they tend to do out there. The howl of the wind died off to a grumble, the rain went away to spoil someone else's day and within an hour I was curled under the overhang of a basalt ledge beside the ruins of Inivae, a village emptied and abandoned during the Highland Clearances of the nineteenth century. High over Calgary Bay, this is one of my favourite spots on earth for moody beauty and utter peace. I'd seen the red deer here in summertime, years ago, and had a hunch that Inivae might be just the place.

It was a long, wet wait. The rain swirled back, and the wind began to complain again among the tumbled stones of the old abandoned houses. I was just making up my mind to give it up as a bad job, when another sound made itself heard above the wind and rain – a deeper and gruffer moan that ended in a hollow retching sound, better suited to Sauchiehall Street on a Saturday night than the wild west coast of a Hebridean isle. I peered round the cliff, binoculars to eyes, and there he was, a king of a stag on the hillside some 300 yards away. The ruff of fur round his neck, coarsened and thickened by the surge of mating hormones, lay streaked and matted, dark with rain, and his hindquarters, red with mud, trickled with water droplets. Neck tensed, muzzle pushed forward and choco-late-brown eye glinting, he opened his jaw and belched out another bay of a challenge, then shook his heavy antlers in a spray of raindrops.

It was an overwhelming spectacle, a display of power and of sovereignty that held me spellbound. A sweep of the glasses showed a bunch of seven or eight hinds half-hidden in the rain curtains. At any other time, they would have had all my atten-tion, but here and now the lord of Inivae held centre stage, easily and majestically. Another bellow to the rival invisible in the mists, another toss of his twelve-pointed crown, and he was stalking upwards and out of sight. I sat pole-axed in the ruined village for a few minutes more, then stumbled down the hillside, drenched through, breathless and overawed.

105

PITAPAT

There's one big pain about gathering the fruits of the hedge-row on an autumn walk if you're a wearer of spectacles. You work your way down a beautiful hedge of blackberries or sloes or elderberries, and you find, invariably, that the best ones are just too high to get at. You hook down the branch with your stick, and bingo! Last night's rain shower descends from the leaves all over your upturned countenance. Your glasses are bespattered. You wipe them off with a hankie already sodden. You reach up for the next tempting bunch of dangling berries… Spit! Splash! Spatterdash!

Every autumn, I bemoan the fact that no one has yet invented automatic spectacle wipers. Why not? Cars have had them since 1903. What's so hard about the technology?

Anyway, inspiration has finally struck, courtesy of a perhaps-unlikely source. Step forward and take a bow, the shade of Philthy Animal Taylor, late drummer and hellraiser with metal monsters Motörhead (the umlaut is non-negotiable). In a splendid back-of-the-tour-bus moment on the band's *Everything Louder Than Everything Else* DVD, Taylor unveils his latest invention. His 'self-contained keeping-cool machine' consists of a padded headband, with a projecting wire holding a tiny battery-operated propeller. Having suitably adjusted the device an inch or so in front of his face, Taylor switches it on and sits back with a grin of pure pride, his bandmates chuckling through their fag smoke as the cooling breeze of prop wash stirs his impressive pompadour.

Now come on, British industry! Can't someone adapt Taylor's creation? Two little propellers with tiny chamois leathers attached, one for each lens? You can have the patent for free, provided I can name it. Brothers and Sisters of the Boot, I give you PITAPAT – the Philthy-Inspired Translucency Attainment Perambulating Ablution Thingummybob. How's that for conciseness?

106

S is for Stick

You see them everywhere – ramblers toting walking poles, stabbing them into inoffensive meadows and flat sea walls and level country roads as through negotiating the high Himalayas. It's a bit ludicrous. But it's also understandable. You can get attached to a walking stick, as I discovered during a dodgy-knees episode.

What I wanted was a stick with character – not too much character, not a ridiculous look-at-me thumb stick or something with a ram's-horn handle and little enamel badges, but a proper useful implement, a stick with stickability, a stick with what our forebears called 'bottom'. I found it in Crete, a white fig-wood *katsouna*, or shepherd's stick, given to me by a friend one Easter thirty years ago, as we prepared to climb a mountain for one of those timeless open-air Cretan feasts.

I loved that *katsouna*. I carried it across hundreds of miles of rough Cretan terrain. It became a true friend, easing my sore knees, saving me from stumbles, whacking nasty dogs, pointing out the way. Cretan mountain people appreciate a good stick. Everywhere I went, the white *katsouna* was a conversation-starter and icebreaker.

'Excuse me, but that is a beautiful stick. Where did you get it? Oh, Kritsa, eh? Who made it? Stelios Aphordakos, eh? Well, well! Yes, I thought it must be one of his. How could I tell? Well, you know – one grows an eye for these things…'

The fig-wood *katsouna* came back to England with me. This was true love. This was the stick that would be with me till the day I died, the stick that would be buried with me. And then? Then I left it in the luggage rack of the 10:30 train from Paddington to Bristol Temple Meads. Bloody fool. I still miss it.

107

Bummelty-kites and yoe-brimmels

Since setting off from Balcombe railway station, I had been on the lookout. In Alder Wood and Great Barrow Wood I kept my eyes peeled, and all along the banks of Ardingly Reservoir. But it was in Long Shaw Wood, beyond the lake, that I finally spotted them – fat clusters of hazelnuts hanging half-concealed among toothy green leaves. The squirrels of the North Sussex Weald, fooled by a mild late summer, had delayed the start of their harvest, and in this third week of September the long skirts of the wood were richly tasselled with softly furred bunches of nuts.

It doesn't matter how many autumns one has been picking hazelnuts – there's always something magical about that first splitting of the elastically resistant shell between the molars and the savour of the kernel inside, a blotting-paper dryness followed by a milky sweetness. Spitting out splinters of shell, I walked on up the path into East Wood, plucking and chewing the hazelnuts as I went. Their presence here shouldn't really have come as a surprise. The clue was plain to read in the name of the road that had brought me to the wood: Cob Lane.

'Cobnuts', our ancestors called the fruit of the hazel tree, back when a basketful might make the difference between a full and an empty belly. They must have been important in the domestic economy of Ardingly and Balcombe, for the villagers to borrow their name for the lane that led to the free harvest of each successive September. To Dorset country people, hazelnuts were 'hasketts'. In Somerset they were 'hales'; in Leicestershire, 'filbeards'. Cornishmen called them 'victor-nuts', 'cobbly-cuts' or 'witch-halse'.

Hazels were known to be magical trees with power over witches, fairies, afreets and boggarts. Diviners sought out hidden water springs with forked rods of hazel. Hazels stood for fecundity, good luck and the power of knowledge and the second sight. It was not just the hunger of rustics that they assuaged, but the sense of helplessness in the face of poverty, disease and death. They insured against the waning of the year and the diminution of men's potency and women's fertility. In picking hazelnuts, our forebears were not only stealing a march on the squirrels and gathering food to eat, to store and to sell; they were casting an autumn charm for their own immortality and against the outreaching dead hand of winter.

I had set out on this walk with the notion of spending most of the day among the rare trees and beautiful gardens of Wakehurst, the Sussex outstation of Kew Gardens. There are more fabulous exotic trees, shrubs and flowers there than one could shake a hazel stick at, not to mention the adjacent Millennium Seed Bank with its displays of thousands of seeds from all over the world. But it was the everyday fruits of the autumnal English countryside that turned out to be the keynote of the day.

In Horsebridge Wood, west of Wakehurst, big beech trees overhung the path. Sifting through the leaf mould of the forest floor, I found some of the triangular beechnuts already fallen, creamy white, crisp and tangy on the palate. Crunching them brought back furtive schoolboy memories of rolling, lighting and smoking the juicy brown beech leaves later in the autumn, in company with other ne'er-do-wells. Rites of passage…

Infinitely more palatable were the blackberries I picked from the field hedgerows on my way back to Balcombe. 'Cockbrumbles', rural East Anglians named them; 'lady's garters' in the Scottish Borders; 'black blegs' in Yorkshire; 'bummeltykites' in Cumbria. 'Yoe-brimmels', said hedge harvesters in my native Somerset. If you didn't pick them before Michaelmas, the Devil would pee on them and they'd taste nasty. But Michaelmas was still a fair few weeks off, I reflected, swallowing the juicy yoe-brimmels and reaching gingerly between the prickles for the next handful.

An end-of-the-earth kind of place

After a morning of furious rain, a blowy afternoon of blue skies had set in over the Kentish coast. The yellow-horned poppies flattened self-protectively to the shingle of Dungeness had clung on to their big papery petals since early summer, but now they went whirling off, one after another. Trudging into the wind, a tiny speck alone on the world's largest shingle beach, I longed for a pair of baxters – the wooden overshoes in which locals used to navigate this dry and slippery ocean of pebbles.

There is nowhere in Britain like Dungeness – nowhere with such a remarkable combination of wild empty spaces and man-made intrusions and eccentricities. Here on the south-eastern tip of Kent, poking out into the channel, is a vast arrowhead of shingle that plays host to hundreds of rare bird and animal species. Lonely, unspoilt, bleakly beautiful – these are the impressions that stick in the mind under Dungeness's enormous skies and sweeping winds.

Yet there, too, are the giant grey blocks of twin nuclear power stations, ranks of pylons striding to the horizon and a spatter of shack-like dwellings shaped and decorated exactly as their owners please. Dungeness forces you to rethink your definition of 'wild'. Unsullied, untouched by human influence? Certainly not. Strange, compelling, an end-of-the-earth kind of place? By all means.

Out there on the rolling back of the beach, the parallel ridges of shingle heaped up by storms were plainly outlined, their spines bushy with the pale green leaves of sea kale and darker ones of viper's bugloss. These fleshy, crinkled leaves were reservoirs of moisture in this driest of dry places. Rainwater lay pooled a few feet down under the pebbles where the plants' long tap-roots could reach it.

Rounding the point of the Ness, sea anglers' rods made a whipping geometry against a clearing sky. I trudged north to where the Dungeness fishermen were overhauling their boats and gear. Several dozen boats lay up on the shingle, surrounded by storage huts, tangles of green-and-white netting, home-made railway tracks, bulbous pink floats, fish boxes and rusty winches. The Dungeness fishing families – Richardsons, Tarts, Oillers – still make a decent living from this remote shore and remain, to some extent, a tribe apart.

'I'm an Oiller,' said the fisherman I chatted to. 'Been at it twenty-five to thirty years, fishing for cod, plaice, mackerel, herring, dab – you name it. Just sold my nice old clinker-built wooden boat and got this fibreglass one – not nearly such a good sea boat, but at least she doesn't leak.'

There are still twenty or so wooden boats working from Dungeness, stout in the beam, with little mizzen sails to keep them head to the wind. Boats, huts, shingle ridges and windy green sea might have been placed for the canvas of an Impressionist painter. The small scale of that composition, the quiet accompaniment of waves on shingle and wind in grasses, made the power-station backdrop of giant grey cubes and striding pairs of pylons seem all the more bizarre.

I went round the nuclear installation in company with two cheerful elderly couples – 'We just wanted to see, you know.' Pipes, wheels, tanks, dials: these looked innocuous. Mighty blue, green and silver beasts crouched mumbling in the Turbine Hall. There was something named the Main Exciter, something else called the Macerator that chopped up any fish unwise enough to get sucked in with the coolant sea water. I saw humpbacked pumps like huge green nautilus shells and a foaming white cataract of a sluice. The reactor core, sufficiently hot to make enough steam to light up the entire south-east of England, lay quietly hidden under a blood-red floor. It was a tour in primary colours, with primary-school explanations that suited me just fine.

Out in the strong, salty wind again, I set my back to the monster and its skeletal striding army and walked all the way to Camber – and didn't see a soul.

109

Wild magic of the Sperrins

'I take groups of people of all ages and stages out walking all over this area,' said Martin McGuigan, 'and I can honestly say I enjoy every single outing. There's something about the Sperrins – they're not exactly mighty mountains, you know, but they do have a kind of magic, a wild magic, to them.'

Up on the saddle of Crockmore, we swung to the west, a gentle climb on a rain-sodden green road that bought us to the summit of Crockbrack, where a big wind was blowing. The view simply stopped us in our tracks. There can't have been less than a hundred miles in view, with the olive-and-grey shoulders of the Sperrins dominating the middle ground. In the far distance rose the pale blue back of the Inishowen peninsula, thirty miles away across the border in far-off County Donegal, dissolving and reconstituting as the rain-water brush of the Celestial Scene-Shifter washed it in and out of the picture.

I would rather have had this watercolour drama of weather than the clear-cut acrylic perfection of a regulation sunny day, and said as much to Martin as we squelched off the ridge and descended beside a rackety old fence into the head of the Drumderg River's tight little glen.

'I find that walking is really a form of meditation,' Martin mused. 'I love walking on my own, just turning things over in my mind, taking everything in all around me. Walking here at night, too – it can be scary, all right, but it's then I find the five senses all open up in a wonderful way.'

The retreating glaciers of the last Ice Age and ten ensuing millennia of weathering had kindly provided us with seat-shaped rocks on which to munch our sandwiches in a green cleft at the head of the infant Drumderg River. Goat's cheese and tomato – is there a finer filling anywhere on God's earth?

Idling in this cleft of the eastern Sperrins, with the hill burns trickling and a stonechat gushing out his metallic little call, I reflected on the marvellous-but-eerie emptiness of the range. It wasn't exactly holiday weather, admittedly, but if this had been the Coast-to-Coast path or some interstice of the Lake District we'd have been sharing our picnic perches with half a dozen other Brothers and Sisters of the Boot. Yet here, in one of Ireland's finest mountain settings, we had hill, stream and birdsong exclusively to ourselves. Perhaps it was a legacy of the late and unlamented Troubles, or maybe the eyes of the mainland walking world were simply fixed on landscapes less rain-blurred and more exotic, but the Sperrins seemed caught under a cloak of invisibility. Long may that continue, I thought with selfish pleasure, as I brushed the last crumbs of goat's cheese from my knees.

110

Solitary mooch with a beautiful killer

You don't always want the flowery dunes and the sun-kissed sands, do you? Sometimes all you're after is a bit of a solitary old hands-in-pockets mooch beside the seaside and, at times like that, the cheerful aspect of nature ablaze with colour just doesn't suit the mood. For a lonesome stroll on a brooding coast, there's no beating the sombre acres of Dunwich Heath on a September evening, when the light is just beginning to go and the first nip of autumn is stealing into the air. For one thing, you're most unlikely to bump into anyone else; for another, there's always the chance that nature will pull one of her spectaculars and present you with a genuine once-in-a-lifetime treat.

I wasn't expecting anything in particular that cold evening, just the downbeat pleasures of solitude in a lonely place. The coasts of Suffolk were once all heathland, a gently rolling landscape of heather and scrub that came into being once the post-Ice Age forests were cut down and sheep introduced onto the sandy plains of this low, pebbly coast. Now these 'sandlings' have mostly gone, having been developed or farmed to extinction. The best of what's left of them is carefully looked after by bodies such as the National Trust, the organisation that maintains Dunwich Heath in all its wild glory for bird-watchers, for insect-fanciers and for walkers like me who love such unspoilt and open landscapes.

When the big grey bird came ghosting low over the heather and passed across my binocular lenses, I almost missed closing in on it in my excitement. I'd been straining my eyes staring at a bare patch in the heather, wondering if that darker bit might be a rare glimpse of a nightjar (it wasn't, though Dunwich Heath does boast a few), and I simply wasn't prepared for the magnificent, heart-stopping manifestation of a male hen harrier in full flight some forty yards away. I dropped the binoculars in the mud, scrambled for them with many a bad word and caught the hen harrier again just as he disappeared over the birch trees. A moment of sheer, abject mortification. Then he reappeared, still gliding low above the heath as though he'd been teasing all the time, and gave me the father of all fly-pasts, slow and majestic.

Hen harriers are our most endangered species of raptor – carnivorous birds that hunt and grab their prey. Their name was given them in medieval times, when, far more numerous than today, they would enter farmyards to seize domestic hens, a helpless target for such capable hunters. Hen harriers go to the uplands to breed each spring on the remote heather moors of northern England, Wales, Scotland and Ireland. The trouble is that grouse breed there too, and their chicks are highly tasty little bundles of protein on legs. Shooters and gamekeepers are on the grouse's side, and some of them deal with hen harriers with what Bruce Willis would term 'extreme prejudice'. What with that and the difficulty of finding truly wild and undisturbed breeding grounds, the current UK population of breeding pairs of hen harriers hovers around the 630 mark.

Sightings are rare, but stunning when luck does come calling. Hen harriers are lovely birds, especially the male, smaller than the brown-speckled female but infinitely more striking-looking. My harrier this evening gave me every opportunity to admire him as he passed and repassed, quartering the heath in search of young rabbits or voles caught out in the open and crouching terrified and motionless among the heather tuffets. A smoky-grey body with a pure-white waistband, a long square-tipped tail that adjusted delicately to every tiny alteration in the air and black-fingered wings held in a low vee – these were the suave habiliments that sheathed this quiet and deadly efficient hunting machine.

This particular hen harrier can only just have returned from his upland summer grounds to the broad acres of Dunwich Heath, where he would spend the winter well supplied with food and with cover. I watched him, fascinated, as he floated with occasional flaps of his wings across the heath, this way and that. A pounce with outstretched talon into a heather clump produced nothing; perhaps the living had been too easy in summertime, back among the grouse chicks of Yorkshire or Gwynedd, and he needed to sharpen up his act a little.

Half a minute more, a final deliberate flap or two of the broad black wingtips, and the beautiful killer in ghost-grey was gone. Then I let the binoculars drop and discovered that I had been holding my breath throughout the show.

111

Ancient oak

The Great Oak of Eardisley was mentioned in the Domesday Book. It must be a thousand years old. Now it stands on its little Herefordshire green like an arthritic giant, knotted and knobbed all over. The limbs that once upheld a glorious 100-foot autumn canopy are truncated, this one split away by its own weight accumulated down the centuries, that one burned off by a lightning bolt before the Battle of Waterloo, others amputated by the surgeon's saw.

The mighty tree shelters spiders, beetles, wood wasps, caterpillars and grubs from oncoming winter. Squirrels still hide its acorns, as they did a thousand years ago. But the giant's strength is not what it was. The whole heart of the oak has gone, burned and rotted away to leave an empty casing, into which I creep out of the rain.

A final, fatal bolt from the blue, some debilitating disease or a total collapse of the enfeebled structure might yet level the Great Oak of Eardisley. But I wouldn't bet on it. My money is on the god-like tree outlasting sickness, baldness and fire from the heavens. It will certainly outlast this naked ape, crouching at its heart with his impudent questions.

112

Staving off the sea

A gold October warmth in the air, and one of those pearly, peachy light effects that autumn spreads so seductively across the Sussex Downs and their fringing cliffs and sea. Farms, ploughlands and flinty lanes lay muted and pastel – a soft-focus dream of a day. Up on Beachy Head, a couple stood outlined at the summit of the great cliff, kissing as if they'd never stop. I shifted a few feet to larboard so as not to inter-rupt their raptures and gazed my fill over one of Britain's finest coast views.

When you try to picture the sheer number of foraminifera, tiny shelly organisms, that died and floated to the bed of the Great Chalk Sea 100 million years ago to form these mighty ramparts of chalk cliffs, and the length of time, some 30,000 years, that they were settling silently, layer upon layer – it just about beggars belief. There are 530 vertical feet of chalk climb-ing from the shore at Beachy Head, the tallest chalk cliff in Britain, and perhaps that much again going down below the sea. Looking gingerly over the edge, I found myself holding my breath – the subconscious readying me for a plunge, perhaps? Way down there rose the red-and-white striped rocket shape of Beachy Head lighthouse, its foot planted in the sea, its back guarded by the huge white wall of the cliff. The lighthouse is more than 150 feet tall, but it looked com-prehensively dwarfed by its surroundings.

I left the lovers still romantically silhouetted, still kissing away fit to beat the band, and set out along the clifftop path. Ahead, the line of the cliffs undulated in hollows and por-poise-backs, a thick ribbon of green and white that sinuated into the far distance, where the bold frontages of the Seven Sisters plummeted down hundreds of feet into the smooth-glazed sea. They looked immensely sturdy, as if they could resist the erosive power of the waves for ever. Yet their strength was all a chimera. These cliffs were crumbling into the sea at a great rate, several feet a year, in falls that stained the shallows white.

Between Beachy Head and the Seven Sisters rose the great whale-jaw shape of Belle Tout, crowned by a lighthouse. You'd think a lighthouse, of all buildings, would stand for perma-nence and long-term resistance, wouldn't you? Yet in March 1999, this pre-Victorian tower, now a private dwelling, was moved more than fifty feet inland to save it from tumbling over the fast-approaching cliff edge. Up beside the old light-house, I stopped to savour the panorama of cliffs and sea, then I dipped down the slope of the ground into Birling Gap.

To save or not to save this delectable tiny hamlet at the edge of the cliffs? Left to its own devices, the sea will have it all in the not-too-distant future; 'That's nature's right and proper course,' say landowners the National Trust. 'But what about our beloved village, our much-adored houses?' reply the inhabitants. 'Can't we build a solid sea defence on the beach below to stave off the storm waves?' It's a debate that is being sparked in low-lying coastal areas all round our shores, in this era of rising sea levels.

I stopped for a pint and a sandwich at one of the tables outside the Birling Gap hotel; the day was just warm enough for that. Then I found a path through bird-haunted scrubland

and long swells of farmland, a low-level stroll back to Beachy Head, with those spectacular giant cliffs out of sight – but still rearing skyward in the mind's eye, long after this dramatic, thought-provoking walk was finished.

113

Dunwich shore and Dingle Marshes

A cold, blowy autumn afternoon had settled over the Suffolk coast. Black-headed gulls screamed as they whirled above the roofs of Walberswick, and the wind whistled vigorously through the broken arches that enclosed the east end of St Andrew's Church. I made a short tour of this most beautiful and melancholy building, but my thoughts were already marching on down the tideline, where wigeon would be clouding half the sky and marsh harriers flapping their long dark wings above the reed beds. Any walker coming to this coast in winter can expect to see wild birds, and plenty of them, settled into safe haven to ride out the roughest season of the year.

Temptation was strong to ride out this short, dark afternoon myself, over a cup of tea and a slice of shortbread in Walberswick's Parish Lantern tea shop. I resisted, manfully, and plunged out along the great shingle bank that runs south along the gradual curve of the Suffolk shore.

To my right lay the level green grazing of the Dingle Marshes, cut with glinting fleets of fresh water where flocks of wigeon and teal bobbed quietly at anchor. Persil-white little egrets flapped hesitantly away, as if asking themselves just what the hell they thought they were doing, relocating from the sunny south to such a bleak and moody place. On my left, the cold, grey North Sea fell rhythmically on the shingle of the tideline. Far ahead loomed the white rectangle and dome of Sizewell nuclear power station, and nearer at hand the low, wooded cliffs at Dunwich.

'Just closed, sorry,' said the chef in Dunwich's beach café when I arrived, red-cheeked and wind-blown from the three-mile shingle trudge. I hung on to the promise of Walberswick's Parish Lantern and its steaming teapots and made inland for the ragged remnants of Greyfriars monastery. Its few broken walls of flint clinging to the clifftop, and a corresponding fragment of a leper hospital on the coast road below, are all that remains of the great maritime city of Dunwich, once the pride and glory of the East Anglian coast.

Medieval Dunwich was a city of pomp, circumstance and power before nature took her inexorable hand. Dunwich was founded on a muddy harbour and crumbling cliffs. The harbour silted; the cliffs were rapidly consumed by the sea. Monasteries, houses, churches, squares and quays all slipped away, a parable of pride and retribution. What remains – one or two snippets of graceful flintwork, the odd angle of wall – only emphasises the poignancy of this most extraordinary place. The fate of Dunwich offers a foretaste of what rapidly rising sea levels will bring about in many other settlements along our coasts during the coming century.

Ominous, Blakeian clouds had been building apocalyptically on the southern skyline, and now they came charging across, dumping their freight of rain and recalling me to the present. The sun had somehow dipped nearly to the horizon while I had been dawdling in Dunwich. Time to strike out north across the Dingle Marshes on the homeward stretch. A broad gravelled track ran through the skirts of Dunwich Forest, overhung with scrubby oak, hazel and silver birch. The rising wind hissed in stands of Scots pine, and the sky swirled with bursts of rain. In the half-light of dusk, I hurried past the lonely outposts of Dingle Stone House and Great Dingle Farm. The names of their attendant hillocks – Fen Hill, Sandymount, Broom Hill – caught the character of this sandy, scrubby piece of country, where any slight rise above the marsh merits a distinguishing name of its own.

Out in the windy wastes of Oldtown Marshes, I pulled up short beside the brick stump of Walberswick windpump. A mass of black-headed gulls was spiralling over the sea. What had spooked them? I swung the binoculars up, and there in my field of vision was a big hunting bird with long dark wings – a marsh harrier stoking itself up on mice and rabbits before departing for its Mediterranean winter quarters, skimming dramatically across the silvery smear of a rising crescent-shaped moon.

114

T is for Thermos

… and thermals, too, and thin layers, and thick overtrousers and all the other stuff my dad would never have dreamed of taking with him on a winter walk.

It's funny, when you come to think of it. Now the season of murk and miry muddiness is upon us, I've got them all out of the drawers and cupboards – the thermal vest and long johns, the thick gloves and the thin ones, the woolly hat and scarf, the gaiters and head torch. I go out swathed like a yeti, carrying stuff on my back that never leaves the knapsack. I come home sweaty, tired and exuding a certain 'essence of overdressed gentleman'.

Dad was an active winter walker until he was well into his eighties. He climbed hills, walked fells, tramped long distances in rain and snow, wind and wuthering. And he did it dressed very simply – cord trousers, a battered old anorak, thick socks and a pair of well-greased Doc Martens. He carried a right-angle ash stick and one of those webbing satchels that ex-army blokes used to tote. Total contents of same: a plastic bottle of weak lemon squash, a pair of Ryvitas with a thin slice of cheddar in between. Maybe a piece of flapjack, if Mum could sneak it past his guard.

Very late in his life, he made concessions – thermal long johns, gloves, a ratty old scarf. But I like to picture him as I best remember him, wet hair plastered across his head, snow on his old boots, ripped anorak flapping in the wind, shoulders well back like a good naval man, striding uphill, not braving the weather, not challenging it – but *ignoring* it, as he would have ignored an ill-mannered drunk in the street. A class act.

115

Stranger on the shore

The labours of landbound Lancaster, ten miles from the sea up the River Lune, to carve a niche for itself in the lucrative eighteenth-century transatlantic trade gave birth to twin ports on opposite sides of the Lune estuary – Glasson Dock and Sunderland. Glasson, three miles north of Cockersand Abbey, opened in 1787 as a handsomely built sandstone harbour importing all kinds of exotic items from the West Indies – sugar and rum, hardwoods for Robert Gillow's furniture manufactories, raw cotton for the weavers and later for the mills. A canal cut to join the main Lancaster Canal in 1826 ensured access to the town at all states of the tide. Gillow's fine furniture was shipped abroad through Glasson Dock, as were the woollen and cotton goods made throughout Lancashire.

On a wildly blowing morning, I drove down a winding side road to Glasson Dock. A blue-painted little freighter, *Claudia*, lay at the east quay being loaded for the Isle of Man. Further along the quay, a big yellow heap of fertiliser had been dumped. They were expecting a load of sand from Germany later in the day, said the gnarled man I got chatting to. The old dock might be out on a limb, he couldn't deny that, but there was life in her yet.

Heysham for size,
Middleton for grips,

Overton for dancing schools,
And Sunderland for ships.

The old rhyme made it pretty plain what visitors to the Lune estuary's settlements should expect. There were no dancing schools at Sunderland, the older of Lancaster's twin estuary ports. The Quaker merchant Robert Lawson built the port in 1715, using stone from Cockersand Abbey, to muscle in on the Barbados and Jamaica trade in rum, sugar and ginger. The very first bale of raw cotton to reach Britain – so soon to be transformed by textile manufacture – was landed on this plain little quay. It lay there for over a year; no one had the faintest idea what the strange substance could be.

Sailors called Sunderland 'Cape Famine', in dread of being kept liquorless and loveless at anchor offshore. But Sunderland prospered all through the eighteenth century, until competition and silting put an end to shipbuilding and trading there. It is hard to believe, looking at the little strip of disused quays and the scatter of houses, that this was once one of the busiest and most important ports in the kingdom.

A country road leads south from Lancaster beside the estuary, towards Sunderland – a bumping, snaking road that I had been warned might be flooded by the high tide expected at noon today. At the roadside Golden Ball pub, they had sandbagged the doors, and the tarmac surface of the road was snaggled over with hanks of bladderwrack left by midnight's flood tide.

Down on the point of Sunderland's narrowing peninsula, the mud-smeared road wound across undefended saltmarshes towards the cluster of houses under their dark, wind-whipped trees. In the creeks, the water bubbled as if a powerful pump were at work in the muddy depths. Wavelets of sea water were already slapping the side of the road, and they came sweeping across as soon as I had passed, islanding Sunderland. I would have to stay there now, for at least a couple of hours, marooned among the big old sandstone warehouses and handful of houses along Lawson's quay.

'When the tide's over the road and we're cut off,' said a fisherman in a cap and faded red smock, looking out over miles of grey-brown water from his doorway, 'well – it's just really lovely down here.' Stark enjoyment, bleak beauty – sea, creek, green marshes, silvery muds, a few bobbing fishing boats and yachts, all to the sound of wind in tree branches and an excited piping of oystercatchers and redshanks on the advancing tideline.

I walked with head hunched down across the windblown neck of the point, looking for Sambo's grave. One among many black people, servants or slaves, brought to Britain from the West Indies, Sambo landed at Sunderland in 1736 and died shortly afterwards – of a broken heart, locals said, but it was probably pneumonia brought on by the change of climate. In a corner of a green field I found his gravestone, inscribed, 'Here lies poor Samboo, A Faithfull NEGRO who (Attending his Master from the West Indies) DIED on his Arrival at Sunderland.'

A sprig of yellow gorse had been laid on the grave. The wind shook the grass of the little enclosure. A strange and poignant resting place for the lonely stranger from a foreign land – still remembered here with flowers and prayers – who lies with his head to a lichened Lancashire sandstone wall and his feet to the wild and rainy Irish Sea.

116

Autumn on the Severn

As summer slips into autumn, another big tide is forecast, a forty-five-footer. That means a decent tall Severn Bore, especially upriver, where the estuary narrows into sharp bends that will squeeze the wave's crest even higher. We gather at Weir Green after dark, a small knot of onlookers, and gaze intently downstream by the greasy light of a full moon and the glow of the distant floodlit cathedral at Gloucester.

The river looks as thick as blood tonight, mysteriously agitated from within. Oily surges pulse upstream towards the city; counter-surges tug seaward, carrying eels that lie entranced on the surface of the river, matt black coils on the silver water.

A low roar comes to us from round the bend of the Severn – a cold whisper of a stir in the air around our faces. Peering downriver, we see a tidal wave of turbulent water crested with foam, six or seven feet tall, driving towards us as fast as a running man.

Water slaps the bank below our feet, breaking off chunks of mud. Instinctively, we step back. Spray bursts round us as the bore passes majestically through the track of the moon, sighing and seething, dragging a train of deep troughs as though ploughing the river. There is something kingly about this big salt wave twenty miles inland: a pagan progression, homage received, largesse scattered in the form of eels, tree boughs and bobbing barrels.

*

We make an October pilgrimage up the Welsh shore to Gloucester, then back down the English bank to the sea, to catch a portrait of the whole estuary as one. The landscape changes, steepens and grows lumpier as it goes upriver. But certain keynotes sound everywhere: eccentrically designed and decorated individualists' houses crouching at the ends of the long lanes, for example, and isolated old waterside pubs by the sites of long-abandoned ferries. Salt-rusted freighters moor under red river cliffs; apple and pear orchards cling to the slopes of small rounded hills; and the estuary fields lie corrugated by the furrows of medieval strip farming.

A sedgy land, hedged and ditched against disaster, swollen with autumn rain, fertile and secret. Plums lie all over the path that leads to a Norman church doorway at Great Porton. Two men laze on the old wharf below Lydney, oblivious to the mist as they contemplate brown mud turning silver in low evening sunlight. Formal Dutch water gardens, restored to their 300-year-old glories of geometry, glint by the road through Westbury-on-Severn.

On the English bank, goldfinches flirt their tails in the hedges among hips, hops and haws. At medieval, moated Wick Court, we watch an enormous Gloucester Old Spot sow and her seven rubber-snouted piglets ecstatically crunching sour little cider apples. From the crest of Barrow Hill behind the farm, we look out over twenty miles of estuary country, from Westbury spire down into the south, where the Severn snakes as a broad grey highway of water under the twin bridges, towards a gleam of sun on the sea beyond.

117

Roasted crabs

When that I was and a little tiny boy, I was mightily fascinated by William Shakespeare's wonderful winter poem in
Love's Labour's Lost, the one about Dick the shepherd blowing
his nail and greasy Joan keeling the pot. Keeling? All greasy
Joan was doing was stirring her pot; I understand that now.
But to this youthful son of a naval household, 'keeling' called
to mind the disturbing image of the keel-hauling punishment
– being pulled across the barnacle-encrusted bottom of a ship
from one side to the other, the nastiest fate that could befall a
jolly Jack tar. I had a sort of confused mental image of a clammy
she-devil sweating over a great cauldron full of flayed sailors.

The more you read on, the knottier things got. Even more
intriguing than the bit about coughing drowning the parson's
saw (what was he doing with one of those in church – dealing
with some deathwatch beetle?) was the line 'When roasted
crabs hiss in the bowl'. I liked roasts, especially roast beef.
They were winter Sunday fare. Roasts usually lay on a plate,
rather than these roasted crabs in their bowl, but maybe the
bowl and greasy Joan's pot were one and the same thing. Had
she keel-hauled these crustaceans and then roasted them?

It was a plausible scenario. But it only raised more questions.
If Joan's bowl was full of crabs, where were those wretched
skinned sailors? And anyway, crabs don't hiss – especially not
after being flayed and roasted. Would you?

Pondering this in logical maturity, I remember that autumn's yellow, green and red crab apples are lying all over the footpaths, going to waste. I think I'll take some home, keel-haul them with the carrot peeler, roast them in the Aga and stick them in a bowl. If drowned in enough good liquor, they're unlikely to hiss, but they will spice up my Christmas home brew.

118

Bolving, soiling and Jacobson's organ: courtship of the red stag

Martin French deserves a medal. Not only did he get up in the cold and dark to see me off from his Bark House hotel at Oakfordbridge, but he put porridge, bacon and eggs on the table at six in the morning. They make them tough down there on Exmoor. Ranger Richard Eales was nursing flu and the effects of a kick from an overexcited Exmoor pony, but he turned up for our dawn rendezvous at Exmoor National Park headquarters in Dulverton in his usual form – humorous, observant and passionately knowledgeable about red deer.

From West Anstey Common, Richard and I surveyed the ground around Lyshwell Farm. The farmer, Raymond Davey, enjoys seeing red deer, so Lyshwell is a likely spot to find a sample of Exmoor's herd of some 4,000 of these beautiful and impressive creatures. Red deer have been native to Britain since shortly after the last Ice Age. Stags and hinds spend most of the year apart, but in autumn they come together briefly for the rut, or mating season. That's when the wooded combes and farm pastures of Exmoor echo to one of the most thrilling sounds in nature: the roaring of the stags.

As Richard and I watched from the high common, a deep dog-like bark rose from the oakwoods in the combe of Dane's Brook far below.

'A hind,' said Richard. 'She's spotted us, and she'll be

warning the others.' Then came the sound we had been waiting for – a grating, throaty roar from the direction of Lyshwell Farm. 'Ah, he's bolving,' exclaimed Richard with satisfaction. 'That's the Exmoor word for the roaring. It's a threat and a challenge to any other stag: "I'm here, and I'm in charge!"'

Through binoculars, I made out the stag as he stood by the hedge, head back and bolving, a large figure indistinct in the early morning light. In the field above him, several hinds and two little calves came into focus. Beside them were a couple of prickets, two-year-old stags with two long dagger-blade horns where their antlers would eventually grow.

'When a stag's in his pomp,' Richard expounded, 'he'll have his "rights" – his brow, bay and tray spikes at the base of the antler – and up to three "points" at the top of each antler. That stag we're looking at, he's a fine beast – he's got all his rights and three points on one side, and all his rights and two on the other. Let's have a closer look at him.'

Down in the Lyshwell fields, we crept with bent backs along a hedge to a point where we could see through a screen of twigs. The stag was the size of a racehorse. He stood sideways on, about fifty yards away, a magnificent spectacle against the rising sun – his dark form dazzlingly outlined in dewdrops, his heavily-antlered head thrown back as he bolved. The roar – a mixture of circular saw, Harley-Davidson and outraged lion – echoed out across Lyshwell Wood, projected forth on a puff of steamy breath.

'See how dark his coat is?' breathed Richard. 'He's been wallowing in his soiling pit, peeing in the mud and rolling in it to get a good stinking smell all over. A stag's cologne, that is.'

Among his harem of a dozen hinds, most faces were turned

towards us, but the stag seemed oblivious. He was sizing up one of the hinds and had nudged her a little apart from the others, scenting her hindquarters and lifting his head between sniffs as if pondering a rare old vintage. Hinds are in season for a matter of hours only, so the stag relies on all sorts of clues to tell him the time is right.

'He'll lick up the hind's urine,' murmured Richard, 'and run it along the Jacobson's organ in his upper lip to see if she's ready to be served.'

This hind was ready. It has to be admitted that the red stag is no languorous *artiste du chambre*. Ten seconds, and the embrace was finished. The hind resumed her grazing, the stag his bolving and scenting of other posteriors. But the group of hinds remained uncomfortably aware of us. Soon enough, they began to move off. Richard's nudge was followed by his whisper: 'We'll go down in the wood and catch them there.'

Deep in Lyshwell Wood, the stag's soiling pit lay well trodden, the wet mud exuding a powerful goaty smell. We crept along a sunken path. From the field above came the groans and roars of bolving in several separate voices – not just one stag but three. Peeping over the top, we saw 'our' stag trotting and roaring and another animal making off in disappointment.

'He'll be back,' said Richard, as the herd disappeared into the wood and we straightened our stiff backs. 'There's a lot of hard work for the stags during the rut, keeping the hinds together, seeing off rivals, not to mention the mating. But they must think it's worth it – they've been doing it for about 10,000 years.'

WINTER

119

Innominate Tarn

I reached Innominate Tarn at noon. It had been one of those glorious green-and-gold winter mornings over Lakeland, and I'd idled along from the Honister Pass, sauntering through the thin snow after my shadow in no sort of a hurry. By Black-beck Tarn, the rocks had been too cold and slippery to sit on, but now, at the brink of Innominate Tarn, the weak sun had warmed the boulders just enough to allow me a seat of sorts.

The night's ice crusted the water, a delicate lace hem along the shore. I dipped in a finger, experimentally. You'd have to be the hardest of the hard to bathe in that, as fell-walking heroes of the past were wont to do. Nothing moved anywhere – only a solitary birch leaf, blown in from heaven knows where, that circled its own reflection in the black water beyond the ice. Snow clouds were beginning to gather in the eastern sky, and the cold wind cut through my mountain gear like a blade of glass. But I sat on, hugging myself for warmth and thinking of Alfred Wainwright – the Master, the writer and illustra-tor of the best Lake District walking guidebooks ever devised – whose ashes lie scattered on this spot. If ever these lonely fells had a tutelary spirit, it was the supposedly curmudgeonly Wainwright, a shy man with a soft heart under his crusty carapace.

At last I got up, shivering and dreamy, and went on up Haystacks, Wainwright's favourite fell. The views were muted, the day ominous and dark. But I had Wainwright with me, and I feared no ill. Passing Innominate Tarn again towards dusk, with the first flakes of snow brushing my nose and eyelashes, I saw the birch leaf still circling, still the only moving thing on the silent winter tarn.

120

Strid and strong beer

A misty, muted day of subtle grades of grey, cool and quiet in the lower reaches of Wharfedale. This dale is Yorkshire's gem, come rain, shine or winter vapours. Today, as I stepped out of the Devonshire Arms with the last of my breakfast bacon sandwich in my paw (I'd arrived hungry, and the hotel had leapt, frying-pan in hand, to meet the challenge), it was as if I had walked into one of those time-suspended, floating dreams. Things felt even more dreamlike when the ruins of Bolton Priory swam into view on their bend in the Wharfe, the delicate window arches seeming to hang in mid-air like some celestial ship about to weigh anchor for Heaven.

Two black Labradors, one in a blue collar and one in a red, were racing crazily in and out of the river, while a calm six-year-old girl helped her quavering father across the stepping stones in front of the priory.

'Dadd-*eee*!' she squealed, as her father collected a cold bootful of Wharfe water. 'Don't say bad words!'

I wandered round the pale shell of the twelfth-century Augustinian priory (painted by Turner, apostrophised by Wordsworth), looking for grotesque medieval carvings. My haul: a gurning face, a laughing dog and a golden Green Man leering down from the rafters of the adjacent parish church. Then it was on through the meadows by the shallow and loudly rushing Wharfe, on through Strid Wood along paths beautifully maintained by the Bolton Abbey estate. These woodland paths have been open to the public for the best part of 200 years. They were a great source of delight to the factory workers and millhands of the nineteenth- and twentieth-century industrial West Riding, and the present owner (the 'custodian', as he likes to put it), the twelfth Duke of Devonshire, keeps up the tradition of access to the estate's paths and countryside.

A fierce hissing and rumbling ahead heralded the Strid, a string of collapsed caverns in the bed of the Wharfe through which the river sluiced furiously, thick with bubbles like boiling sugar. The surrounding rocks lay slippery with wet lichen and moss. Many have tried to jump across the Strid; many have been swallowed and drowned.

I stood mesmerised by the thunder and haste of the water, then went on to where the dale broadened out with stone walls and sheep pastures around Barden Bridge. Up on the bank above the Wharfe loomed the many-windowed lichen-green ruin of Barden Tower, as grim and haunting as could be against the pale winter sky. Here, in the late fifteenth century, lived Henry Clifford, the 'Shepherd Lord', a reclusive and studious astronomer who turned his back on his inherited residence of Skipton Castle.

From Barden Bridge, the Wharfe flows in more open country. The valley widens into a green landscape of stone-walled fields and clumps of trees that shelter greystone farmhouses and barns with high-arched doorways. There were herons and diving ducks along the river, careless of the rain; I, too, hardly gave it a thought until I stamped into the warm, dry hallway of the New Inn at Appletreewick and realised that I was literally soaked through to the skin.

I hung my sodden things to steam dry and asked about a

bite to eat. They had stopped serving lunches, but obligingly found me a cheese sandwich and a pint of beer. The sandwich was great, and as for the beer... if I had wanted to stay out of the rain and sample specialist ales till wheeled home in a handcart, the New Inn would have been the place to do it.

Just looking at the pub's beer menu made my head reel. There were Belgian fruit beers made with peaches and cherries; Trappist ales from the Low Countries with 'subtle chocolate tones'; smoked beers with the savour of moist beechwood logs; and Samichlaus, brewed only on 6 December, the strongest beer in the world, 'only appreciated by very seasoned palates'. I took my seasoned palate away before temptation could capture it.

Returning down the east bank of the roaring Wharfe, I turned aside to climb into the 'Valley of Desolation' – a lonely declivity rising between moorland peaks to a crashing waterfall. There I stood and stared my fill over lower Wharfedale, where trees and river were wrapping themselves once more in shawls of evening mist.

121

U is for Umbrella

... that quintessentially British piece of outdoor equipment – characterful, stoical, faintly but unmistakeably laughable. What could be more indicative of our national mettle than something all stiff and buttoned up that transforms itself at the press of a stud into a ramshackle piece of pure ingenuity, unfolding clumsily into a great flapping sail liable to be blown inside out or clean away by any decent wind? That happened to me when I tried walking with a brolly at the Devil's Punch Bowl – a moment's glorious shelter whipped away in abject wreck, with a whipcrack noise like a thunderstorm localised in my right hand.

The umbrella represents a triumph of hope over reality – particularly in the grasp of a walker in this country. You need your hands, free and unencumbered, for lowering barbed wire, for opening gates, for the zipping and unzipping of anoraks, for flailing at farm dogs and scratching heads over maps. How can you wrestle simultaneously with an apparatus so diametrically opposed to anything common-sensical, an instrument seemingly designed to pinch your fingers and challenge your dignity as it wraps itself round your head like a demonic heron? And don't even think of putting it to dry by the pub fire – because it's *bad luck to open an umbrella indoors!*

How splendidly British! Yet... it was the Chinese who invented the contraption, the diligent and dexterous Chinese,

3,000 years ago, while we were skulking round our rain-soaked island encased in sodden wool. I suspect they may have done it just to get at us. Someone, somewhere, needs to invent something to get our own back. I have a half-formed plan for an electrified noodle bowl, or a set of mah-jong tiles with symbols that rub off on your fingers. Any advance on that?

122

Galoshes

'The Mole's cap was missing from its accustomed peg. His galoshes, which always lay by the umbrella-stand, were also gone.'

So begins one of the most thrilling episodes in Kenneth Grahame's *The Wind In The Willows*, when Mole slips out of the Water Rat's house on a chill winter's day, to visit Badger, and finds more than he bargained for in the snowy depths of the Wild Wood. Ratty tracks him easily, though. 'The galoshes were new, just bought for the winter, and the pimples on their soles were fresh and sharp. He could see the imprints of them in the mud, running along straight and purposeful, leading direct to the Wild Wood.'

I must have read that for the first time when I was about seven, and my eye snagged straight away on the word that stuck out like a thorn from the smooth stem of the story. Galoshes! It sounded sort of squashy and splashy. What could they be? Some sort of shoes, obviously, because their soles left prints in the mud. And those soles had pimples – what was that about? I knew what pimples were, nasty things you got on your face from eating sweets between meals. But shoes with pimples?

I don't think I have ever actually established what galoshes are (or if you can have one galosh on its own). Yes, of course I could Google them and find out in a jiffy, probably order myself a pair of bright scarlet ones in hand-tooled Skivertex. But I quite like leaving that childhood image undisturbed – squashed-up winter shoes that a Mole might wear for sploshing around in.

So that's what I'll pack up in the old kitbag of the imagination, if this winter proves a squelchy one. Galoshes. With pimples, fresh and sharp.

123

My bedside Essex

I lived in an Essex marshman's house for years. I went punt-gunning down silvery creeks at dawn; I rowed the moody Thames looking for a place to hide my convict acquaintances. I almost drowned on the tidal causeway to Horsey Island; I fought and drank contraband brandy with the smugglers of Mersea. On Wallasea Island, I ran from the witch called Old Mother Redcap with my heart in my mouth. All this without stirring out of bed – all this as a boy, late at night, courtesy of what I read and imagined in Charles Dickens and Sabine Baring-Gould, in Arthur Ransome and J. Wentworth Day.

If reading was a powerful key to the landscape of rural Essex, music was the agent that kicked the door down later. Ian Dury was the original Upminster Kid, and his wonderful, funny and very rude lyrics made me fonder and fonder of my fantasy Essex. Side by side with the Upminster Kid, I drove around 'in a two-tone Zephyr with a mean and nasty grin'; I held down a love rival for 'Harold Hill of Harold Hill' to operate on 'with his Black and Decker drill'; and, in the company of Billericay Dickie, I lay on the couch 'with a nice bit of posh from Burnham-on-Crouch'.

But it was Canvey Island's R & B kings Dr Feelgood, and especially their songwriter and guitar player Wilko Johnson, who really drew me to this grittier side of Essex – what would have been the classic Essex stereotype of kneecappers and slappers, if it hadn't been for Johnson's wit, the panache of his rhymes and the endearing fact that all his wannabe big shots were really small-town losers. Johnson's sharp little songs such as 'Roxette', 'Sneakin' Suspicion' and 'Walking On The Edge' drew portraits of Canvey Island every bit as economical and pungent as a Raymond Carver short story or a burst of Mickey Spillane.

By the time I actually moved to the region, I had a rich mental picture of Essex as a county of two halves: Wilko Johnson-land along the Thames estuary, all smoky boozers and oil refinery flares; and moody marshes out to the east, smeared with tidal mud and bristling with smugglers and madmen. What I found were landscapes as diverse, shifting and atmospheric as could be – the Dengie peninsula, for example, round whose seawall path I could literally walk all day and see nobody. The folded hills around the Stour valley. The maze of creeks and marsh islets in the Walton Backwaters. The heathy commons and the ancient woodlands around Danbury.

The more you walk in Essex, the more you explore the footpaths and green lanes, the more you fall under the spell of these landscapes. Their low aspect, their long and flat horizons, their margins where sea and land intertwine, are an endless source of nourishment and of stimulation for mind and spirit. We all need empty horizons, lonely shores, forgotten woods, huge skies with nothing but a tree or a church tower sticking up into them – places where nature just carries on doing what she does without caring if we are there or not. Places we don't make a mark or leave our stamp, places we can feel truly and properly insignificant. Places to feel a thrill of loneliness. Places that make us disappear.

124

Moody, muddy Dengie

The blunt-nosed Dengie peninsula, pushing out east between the parallel estuaries of Crouch and Blackwater, is less than an hour's journey from central London. Capital-dwellers in search of an atmosphere in variance with their everyday lives hunt in vain for it in the Chilterns, the Cotswolds, the South Downs. Dengie, the wildest and least urbanised place any stressed Londoner could dream of, a moodily haunting retreat on the capital's own doorstep, remains overlooked and ignored.

Two agreeable small towns form the gateway to Dengie. On the north, Maldon with its red-sailed barges and steep streets stands at the landward end of the Blackwater estuary. Burnham-on-Crouch in the south, red-roofed and full of creaky old-fashioned shops, lies halfway down the Crouch's narrow estuary. East of these two towns is where the Dengie begins – a huge flat plate of 11,000 reclaimed acres of marshland, every inch crammed with crops, its margins bounded by forty miles of sea walls and uncounted acreage of lonely salt marsh and mudflats.

The old marsh farms – Westend East Wick, Wraywick, Bridgewick, Landwick, Weatherwick – perch out along the rough roads in the vast emptiness of Dengie. They retain that Anglo-Saxon 'wick' ('dairy farm'), recalling the ancient practice of fattening sheep on the marshes for their milk and cheese. The only analogy that really captures the isolation of these easternmost farms of Dengie, marooned in their Brob-dingnagian swathes of crops, is of ships at anchor in a dark green sea. Beyond the sea wall stretch the marshes – a drab brown-and-pale-green tableland of vegetation packed tight above thick Essex mud. In those mud flats live countless millions of invertebrate animals, a food store for coastal ducks, geese and wading birds.

I first set out to walk from Bradwell to Burnham on a November morning: intense cold, a threat of snow in a yellow sky, a skin of ice on the creeks. Once I was past the grim grey cubes of Bradwell's nuclear power station, the dark-bellied brent geese dominated the day. Freshly arrived from Siberia, they brought with them the feeling of winter, with their characteristic hound-like bark and tideline grazings.

A crook-winged tern sailed the south-east wind, balancing against it with infinitely subtle adjustments of tail and wings. Out beyond the gleaming muds of St Peter's Flat, a red-sailed barge was beating up towards Maldon, its shivering sails and heavy lurches in the choppy seaway a crude echo of the tern's instinctive mastery of wind.

That wind buffeted me and brought spatters of rain as I trudged south in glorious isolation. Marshhouse Decoy Pond lay hidden behind its trees. Seventeenth-century marshmen borrowed the idea from the Dutchmen who were draining the East Anglian fenlands at that time: lure wildfowl to the pond with grain, use dogs to herd them into the deadly nets and wring their necks for the gentry's larders.

It is about sixteen miles by sea wall from Bradwell to Burn-ham-on-Crouch, a long walk when you are pushing into a blustery south-westerly half-gale. I saw not a soul during the day and heard nothing but the wind, bird-cries and the distant rush of waves that grew steadily louder as the tide came in.

The shore birds of Dengie see few humans. Near Holli-well Point, down in the remote south-eastern corner of the peninsula, turnstones and plover continued to patter uncon-cernedly along the cockle-shell beach even when I sat down to watch them ten feet off. Wrapped in the silence and loneliness of Dengie, I could not quite believe that central London was less than an hour away.

Flint and clay

The two-inch-long scraper made a tiny clinking noise as it came into contact with the toe of my boot – just enough to make me glance down. Otherwise, I'd never have noticed it in the ochre-coloured furrow of the ploughed field. The scraper must have been lying at least 6,000 years in the Suffolk clay, but its delicately scalloped edge was still acute enough to slice through sinew, flesh or skin. It wasn't hard to picture its original owner, some Stone Age farmer or hunter-gatherer in the valley of the River Box, searching in vain for the painstakingly handmade tool that had somehow fallen from his grasp and now lay disguised among a thousand other faceless flints.

I left the shallow river valley and climbed the lane to Stoke-by-Nayland, testing the sharpness of the little scraper against my thumb. It would be something to talk about over the teacups with my friends in the house they'd recently moved to – a timber-framed ploughman's cottage that dated back to the Wars of the Roses, a house that had spawned twenty generations of labourers to work the heavy, fertile land along the borders where Suffolk and Essex meet.

Everything that goes to make up the landscape of this delectable corner of East Anglia – the productive soils of the low, rolling fields, the pastures and cornfields, the dozens of streams and rivers, the clumps of ancient oak wood – is bedded on the twin foundations of flint and clay. And they in turn rest on a great wedge of chalk laid down some 100 million years ago in seas as clear and warm as a Tahitian lagoon.

Walking the East Anglian farmlands on a cold winter's day in the twenty-first century AD, it was curious to think of the tropical sponges whose liquefied skeletons, hardening in the chalk bed of those turquoise seas, formed the flints that I had been carelessly kicking aside with every step. Even stranger to picture the towering, mile-thick Ice Age glaciers inching their way ponderously eastward across the land 10,000 years ago like blind beasts, melting as they went and spewing behind them the trail of rocks and clay crunched up with chalk that created the wonderfully productive soil called boulder clay.

The great wild oak woods of Suffolk owed their vigorous spread to the fertility of that thick carpet of lime-rich clay – and their decline, too, as men moved in and began to cut down the trees to make way for the golden grain. You can catch a hint of the atmosphere of ancient wildwood in Bradfield Woods near Bury St Edmunds or Wolves Wood near Hadleigh, carefully maintained remnants of primitive woodland that ring with birdsong. Out in the pastures and barley fields, though, it's strictly business – the immemorial business of raising cattle and corn that absorbed the occupants of the Stoke-by-Nayland ploughman's cottage and countless others like them down the long millennia.

It's not just the livelihoods of Suffolk men and women and the vegetation of their countryside that have been shaped by the geology that underpins the county. Unlike the limestone of the Cotswolds, the sandstone of Devon or the gritstone of the Derbyshire dales, Suffolk's ground has almost no building stone. Clay and flint are what there is, together with the trees that thrive so well in this rich soil. And it's timber from the woods, straw from the harvest fields, reeds from the river valleys, the stiff boulder clay and the dark nuggets of flint that nestle there that have produced the beautiful vernacular architecture of the region.

Timber-framed farmhouses, many dating back to the Middle Ages, are a familiar sight everywhere you go on the borders of Suffolk and Essex. Braced by wooden beams, their walls are made of hazel-twig lattice bound together with straw and clay. The plaster that seals the walls is sometimes richly pargetted or adorned with relief decorations; the roofs are made of fired clay tiles or thatched with straw or reed. The rough and beautiful timberwork of the great barns – 'Cathedrals of the Harvest', as they are called – was refined in the interiors of famous Suffolk parish churches such as Long Melford, Lavenham and Hadleigh, where the art of knapping local flints and combining them with imported limestone was brought to perfection in East Anglia's medieval heyday.

Such deep foundations make for a landscape that changes remarkably little. The gnarly oak trees, the wind-rippled cornfields and huge cloudy skies full of light that John Constable caught in his great Suffolk landscapes are all still here. In the end, it's flint and clay that every lover of this locality comes back to – the edge of a Stone Age implement rasping against the thumb, or a rusty Victorian ploughshare picked up among the furrows of a stiff clay field.

126

V is for Vixen

... specifically the very beautiful animal who came at me out of a moonlit cornfield. Foxes are ten a penny in Bristol, where I live – in fact, at night-time, you're more likely to see a fox slinking over a wall or trotting lightly along the gutter than you are a dog or a cat. I spot them all the time: gleaming red presences in the car headlights, smoky grey shadows under the street lamps. But this fox, this big sleek vixen parting the barley like a ship in a silky ocean, was a different class of beast entirely.

Any summer night's walk has its own enchantment, of course – this one especially, a sea wall ramble along the edge of the great pebble ridge of Chesil Beach with a calm sea whispering among the stones. And there's no doubt the vixen was lent glamour by the light of a harvest moon at its fullest, hanging like a Chinese lantern over the Dorset coast. The diffuse-but-intense radiance made her eyes coruscate like emeralds and laid a pearly sheen along her sinuous back.

Like any sensible wild animal, she froze stock-still as soon as she caught sight of the ominous shape of Man the hunter, Man the chicken-avenger, outlined above her against the stars. I don't suppose it was more than seven or eight seconds that we stared one another down, but I felt the hair rise all up the nape of my neck. A rustling swirl in the barley as she turned, a last glimpse of those glittering eyes looking over her shoulder and then a dark wake retreating through the corn. I didn't see her again. But the moment has lived with me.

127

Song of the mermaids

Wild and wintry weather was tearing across the flat north Lincolnshire landscape, showering the huge ploughed fields and ruler-straight roads with whirling leaves and bursts of rain. Lovely weather for ducks – and for grey seals, according to Claire Weaver, Natural England's adviser on wildlife management for several of the Sites of Special Scientific Interest (SSSI) along the Lincolnshire coast.

'The seals don't care,' she observed, as we set off along the fenced path through the dunes of Donna Nook, heads down against wind and rain. 'They've got just two things on their minds at this time of year – giving birth and having sex.'

The UK is home to something approaching half the world population of grey seals, and the window of opportunity for them to pup and mate is a narrow one. They have to come ashore to do both, explained Claire. But on land they are slow, clumsy and vulnerable, particularly when all hyped up and distracted by birth and sex hormones. So nature squeezes both activities into a very tight time frame. The cows, having delayed implantation of last year's fertilised eggs for seven months, have been carrying developing pups since late spring. They give birth a couple of days after they reach land, wean their pups for three weeks and then mate and get back to sea in as short order as possible. By that time, they are literally starving; they don't eat while on shore, and drop about 40 per cent of their body weight.

The enormous flat expanse of salt marsh and mudflats at Donna Nook, on the southernmost edge of the Humber Estuary, the Lincolnshire grey seals' chosen pupping and mating ground, is not only an SSSI and a National Nature Reserve managed by Lincolnshire Wildlife Trust – it's also an MOD bombing range. Juggling things so that aircraft can practice, seals can perform their functions undisturbed and the public can enjoy the spectacle safely is a complicated business, but National Nature Reserve warden Rob Scott, his solo assistant and dozens of volunteers make a wonderful job of it. The fenced path conducts you along the edge of the salt marsh, and there are the seals, hundreds of them, some close enough to touch – if you don't value your fingers.

'They're wild animals,' Claire reminded me, as we stood looking down at a snow-white pup cuddled up to the fence, 'and they can give a nasty bite.'

There is something very Walt Disney about grey seals – the adorable huge-eyed pups in white coats, the sleekly dappled mothers and big bruiser males with ripples of fat round their scarred necks. 'Ooohs' and 'aaahs' were in the air. At first glance, all the adults looked utterly docile, a collection of fat slippery slugs marooned in the mud. But nature is a ruthless driver of behaviour. The bulls went slithering and undulating forward to confront one another with open-mouthed roars, occasionally tumbling over in actual combat as they bit at one another's necks. Young males not yet bulky enough to ring-fence a harem made nuisances of themselves, teasing the seniors by invading their personal space to provoke deep roars and impressive displays of sharp teeth.

A couple of bulls tried their luck with the cows, but were warned off with snarls. It was a little early in the season for mating; the first pups had only been born three weeks before.

Now there were well over 400 of them, ranging from the newly born (in coats still stained bright yellow by amniotic fluid) to three-week pups already losing their lanugo, or baby coat of white.

The cow and pup pairs lay high up the salt marsh or in the dunes, well away from the roaring and splashing on the mud-flats. I watched a well-grown pup nuzzling for its mother's tiny teat while she guided it with flaps of her flipper. Seal milk is fabulously rich in fat, so while the cows and bulls starve and diminish, the pups put on weight like super-sizers, nearly four pounds a day.

'They need to,' said Claire. 'When that cow goes to mate and then back to sea, the pup'll be fending for itself for the next fortnight, living on its blubber until it gets into the sea and starts fishing for itself.'

It was a mesmerising sight – the rain-freckled marsh and mudflats covered in grey seals, apparently inert but in reality working overtime to respond to the timeless imperative of the reproduction of the species. As I watched, I became aware of the extraordinary noise the seals were making, swelling like a chorus behind a show – a mooing, roaring, groaning and banshee wailing that our seafaring ancestors told each other was the song of the mermaids. Eerie, ghostly and spine-tingling, it haunted my inner ear for the rest of the day.

128

Starling roar

At half past four on a November evening, I waited with my binoculars at the crook of the lane that leads from Westhay out to the vast, flat peat moors of the Somerset Levels. I didn't really know what to expect. The largest congregation of birds I had ever seen on the wing together was a cloud of dunlin on the Norfolk coast, estimated at 15,000. At the time, that had seemed an overwhelmingly large number of birds. I couldn't begin to imagine what a couple of million starlings might look and sound like.

As the dusk began to thicken, the starlings appeared: thin lines of thirty or forty birds at first, then congregations of several hundred, and finally armies many tens of thousands strong, sweeping across the sky in vast dramatic waves of closely packed birds to join the gigantic assembly already swirling above the trees. Their aerial meeting place was right over Westhay – right over my head.

The cloud they formed was like a sky beast with a life of its own. At one moment it flew balled into a solid black clot, the next it was stretched out like a rippling silk scarf three miles long. It thickened and thinned as though a giant magnet beyond the setting sun were drawing iron filings across the sky. It sped to the west, rose several hundred feet, turned as if directed by a celestial choreographer and plunged towards the lane, where I stood transfixed.

The willows and apple trees blackened instantly. They bowed their branches to the ground, laden with starlings like heavy fruit. A shower of droppings splattered across lane and hedge, whitening my coat and shoes. I felt the wind of several million wings and heard a roar in the sky like a jet engine. Black dots buzzed and whirled as the starlings came streaming through the village. And into the blizzard of birds, chugging against the tide, went a farm tractor driven by a hooded figure, dark and hunched as if in a dream.

Where the birds put down for the night I never saw. They went barrelling away towards the sunset again and dropped into the dark somewhere.

Once you have seen one of the great winter starling roosts in action, you have to go back for more. So, this winter, I found myself on a cold January evening back at Westhay – in a bird hide out on the moor itself this time, staking out the very reed bed I'd been told the starlings would overnight on.

They came on cue across a low, intense sunset under a sky of white-edged snow clouds. Wave after wave of starlings skimmed the reed beds and wet woods of the moor, until the whole northern sky over Mendip was crammed with birds. The aerial currents ebbed and flowed, this way and that. It was astonishing that there were no mid-air collisions.

After half an hour of rippling communal rollercoastering, the immense mass of birds made a final pass across the last glow of daylight and came in to the reed bed. The whole flock dropped to the reed stems in a couple of minutes, and there they shifted, rose and fell with a deep bass thunder of wings and a piercing shrilling of voices. Gradually the roost settled, until the roar of movement had subsided and the shrieking had muted to a sound like the trickle of a shallow river over stones.

The sunset shrank to a glowing bar of gold behind a stand of silver birch. Darkness closed down over Westhay Moor. I lingered by the reed bed, unable to leave, mesmerised by the sound of three million starlings settling in for the night.

129

Land of the dragon

Staring up from thirty feet below, I couldn't help noticing that venerable Ina, king of the Anglo-Saxons, had an icicle on the end of his nose. So did his elegant consort Æthelburgh, standing alongside. In fact, glancing along the great array of sculpted figures both secular and sainted that filled the niches in the west front of Wells Cathedral, they all looked half-frozen, grey-faced and grim. Then the wintry sun found a chink in the yellow snow clouds over Somerset, and suddenly prelates, bishops and kings were sparkling as if the Celestial Scene-Shifter had showered them all with diamonds.

The great early thirteenth-century facade at Wells is often called the finest west front in Europe. The huge Gothic cathedral rides the tides of history among the ancient houses of this delectable small city like a vast liner moored among skiffs. Today, the swans around the Palace of the bishop of Bath and Wells lay huddled up for warmth under the curtain wall, while Muscovy ducks and hybrid mallards waddled cautiously across the ice of the frozen moat. A film of powder snow crusted the mosaic made by local schoolchildren and installed beside the moat in 2001. It depicted in spiky detail the slaying of a dragon by bold Bishop Jocelin at around the time the west front was being constructed – a feat of heroism, legend says, that must be celebrated every fifty years, lest the beast should return from its lair under Worminster Sleight.

I shoved my gloved hands deep into my pockets, turned my back on the whitened roofs of Wells and forged up through the leafless oaks and sycamores on Tor Hill. The East Mendip Way hurdles these southern flanks of the Mendip Hills, and I found the path a great companion, running purposefully eastward with its ruts glazed with thick white ice and its hedges glittering with hoar frost. Up on King's Castle Hill, the bare trees hunched together as if for warmth, their twiggy shapes a delicate mauve under the lightless, snow-laden sky. In spring, the undergrowth on this hill is bright with bluebells and the brush-like yellow heads of wood goldilocks; in autumn, with the crocus-shaped flowers of meadow saffron. That day, it lay shrunken and brown, sufficiently thinned by the fingers of winter for the eroded ramparts of an Iron Age fortification to show through at the nape of the hill.

From the long ridge of Lyatt, a far view unfolded southward over the low-lying wetland and moorland of the Somerset Levels, away past the round tump of Glastonbury Tor with its pimple of a summit tower, on over the Polden Hills towards the pale blue curves of the Quantocks and Exmoor beyond the Bristol Channel. I walked faster to generate heat, crunching over dead nettle heads and ancient field boundary banks across the former sheep pasture of Furzey Sleight, kicking up frosted leaves in Sleight Lane – hereabouts, a sheep walk is a 'sleight', an Old English word that would have been familiar to the ears of Ina and Æthelburgh. Then I made downhill by way of West Lane, a proper old muddy and rutty field lane that snakes down the slope of Mendip to reach the former mill town of Croscombe, lying in the valley bottom along the River Sheppey.

Long gone are the days when the streets of Croscombe rattled with silk and corn mills and the Sheppey ran brown, foul and stinking from its bankside tanneries and leather washeries. Now the village lies quiet, a treat for a walker's eyes and ears. I crossed the sparkling Sheppey and climbed the steep lane to the southern ridge of the valley, where a blackbird sat songless on a frosted gate bar, outlined against a sky already turning orange with evening. On the far side, the hidden valley of Worminster fell away, a silent green cleft. Up over the back of Dulcote Hill I went, brushing through sapless brambles in the skirts of Dulcote Wood, to come suddenly to the brink of the great bitten-out quarry, recently redundant, that hollows the back of the hill.

A peregrine was cutting the air before the quarry ledges. I let my eyes follow its upward swoop and pondered the question that preoccupies many in this roadstone-rich part of the world: what to do with these worked-out delvings in the hills? Fill them with industrial units, with hundreds of workers and lorry movements, or leave them for time and nature to work on? Or try the experiment that's ongoing at Dulcote Hill: build a ready-meals factory in one half of the quarry and leave the other undisturbed for the established residents – peregrines, orchids and great crested newts. It's an ambitious plan, a commendable vision, and – rather against expectation (mine included) – it seems to be working.

I lingered a moment, looking down over Worminster, the 'town of the dragon', and the sleight under which the old monster still lies and bides its time. Then I dropped down through the trees and made for the distant towers of Wells.

130

A pot of bile

I do love Alfred Wainwright, supreme creator of walkers' guidebooks, for reasons some might think perverse. Not so much for his pre-eminence in the Lake District, nor for his role as guide, philosopher and friend along the Coast to Coast walk. What I really treasure is Wainwright playing Job's comforter, the cantankerous northerner salting his practical instructions with the driest and grimmest of pessimistic drollery. And A. W. was right at the top of his game in that particular vein when he wrote what I consider his best work, his *Pennine Way Companion*.

I've written a dozen walking guidebooks (total sales: roughly 1,000 times less than Wainwright's), and I must have read hundreds. Every one of them, mine included, is a pallid, crowd-pleasing thing compared with the Master's little masterpiece. Other guidebooks don't snap at the complacent reader's heels. They don't send the walker on his way with the cheery observation that 'you are going to suffer ... you are going to feel miserable and wish you had never heard of the Pennine Way', or preface each page with a biting aphorism – 'ghastly'; 'a wet and weary trudge'; 'you will question your own sanity'.

I treasure A. W. for his gritty honesty, black jokes and bilious humour. The Pennine Way, toughest of routes, makes fools of kinder writers. What you need at your elbow in a howling February gale on Bleaklow, when you're up to your knees in peat slutch and bog water, is Wainwright, muttering, 'Cheer up. There's worse to follow.'

Forget those guidebooks that glow with positivity. Give me Wainwright and his pungent pot of bile. I only wish I had half the chutzpah of a man who could growl at his readers by way of valediction: 'You won't come across me anywhere along the Pennine Way. I've had enough of it.'

131

What's under the jacket

I love Ordnance Survey maps with a passion. Those bland-looking covers, crimson Landrangers and orange Explorers, conceal a fabulous treasure chest of landscapes, stories, mysteries and adventures. But I have to admit that they are awkward devils to handle. When you're wrestling with OS 1:50,000 Landranger 152 ('Northampton & Milton Keynes') on a Saturday morning in bed with a loaded tea tray, a pile of post, a heap of newspapers and four other maps in various stages of unfoldedness, you can get surprisingly stroppy, even with a thing as basically wonderful as the Ordnance Survey.

Jane and I were hunting for a winter walk, something that we could do together in the few short hours between a December dawn and dusk. Where had neither of us walked before? How about Northamptonshire and the never-yet-opened Landranger 152?

In the hard currency of the walker's world, Britain's Ordnance Survey is the gold standard. No maps across the face of the earth can match the OS for detail, clarity and accuracy. But OS maps are not just coldly functional tools. They paint a vivid picture in the mind's eye. Flat rectangular blocks of green become curvaceous hilltop woods. Brown contours bulge and ripple into mountains and valleys. Dotted lines lay a network of green lanes and country footpaths across the paper landscape.

There are warning signs too: spidery snares of electricity cables to ruin the view, scarlet slashes of noisy main roads, the acne rash of a rubbish dump or spoil heap.

'Not here,' whispered Landranger 152. 'See the M1 over there, and these sprawling estates around Milton Keynes, and that pylon web tangled all round Castle Ashby? You can do better than this.'

I left Landranger 152 to the toast crumbs and tea puddles and went looking for a friendlier welcome. Well – what about the Cotswolds, nice and close to our Bristol home?

'Yes, come in, how nice to see you,' cooed Landranger 150. 'Let me recommend Stanton, Stanway and the Cotswold escarpment – no pylons, no A-roads, no urban sprawl. Need more details? Have a chat with my big brother, 1:25,000 Outdoor Leisure 45, why don't you?'

We swept maps, tea tray, letters and papers off the bed and got the orange-coated OL 45 laid out flat. At twice the scale, the promise that the Landranger had held out became a certainty signed, sealed and delivered. A mighty slope of escarpment that must have great views out west; racehorse gallops near the hamlet of Ford; plenty of woodland walking; the villages of Stanton and Stanway, far from any main road. The green diamond symbols of the Cotswold Way National Trail guaranteed a clear, waymarked path for at least half the walk; other footpaths and bridleways completed the route. A ten-mile circuit, with a pub to start from and another halfway round for a lunch stop. Bingo! Where are those walking boots?

The true delight of map-planned walks is that, however enticing the pictures that imagination lodges in your inner eye, you just can't tell what it's going to be like when you actually get out there on the ground. We could never have foreseen the magical moment at the start of the walk when trainer Jonjo O'Neill's racehorses came thundering out of the Cotswold mist, nor the beautiful shapes and colours of the fungi we found growing in the woods, nor the thrill as a dozen pheasants, in flight from shooters in the fields, came hurtling towards us with a whirr of wings and settled in the bare beech branches over our heads.

Stanton and Stanway turned out to be golden dreams of villages in honeycomb-hued Cotswold stone. From the crest of the escarpment, we gazed out into a peach-coloured sunset over the Vale of Evesham. Just as good as all this – maybe better – was the hot cup of tea by the Plough Inn's fire at the end of the walk, as we folded the secrets and pleasures of the day back inside the workaday orange jacket of OL 45 once more.

W is for Willy Knott

… and other place names that get the humour juices flowing. A few years ago, I bought the Ordnance Survey's *Gazetteer of Great Britain*, a thumping great tome whose 791 pages consist of nothing but multiple columns of print so miniaturised that even literate mice would have to fetch the specs out. But what treasure lies here! I solemnly swear that I haven't made up any of these names – there they are in black and white, if you have the eyesight of a goshawk and the patience to unearth them…

Howl Beck, Roaring Middle, Groan, Moan and Yell,
Whisperdales, Mutterton, Silent Pool, Dumbrell;
Quaking Pot, Shivering Knott, Trembleath, The Scares,
Bold Burn, Brawlings, Dasher and Dares.

Leapingwells, Lightfoots, Dartmeet, The Runn,
Stamperland, Heavitree, Weighton, The Ton;
Bawdy Craig, Randy Pike, Nudge Hill, The Wink,
Stiff Street, The Risings, Soften and Sink.

Booze Moor, Tipple Cross, Drunken Bottom, Nutters,
Illers Leary, Heave Coppice, Sickers Fell, Gutters;
Gobley Hole, Gannets, Gulpher, Greedy Gut,
Shattering, Shitlington, Shothole, The Shut.

Covid Winter: Skirrid in the Sky

The River Severn's estuary is at a fantastically low tide as we cross the 'new' bridge on a day of no cloud whatsoever. Yet another lockdown looms at the butt end of this pandemic year, and Wales is rumoured about to be declared out of bounds again. Just time to squeeze in a classic winter walk before that comes to pass.

Looking seaward through the stroboscopic flicker of the bracing wires, we can see the tidal outcrop of the English stones fully exposed and slathered in red mud. Downriver, the little hump of Denny Island off Portishead stands marooned in a huge desert of sand. Other sand- and mudbanks lie around the widening tideway like beached whales. Unwary strangers might even suppose you could cross the five miles from the English to the Welsh bank on foot and do no more than bespatter your spats. And maybe you could, if you were able to walk on water while negotiating quicksand, slow mud, sudden drops, fathomless pools and the second-highest tidal range in the world sneaking round the corners to cut you off.

Over in Wales, we hightail it to Llanvihangel Crucorney, a place with a name whose sound put the immortal walking writer John Hillaby in mind of 'a toy train scampering over points'. Llanvihangel Crucorney lies in the River Monnow's valley, which forms the eastern boundary of the Black Mountains and Brecon Beacons. It's a great jumping-off point for walks westward into those mountains, but today we are aiming east to climb the Skirrid (Ysgyryd Fawr, the 'big split one'), a tall hill that lies north–south with its head cocked and spine raised like an alert old dog.

The Skirrid is made of tough old red sandstone lying in a heavy lump on top of thin layers of weaker mudstone – hence its history of slippage and landslides. We come up to it in cold wind and brilliant sunshine across fields of sheep, skirting its western flank through scrub woods, gorse bushes blooming yellow and holly trees in a blaze of scarlet berries, with the dark purple crags of the northern end hanging over little rugged passes of landslide rocks fallen in a jumble.

The ascent is short, steep and stepped, but it's the sort of 'starter mountain' that families with six-year-olds can manage. Many are out: mums, dads, children, students, 'maturer' folk such as us, all hurrying to revel in the glorious winter sunlight before the reintroduction of lockdown in Wales comes into force.

Once at the peak, in this unbelievably clear weather, we gasp to see the landscape laid out in pin-sharp detail 1,000 feet below and fifty miles off – Malverns, Black Mountains; farmlands rising and falling towards Gloucestershire and the Midlands; the slanting tabletops of Penyfan and Cribyn over in the Brecon Beacons; Cotswolds, Mendips, Exmoor; and the South Wales coast trending round into far-off Pembrokeshire.

Nearer at hand, a grey streak of softly glimmering sea shows the tide rising in the Severn Estuary past Brean Down's promontory, the slight disc of Flat Holm and the hump of her sister island Steep Holm, their lower edges lost in mist so that they look like floating islands in some fabulous sea.

134

Fight for the footpaths

Not far into our walk from the Wiltshire village of Heddington, we came across an all-too-familiar scene – a mile or so of pasture through which the footpath ran unwaymarked over neglected stiles, to stop short at a done-up farmhouse, where the right of way passed across the farmhouse garden. An unguarded electric fence blocked access to the unmarked gate leading into the garden. All signs and waymarks were missing, giving the impression that there was no right of way. We hollered for the owner, who first sent the dog out, then somewhat shamefacedly emerged from the house and admitted that, yes, the path did cross her garden. No apologies for the electric shock that Jane got crossing the fence, however.

It's become very noticeable in recent times how many rights of way have been obliterated or obscured, waymarks and signposts removed and obstacles erected around nice country houses whose new owners have done the property up to the nines and decided unilaterally that the rights of way they accepted when they bought the house can be quietly abolished. It's reminiscent of the land grabs and right-of-way abolitions during the Enclosures of the eighteenth and nineteenth centuries. Wiltshire's a particular culprit, for some reason, and Essex is not far behind, as London escapers buy up old farmhouses and turn the surrounding acres into horse paddocks with powerful electric fencing. Only super-confident walkers, or those suicidally insistent on their rights, are going to face crossing a dozen rickety stiles in quick succession (if the stiles are even there), risking a nasty 8,000-volt electric shock and a bite or kick from the large and unpredictable occupants of the paddocks, when there are no waymarks to reassure you that this is the route. No, mate, never heard of no footpath here. Better go back the way you came. Or get round by way of the road and brave the hurtling land cruisers on those picturesque bends.

One of Britain's greatest national treasures is its network of public footpaths – an almost unbelievable 140,000 miles of them. But only the officially designated National Trails – the footpath motorways of the nation, the ones with the highest public profile and greatest footfall – are being properly looked after, their stiles and kissing gates maintained, their signage checked and renewed. 'Lesser' paths are down the pecking order, while the everyday footpath that joins farm to farm and field to field is a very poor relation, in dire danger of being planted over with impenetrable crops of maize, or having its footbridges removed and its gates immovably tied with binder twine or barbed wire by the landowner.

Poverty of resources at County Hall has led to the laying off of many of the county footpaths officers whose job it is to keep this wonderful and unique network of paths open by making sure that householders, landowners and farmers do toe the line about maintaining access. The Ramblers organisation does the best it can, but it can't keep up with the decline in the grassroots footpaths of the network. Yet it's these humbler paths, the local links, that make a proper interconnected network of those 140,000 miles – the envy of walkers, hikers and ramblers the world over.

We everyday walkers with our secateurs and our

undergrowth-trampling boots are the sharpest weapons this country possesses in the fight to preserve what amounts to an irreplaceable national treasure. Keep snipping those brambles! Keep walking those paths, folks!

The rough embrace of winter

A beautiful winter's morning shortly before Christmas – one of those crisp, smoky mornings with ice skinning the puddles and a sky of unbroken blue over the leafless woods, when nature calls you imperiously out of doors, then smacks you in the face when it has got you there. Setting off from the West Berkshire hamlet of Lower Green, eyes running with chilly tears, breath pluming out like a leaky locomotive, I gasped with cold and asked myself what the hell I thought I was doing. Five days ago, I had been basking in 35°C heat in tropical north Australia, and this thermometer plunge into the minus zone was a shock and a half to the system.

Out in the fields, rooks strutted the stubble rows, their fat feathery thighs making them roll like drunken sailors; my boots cracked milky panes of ice in the ruts; brambles hung whitened and stiff in the hedges, each spiny leaf tipped with a droplet of half-melted frost. All the pleasures of walking the English countryside in winter came flooding suddenly in on me. After weeks of energy-sapping heat on baking Queensland beaches, I welcomed the rough embrace of winter stinging my cheeks and rasping in my nostrils – a brisk exhortation to stride out and get the blood coursing round the body.

Up the steep breast of Inkpen Hill I slogged, puffing out steam, stripping off scarf and then woolly hat as the interior radiators were turned full on by the hard exercise. Up at the top, there was all the time in the world to pause, pour a cup of coffee from the flask and take in the quite stupendous view. I gazed north, twenty or thirty miles across the plains of Berkshire and Wiltshire towards the White Horse downs and the distant Cotswolds. The windows of deep-sunk country houses flashed among spinneys and copses that in the full leaf of summer would shield them from sight. Unknown villages and farms I would never visit spread their bare fields in subtle winter colours of cream and powder blue. Sheep moved slowly along the crest of the down, their fleeces turned to spun gold in the low sunlight.

The black T-bar of sinister Combe Gibbet, by contrast, stood stark and dark on the humped back of a Neolithic burial mound. The original scaffold, set here on the skyline so that everyone for twenty miles round would see it, was used only once: in 1676, the bodies of George Broomham of Combe and his lover, Dorothy Newman of Inkpen, were suspended from either cross-piece and left to rot as a grim warning, after the pair had been hanged for the murder of Broomham's wife, Margaret, and his son, Robert. It was a man known locally as 'Mad Thomas' who blurted out that he'd seen the victims being drowned in a pond; they had stumbled by evil chance across the lovers, in flagrante delicto on the down.

Beyond Combe Gibbet rose the green inverted bowl of Walbury Hill, bisected by the ancient trackway I was following. The works of our distant ancestors litter the long ridge of the downs hereabouts: burial mounds, ditches, rutted tracks and the high-piled ramparts of Walbury Camp. It is easy to see why Iron Age men fortified this hilltop – at 974 feet above sea level, Walbury Hill is the highest chalk hill in Britain. Anyone commanding this site would be able to see strangers, whether friend or foe, approaching from any direction in plenty of time to prepare an appropriate reception.

From the old hilltop stronghold, I dropped down into the sheltered valley where Combe hamlet sits. In the south wall of the flint-built Church of St Swithun, shadowed by mighty old yews, I found a tiny stone head, carved by some humorous-minded medieval mason, an imp-like homunculus with crazed feline eyes and the cheekiest of smiles. The narrow interior, with its fine Victorian glass and elaborate Georgian grave slabs of black marble, breathed peace and stability, a fixed point in a whirling world.

Up on the back of the downs once more, I faced into the cutting wind and forged northwards. Pheasants exploded out of the hedge roots, and a flock of meadow pipits flew swooping and squeaking across the track. Back at the crest of Inkpen Hill, I took a deep breath and went half-running down the slope, through a tunnel of pale elder suckers and back into Lower Green. I felt my cheeks reddening and my grin widening. It was good to be home.

136

Snow bridge

It has been a long, peat-spattered climb to the gritstone edge. The Met Office tells us there'll be more snow by Christmas Eve, but just for the moment there's a thaw, and everything underfoot squelches and slops. All the way up from the reservoir in the valley floor, the walk has been dominated by two sounds – the slurp and suck of our boots in the quaking ground and the distant mutter of the burn that tumbles off the crags at the point we're aiming for.

I've been thinking that the burn's music sounds curiously muted, considering the amount of meltwater that must be rushing down it. And as we reach the crest, and the dark channel of the burn finally comes in sight, a chilly wind smacks into our faces and all is explained. Up here in the north-facing shadow of the crags, where the air temperature is ten degrees lower, a thick band of unmelted snow is plastered to the cliff. The burn drops sparkling off the edge, plunges under the snow and re-emerges 100 feet lower to tumble on down the moor slope towards the valley.

Close to, the snow bridge is revealed as a crusted shell with delicate edges of transparent ice, fretted by the wind into fronds of gleaming glass. There's a strange acoustic reducing the solid hiss of the falling burn to a hollow tinkle, like pebbles being rattled in a china mug. I bend low and look up the near-vertical tunnel to watch the black water sluice. It's as cold as a knife to the ungloved hand, toothache cold in the mouth.

A foot of snow next week, predicts the weatherman, and a proper white New Year. We'll come up again then, we tell each other, and see the fall in all its frozen glory.

137

X is for Xmas

… but also for xenon. Xenon is a heavy, inert, gaseous element, with the symbol Xe and the atomic number 54. But you knew that already, didn't you? It's also described as a noble gas, and odourless to boot.

After exhaustive research, I believe I have discovered a new element, discernible on only one day a year, at about four o'clock on Christmas afternoon. This element certainly shares the characteristics of heaviness and inertia with xenon. Unlike its parent gas, however, it cannot be described as odourless. It is, in fact, the very first 'ignoble' gas ever recorded. 'The inertness of noble gases' says Wikipedia, 'makes them very suitable in applications where reactions are not wanted.' And that is doubly true of the ignoble gases. If ever there was an application where reactions are not wanted, it is after Christmas dinner when everyone is hugger-mugger round the telly.

My new element – a product of collision between xenon and Xmas – I have decided to call 'X-gas'. I have allotted it the symbol Xg and the atomic number 119. Verification from the British Library of Atomic Theoretical Elements Directorate (B.L.O.A.T.E.D.) has been applied for.

Essentially, my discovery of X-gas has solved an age-old riddle. 'γιατί κάνω Βρεταννός πηγαίνω μια βόλτα μετά Χριστούγεννα γεύμα;' pondered Simplicius of Cilicia in AD 555. 'Why do Britons go for a walk after Christmas dinner?'

Simplicius and his ilk – Asclepiodotus, too, and Nigidius Figulus – never dreamed of the existence of Xg 119, of course. If they had known about X-gas, as the scientists of the world will do once my discovery has hit the news stands, they would surely have answered in gladsome chorus, '*Για να εξαγνιστούν των αναξιοπρεπών αερίων*' ('to purge themselves of ignoble gases').

Simples!

138

With George Borrow to Castell Dinas Bran

A lovely winter morning in North Wales, cold but clear under a blue sky, with the River Dee roaring as it powered its way down to Llangollen. A couple of days of rain in the mountains had swollen the river, pushing it hard over the black shale ledges in its bed and making it foam and sluice round the stone cutwaters of Llangollen Bridge. On the north side of the constricted Dee Valley, the shattered walls of Castell Dinas Bran stood proud across the crest of their 1,000-foot hill, a wink of light through one of the arches visible a mile off.

I savoured the sight of the racing river from the bridge, then scurried for shelter under the station awning of the Llangollen Railway as the first of a succession of rain-bursts descended. Five minutes later, as I turned east along the towpath of the Llangollen Canal, it was blue sky and bright sunshine once more, with the next slate-grey slab of rain already to be seen building over the Berwyn Hills to the west.

I thought of George Borrow, the inextinguishable enthusiast and romantic, striding these hills and valleys through storm and shine in 1854 on the great foot journeys that would inspire his classic travel narrative *Wild Wales*. Borrow, a Saxon by birth but a Celt in his heart, loved Wales, its people, its language, its history, its poetry, all with a passion that admitted no challenge and no correction, even when – as happened more often than he would ever admit – he got things wrong. Rain, wind, darkness, discomfort: he cuffed them all contemptuously aside, splendidly armoured in egotism and bossy self-belief.

The still black water of the canal was jewelled with floating oak leaves in red and gold. Narrowboats moored for winter lined the banks. A trickle of smoke came from the chimneys of *Florence E* and *Chardonnay*, along with smells of frying bacon. Borrow would certainly have knocked and demanded breakfast, paying for it with a fruity couplet composed on the spot.

On the hillside above, I skirted the farms of Llandyn Hall and Wern-uchaf, and turned up a leaf-strewn lane to the foot of the castle mound. In Borrow's footsteps, I climbed to the ruins of Castell Dinas Bran and sat among the broken walls of the stronghold built on this natural eyrie in the mid-thirteenth century by Gruffydd ap Madoc, Prince of Powys.

When George Borrow made his climb, he was accompanied by a jeering mob of urchins from the town. That didn't prevent him spouting off in Welsh for the purpose of impressing those he found on the peak. Today, there was no one except a solitary raven to share one of the most stunning views in Wales – north to the banded crags of Creigiau Eglwyseg; west to the Snowdonia mountains half obscured by storm clouds; and south over Llangollen sheltering under the tremendous wall of the Berwyns, with the River Dee snaking between the houses in a thin ribbon of silver nearly 1,000 feet below.

139

Angling and quanting:
the Norfolk Broads in winter

The heron had been following our boat down the River Bure since we set out from Wroxham on this sunny, glittery winter morning. In a quiet backwater, Richard Furlong threw him a herring head.

'Come on, old boy, come in the boat like you usually do!'

But the wily heron was suspicious. He gobbled the fish head willingly enough but kept looking sideways at me out of a cold yellow eye and would not take his customary flight to Richard's hand.

Winter in the Norfolk Broads moves in slow time. It's a season for short days of birdwatching and exploring the uncrowded broads and their interconnecting rivers and dykes; for spending bad-weather days enjoying the indoor pleasures of the region's treasure of medieval parish churches and its firelit pubs; and for leisurely, well-wrapped-up fishing expeditions when a frosty sun shines.

If you want a guide and mentor to help you make the most of a midwinter angling sortie in the Broads, Richard is your man. I put myself, a clumsy once-a-year fisherman, in his hands, and within five minutes knew I was in the presence of a master.

'See those roach topping the water? That means there's a pike among them.' Richard pointed to a tiny swirl on the surface of a side creek. We cast out a fresh smelt – 'Float-ledg-ering dead bait with a pierced bullet and two triple hooks, if you want to get technical,' said Richard – and waited, not for long. The float bobbed under. 'Hold on,' Richard instructed. 'Let him get it properly between his teeth. He's just sitting under the bank thinking about it at the moment... now, strike!'

I jerked the rod upwards, and a heavy tug on the line told of a hooked fish hidden in the river. I drew him to the boat side, and Richard lifted him inboard: a gleaming olive-green pike with a porcelain-white belly and scarlet gill rakers. He lay in my hands, cold and solid, his glazed brown eye staring.

'Four pounds, about,' estimated Richard, as he slipped the pike back into the river. 'Only a little 'un. But a nice feeling, eh?'

*

'You've got to look after the reed beds,' said Eric Edwards as he quanted me from Toad Hole down the Turf Fen dykes the following morning. 'Thatchers buy reed and sedge, and they only want the best. You've got to cut the reed beds properly, not too much and not too little. If you don't keep them cut, they fill in and go to woodland.'

It was a cold old day for quanting, or punting, along the River Ant and its marshes, a morning of pearly mist that nipped the cheeks and fingers.

'When I started as a marshman back in 1967,' Eric told me, 'it was really hard. Every bundle of reed and every tool had to be carried by hand or boat off the marsh. I'd come home every night frozen, with my hands cut to ribbons. But I had a good old Norfolk boy to tell me and teach me.'

A few strokes of his scythe, honed to razor sharpness, and Eric had felled enough reeds to make a bundle. Expertly he gathered, tamped and tied them, ready for the thatcher.

'It's a real physical job, cutting reed and sedge in winter. Youngsters today don't want to work like this, but they miss out on the true nature of the Broads, the mystery and magic.'

The Turf Fen windpump loomed in the mist, its sails held stiffly in a skeletal cross. Somewhere ahead, geese were gabbling – refugees from northern Scandinavia or the Arctic Circle, recently arrived to spend the winter in the milder climate of the Broads. Suddenly, a big dark bird of prey swung out of the fen fog, planing on long upraised wings: a marsh harrier, quartering the reed beds in search of a water vole or unwary coot.

'Wonderful,' breathed Eric. 'The real spirit of the Broads, that big old bird.'

140

3,000 geese at full gabble

A winter afternoon towards twilight at Holkham on the North Norfolk coast. In the brick-and-flint office of Natural England, I sat over a cup of tea, talking pink-footed geese with Victoria Francis, manager of the National Nature Reserves of Holkham and Scolt Head Island. Victoria had reached the mysteries of the evening flight, when she was interrupted by her senior colleague Michael Rooney, calling from outside in the yard: 'Better come and have a look at the real thing!'

It was one of those wildlife sights you never forget. The pink-feet were beginning their evening flight seawards from their feeding grounds in the sugar-beet fields, and they literally filled the sky. A muted roar of massed gabbling swelled from the south, and the vanguard of the flight came into view, a flickering phalanx of bird. They drew the others after them in undulating waves, like a dark Aurora Borealis – hundreds upon hundreds of pink-footed geese, necks outstretched towards their objective, stiff wings vigorously sawing, a mighty aerial army.

The Natural England offices lay perfectly positioned directly beneath the pink-foot flight path. This was the kind of aerial traffic I'd have paid a king's ransom to see over my own house and, judging by Victoria and Michael's grins, they appreciated just how lucky they were. The deafening noise of

3,000 geese at full gabble faded towards the north, its echoes bouncing back from the yard walls.

'They'll be putting down in the freshwater marshes for the night,' said Michael. 'Let's go and have a look at them, shall we?'

The pink-footed goose, according to Victoria and Michael, is an unpredictable beast. You can't tell when or where, or in what numbers, it will appear on the estuaries of these islands each winter – let alone exactly where or when it might choose to flight on any given day. Yet the big dark-headed birds with the pale wings and lipstick-pink legs have captivated generations of bird-watchers, wildfowlers, biologists and plain lovers of a thumping great wildlife spectacle.

No one knows for how many millennia the pink-feet have been taking their southward flight each autumn as General Winter invades their summer breeding grounds in Iceland and Greenland. They arrive in stages, first in Scotland and then in a gradual drift down the British Isles, reaching the mudflats and beet fields of North Norfolk from September onwards. And when they come, they come mob-handed – perhaps 100,000 altogether to East Anglia, with up to 50,000 congregating in the bailiwick of Victoria and Michael. What draws them here are the sliced fragments of sugar beet, left scattered on the land during the winter-long beet harvest. It's rich feeding, and few of the farmers begrudge the pink-feet their gleanings.

Down on the Holkham freshwater marshes, we opened the door on a hide crammed with birdwatchers. Everyone in the twitching world knows of Holkham. We slid onto the benches, hip to hip, and levelled our binoculars out of the slit windows over grassy meadows and fleets of water. Dark wigeon bobbed there, whistling plaintively. Flights of egrets went flapping heavily through. A pair of barn owls quartered the hedges, ghostly white in the dusk. And out between the fleets, the grasslands heaved and crawled as if alive. Our 3,000 pink-footed geese had already put down for the night there.

'Traditionally, the pink-feet spend the night out on the intertidal mudflats, where they're safe from predators and disturbance,' said Michael. 'But a few years ago, they began to use these marshes as a night roost – they're more sheltered than the beach, there's no high tides to shift the geese halfway through the night and no one shoots them. Of course, that's wonderful for us, because we can see them at the roost close up.'

As the evening advanced, and a fragile crescent of new moon appeared in the southern sky, more and more pink-feet came sailing in to roost. In scores and fifties they wavered across the sunset, put their flaps down with a convex curvature of wings, and dropped in among their fellows. The marshes seethed, the sky flickered and swam with geese and the wind was full of clamour. '10,000, I should think,' calculated Victoria, eyes glued to binoculars.

We sat at the open windows of the hide, hypnotised, until our fingers were numb and our eyes grew too strained to see the geese. As we left the marshes, sated, the pink-feet were still dropping in for the night, indefatigable survivors of uncounted journeys.

141

The unspeakable Stiperstones

A cold winter's evening on the Long Mynd, with a powdering of snow slanting in across Shropshire's whaleback hills from the north. I shoved my hands deep into my pockets and walked towards the ridge. Ice crunched under my boots, and a raven carked overhead. The harsh sounds set a suitably bleak and ominous tone for the Stiperstones, silhouetted on the skyline against a smeary red sunset. On this December night, the longest night of the year, Wild Edric the Saxon is said to come to the Stiperstones to meet all the ghosts and witches of Shropshire. It seemed a fitting time to pay a visit to one of the most haunted and legend-rich landscapes in Britain.

Cranberry Rock, Manstone Rock, the Devil's Chair, Scattered Rock and Shepherd's Rock: the five craggy tors of the Stiperstones stand along their hilltop. They are outcrops of hard quartzite, formed of sandstone under giant pressures and temperatures some 500 million years ago, then pushed aloft by volcanic upthrust. They stand amid rough grassland, scrub and heather, carefully preserved from the encroaching commercial forests and 'improved' (chemically enriched but ecologically impoverished) grazing fields.

Our distant ancestors were drawn to the Stiperstones; their burial mounds lie all around. From Roman times onwards, lead miners delved in the mineral-rich seams of the locality. Smallholders grazed their animals around the outcrop.

In these wild uplands, superstition was commonplace. Local farmers would place the bodies of stillborn lambs in the trees – if they were buried on the farm, all the surviving lambs would die. For the lead miners, whistling underground was the greatest of offences, guaranteed to bring bad luck. If a miner crossed paths with a woman on his way to work, he might as well return home at once; no good would attend him on that shift.

Through the centuries, the weird frost-shattered shapes of the Stiperstones, so often distorted and half-hidden by mist, fostered a whole raft of strange and wonderful tales. The centrepiece of the group is the Devil's Chair, a craggy mass of lichen-stained quartzite. Most of the legends gather about this outcrop. They say that the Devil was flying over from Ireland with a lapful of stones, intending to block up the Hell Gutter valley, when his apron strings slipped and the load tumbled to earth to form the 'chair'. A portion has fallen away to make the Devil's Window, through which the bold may creep. Those who do so may come to good or ill – no one can predict which. When mist creeps across the ridge to hide the Stiperstones from view, then you can be sure that the Devil is ensconced in his chair, waiting for the outcrop to sink into the earth. If that comes to pass, England will fall into ruin.

Some of the tales have a Christian subtext – maybe they were foisted on the credulous locals by canny preachers. One concerns Lady Godiva, whose heart-rending wailing can be heard as she rides her spirit horse through Mytton Dingle and up along the Stiperstones at the head of a wild rabble of ghosts. It is her eternal punishment for going hunting when she should have been at church. Another story, set on Bog Hill near Cranberry Rock, features Slashrags the Tailor, who met the Devil in the form of a big 'boogeboo' with 'a strong sulphurious smell'. The Wicked One asked Slashrags to make him a suit of clothes. But the tailor, spying the cloven hooves and tail of the stranger, stalled him by agreeing to meet again in seven days. This time, Slashrags brought Mr Brewster the parson with him, and when the Devil caught sight of the holy man, he let out a frightful shriek and vanished in a puff of brimstone.

Wild Edric was a Saxon warlord, it seems, a bit of a chancer who once burned Shrewsbury. He married a fairy wife, who left him to die of a broken heart. If Wild Edric and Lady Godiva were about the Stiperstones with their witchy cohorts on this freezing night, I saw and heard neither hide nor hair of them. I was glad to hunch into my coat and watch the last glow of the winter's day as it dissolved behind a fine curtain of falling snow.

Down in Shrewsbury's reference library the following day, I hunted for a copy of *Shropshire Folk-Lore*, a Victorian book reputed to be stuffed full of Stiperstones legends both spooky and salacious. Eagerly, I turned to the relevant chapter. It was blank. The Stiperstones pages had all been removed – not neatly cut by the knife of some unscrupulous collector but ripped out so passionately that the torn edges had been left in a ragged fringe down the crease of the book. Across the nearest page, the single word 'UNSPEAKABLE' had been dashed in a fiery pencil scrawl. That such passion could be engendered by a few old folk tales is a measure of the raw power wielded by landscapes as dramatically resonant as the jagged, ill-omened Stiperstones.

142

Y is for Yer Tiz

… and the… now, how shall I put this…? The siren call of rural micturition. You know – exoteric evacuation. Ummm… that is, voiding en plein air… I mean to say, a bucolic egestion, or exudation al fresco. Or, in plain English, the need to find a handy bush or thicket behind which to strain the potatoes. Or spend a penny. Or 'go to the bathroom', if you happen to be a resident of the New World.

May I speak frankly? Ladies tend to find such informal arrangements, especially in the colder months, rather more of a trial than gentlemen do, 'for reasons upon which no lady would care to enlarge, and into which no gentleman need trouble himself to make further enquiry' (according to The Duke of Clarence's *A Modeſt Book of Etiquette*). Suffice it to say that, in the absence of conveniently positioned 'bathrooms' along the route of one's favourite walk, the tendency is to hold on until the pub heaves in sight.

In the Mendip Hills above Wells, a perfectly placed venue for a mid-walk flushing of the buffers was the old Slab House, a venerable roadhouse – recently burned down, to universal regret. The Slab House offered a beautifully slick shove ha'penny board, stone-flagged floors and baskets of chips in which truly gigantic sausages were embedded. The beer wasn't too bad, and the talk was all local. But best of all, for eyes watering with the effort of withholding, was the sight of a handmade sign nailed to the door of the noxious shed behind the pub, which proclaimed in good broad Somerset: 'Yer Tiz'.

Here, with a sigh of satisfaction, generations of retentive ramblers were welcome to write their names in water, a deed perfectly expressive of the zen-like insouciance for which such folk are famous.

143

Too much damn trouble

'The camera is beyond repair; it appears to have been inundated with a sticky substance.'

So said the repairer's note attached to my point-and-press Canon. Shutter and zoom were stuck tight, as though they'd been welded with superglue, and the battery compartment was half-filled with the sort of gunk you get in the nether regions of a drainpipe. It was a valuable lesson of a sort, actually. If you hear a funny noise when you're driving, don't ignore it.

We'd just finished a fantastically rainy walk in nethermost Devon. We had mud to the eyebrows and were soaked to the skin, and I chucked the camera into a plastic box on the back seat without putting it back in its padded case. To be absolutely honest, I hadn't put the camera back in its case since the day I bought it. You don't, do you? Oh, you do. Oh, well – *I* don't. It's too much damn trouble to get it out and put it back fifty times over on a walk.

Anyway, I must admit I did hear a clunk and a gurgle immediately after we'd driven over a bump. But I was chatting away, or maybe I was trying to find 'She Does It Right' on my Dr Feelgood CD. Whatever the cause, I didn't stop and look. So, it was only when I got home that I discovered the following back seat disaster scenario:

1. A recumbent soya milk carton, empty.
2. A plastic box, half-full of khaki liquid.
3. My camera, submerged in the tide.

Cameras and soya don't mix. I know that now. So, does my replacement camera live in a nice protective case? No, it doesn't. Still too much damn trouble.

144

Covid Winter: sunrise at the long barrow

We leave the house on Christmas morning as the first crack of light is spreading in the east. No grandchildren opening their Santa stockings in our bed this Covid Christmas, no Christmas table to set, no family sprawling all over the house. All are locked down elsewhere.

Down empty roads and muddy lanes running with water we go, to a little parking space where the puddles are iced over. The first time this year I've pulled on hat, scarf, thick gloves, thermals and padded winter coat.

Across a racing stream on a footbridge slippery with frost, and up a frozen grass slope to the long barrow, darkly silhou-etted on the skyline against a sky already broadened into a peach-coloured dawn, the blue above streaked with dozens of drifting horsetails of cloud.

I worm my way into the cold, damp stone passage that leads back for thirty feet or so into the artificial hillock of the barrow. The floor where I kneel is wet and muddy, the stones hard against my back. The entrance is guarded by a big ammonite embedded in one of the kerbstones. Looking out, the view is south-east up a gentle slope to a wood on the skyline.

It is a half-hour wait, with the invisible sun lighting up the higher features of the village in the valley – the church tower and fine tall buildings. Golden light creeps gradually down the slope behind the houses, and crowds of rooks on the wing are becoming agitated and vocal at the sunrise they can already see from their vantage points fifty feet in the air.

At last, the moment comes. The first shallow arc of the sun rims the hill, spinning like a ball, its intense light diffused behind the ivy-thickened skeletons of the trees. The clouds gleam; the peachiness of the sky leaches into pale blue. A finger of dazzling sunlight approaches down the sloping field, enters the passage and lights up the back wall of the burial chamber in an unbroken wash of light as bright as polished silver, as it has done at every winter solstice since the architects of the barrow aligned it so precisely 5,000 years ago. A reassuring reflection at the end of this pandemic year that has shaken everyday life to its roots and beyond.

145

Boxing Day: go climb a hill

Newly fallen snow crunches and squeaks under our boots as we climb our favourite Boxing Day hill. It's somewhere in the West Country, a small hill, not more than a couple of hundred feet from roots to summit. An Iron Age hill fort surrounds its brow like a royal circlet, and the button on the crown is a Bronze Age bowl barrow. People must have been climbing this hill in sunshine, rain and snow for thousands of years, following the age-old imperative to stand higher than the surrounding land, up where the everyday drops away and all seems sublime.

At the top, it's cold and windy, with distant hills lying like frozen surf waves along the northern horizon. I unship my backpack and pull out my melodeon. With numb fingers, I fumble at the buttons, and slowly a tune emerges, jerky and hesitant, as though surfacing from hibernation. It's the first time I've played it since this day last year – 'The Holly And The Ivy', old-style. My companions take hands and dance, not palely and solemnly, but with red cheeks and a lot of laughter. This is what we do each Boxing Day, come rain, come shine.

There have always been rituals and jollifications on St Stephen's Day, the day after Christmas Day, whether it was giving 'Christmas boxes' of money to one's servants or hunting the wren because, legends said, it was the little bird who betrayed the whereabouts of the fugitive St Stephen to the saint's persecutors. But long before Christianity came to these shores, people would have responded to the same impulse on the morning after the big midwinter feast day. Ooh, too much mead and metheglin last night – what a head I've got! All that roast mammoth, too. Hmmm, this cave is a bit... well, 'fragrant', don't you reckon? Tell you what – get your furs, and let's grab some fresh air. The kids? Oh, they'll be all right drawing on the walls for an hour or two.

Too many pies – and too much piety, back in the days when you couldn't crack a Christmas smile for fear of the Devil. Charles Dickens put paid to that sort of po-facedness nearly 200 years ago with his depiction in *A Christmas Carol* of an open-hearted, open-handed festive season. We've learned to love our Christmas feasting. But we still need, as much as we ever did (and maybe more, with our new mindfulness and health-consciousness), that time-honoured antidote – to get outside and away from the house, to fill our lungs with clean cold air and to go climb a hill to get the blood racing and put a good hot tingle in the cheeks.

My dad would have laughed at the very notion of mindfulness. But he and Mum got my sisters and me outside every Boxing Day for a reviving walk, more often than not up Bredon Hill, half an hour's drive from home. We were sometimes sulky, usually reluctant at first. But now Boxing Day on Bredon Hill is one of my favourite childhood memories – the milky panes of ice in the frozen ruts of the cart track that led up from Westmancote; the plumes of breath in the cold air that turned me magically into a steam engine; and the squashing of the sun into a sullen red ellipse as it sank into a black net of leafless trees. It didn't matter that the countryside lay dark and dead – that was part of the spell.

Hardly a 26 December has gone by since then when I haven't

gone out for a walk in snow or sunshine, far or near, steep or flat, with the kids or without them. And now, looking back, I see that those winter expeditions on Bredon Hill remained the template for all my subsequent Boxing Day walks – until, some thirty years ago, I found this little steep hill with the button on top.

*

Snow has begun to fall again, and the prints of our dancing feet have long since disappeared from the crest of the hill. We are long gone too. By now, we're in a pub not far away – a wonderful old pub, the kind you dream of and rarely stumble across – singing and drinking and watching the local mummers acting out, clumsily and hilariously, the kind of ancient earthy pantomime that has been played in rooms like this since time out of mind. The beer and the singing wouldn't taste the same without the walk as a relish. And the walk would lose half its savour if we didn't cap it with firelight and foolery.

That's the whole magic of winter walking. Long, long may it last.

Z is for Zymurgy

… otherwise known as 'the practice or art of fermentation, as in wine-making, brewing, distilling, etc.' (Thank you, *The Shorter Oxford English Dictionary*, 1972 two-volume edition, still outclassing anything online by a country mile.) And what has the art of fermentation – all right, let's be frank, the art of brewing – got to do with walking? Well, what a stupid question.

Yesterday, I had a wonderful walk in the winter sunshine, a beautiful and uplifting circuit of the south Cotswold valleys around Hillesley. And when I got back to the village, I went into the Fleece and I had a plate of nice hot chilli and a pint of Budding. Yes, I know I didn't need the beer. No, I know it can't be justified on grounds of health, or thirst-quenching or economy, or by any rational yardstick. Yes, nurse, water would be better for me, and yes, accountant, cheaper too. But beer and walking go together like – well, like beer and most pleasurable activities. Why? I don't know why, but I promise to go on researching.

There was definitely something about that Budding. 'Very popular pale ale, with a grassy bitterness, sweet malt and luscious floral aroma,' says Stroud Brewery, the home of the zymurgical alchemists (or thaumaturges – thanks again, OED) who brew it. Bitter and sweet, grass and flowers? You can't say fairer than that.

What's the point?

My teenage son growled: 'What's the point
Of straining every nerve and joint,
Of hiking till your toenails split,
Of walking till you're sick of it?'
'And do we *have* to?' came the cry
From his three sisters, scowling by;
A fair enquiry, in my book,
And worthy of a little look.
Why do I walk so jolly far?
Why don't I do it all by car?
An existential question, friends,
That makes one bite one's finger-ends;
A knotty poser, you'll acknowledge,
Fit for debate in hall or college.
I have cogitated much
On cause and grounds and roots and such,
And here's the crux of what I've learned
(Deep within my brain it's burned):
The very heart and soul, the nub,
The point of walking is... the pub.

Now I was once upright and noble;
I'd sooner suck a stone or snowball,
Sooner mortify the flesh,

Than drink new ale when it was fresh.
Pubs to me were most abhorrent –
I would seek the mountain torrent,
Gather raindrops, quaff the tarns,
Drink at rusty troughs in barns,
Sip the dew from off the grass,
Gulp a melted Häagen-Dasz –
Anything but enter in
A public house, that den of sin,
Siren's lair of sloth and slackness,
Gorgon's hovel, pit of blackness.

Ere I had my pub renaissance,
I ate naught but nuts and raisins,
I drank only Adam's ale –
I was puny, poor and pale,
Good for little, fit for nuffin,
Long of face and short of stuffin.

Picture me, one fateful day,
Battling with the Pennine Way;
By the tempest almost felled,
On the bleak moors north of Keld;
Head bowed down before the wind,
Feet all blistered, ankles skinned;
Sixty pounds upon my back
Fit to make each rib bone crack;
Smeared with peat and soaked with rain,
Lost in bloody mist again;
Night a-creeping o'er the lea,
No one there to comfort me,
Steer my steps or set my brain right

Save the Master, sainted Wainwright,
Guiding me through cleft and canyon
With his *Pennine Way Companion*,
Stained with rain and earth and sun,
Open at page 91.
Though black misery filled my cup,
Though I'd almost given up,
Though my will was growing dim,
Still I kept my faith in him.
Now I fumbled for a match
('Twas the last one of the batch);
Struck it with a trembling hand
As the Master's page I scanned,
Following the dotted line.
There it lay, in print so fine,
As the dark and mist closed in –
Fatal legend: 'Tan Hill Inn'.
Peering forward through the night,
There I spied a wondrous sight –
Lights a-twinkling in the gloaming,
Whispering, 'Traveller, stop your roaming!'
I was absolutely knacked,
And so, my lords, my willpower cracked.
Through the door I dragged myself,
Dumped my pack upon the shelf,
Tottered forward to the bar –
Out, then, like a jaguar
Sprang the barman, and he cried:
'Y'muddy bugger – get outside!'
God, my friends, I nearly died!
I dropped Wainwright with a rustle;
I simply couldn't move a muscle.

Then the miracle occurred!
The landlady appeared and purred,
'Hither, son, and do not fear –
What you need's a pint of beer!'
Then I found my heart's desire
As she sat me by the fire;
Pulled the boots from off my feet;
'Would you like a bite to eat?'
Bound my blisters, combed my beard
(That was nice, though somewhat weird);
Brought me, like a magic wish,
Steak and kidney in a dish.
There, beside the fragrant pudd'n,
Dark and foaming like a good'un,
Stood a glass… I will not fool yer –
It was Theakston's Old Peculier.

Nobles, that was it for me;
That was my epiphany.
Once I'd got the first one down me,
I drank quite enough to drown me;
Scoffed the pudding, then one more;
Went to bed for eight hours' snore;
Rose at seven, ate six eggs;
Felt as if I'd got new legs;
Kissed the lady, took my leave;
And reached Kirk Yetholm late that eve.

There is a message clear for all
Who heed the hills' seductive call –
When dusky eve comes creeping o'er
Benighted bog and moody moor,

When hard-worked feet have swollen so
You cannot feel each heel and toe,
When you are out of power and puff –
In short, when you have had enough –
You know you do not have to wait
Until the hour is growing late;
You do not need to yomp the path
While mortal folk are in the bath;
You're not compelled to keep it up
Till you have drained exhaustion's cup;
There is no need to ford that beck –
Consider cutting short your trek!

Friends, take warning by my tale!
Do not shun good steak and ale!
Cast away that stale Ryvita,
Hurry past the Happy Eater,
Shun that isotonic bottle;
Get some strong ale down your throttle.
When your Brashers start to rub,
Hurl them hence and seek the pub!

If you are a sentient mammal,
Quit the flask and shun the Camel,
Pour yon pallid tea away,
And drink with me the livelong day.
One word of warning to you, sonny –
For God's sake, don't forget your money!
For there is nothing in this world
So guaranteed to get toys hurled
Out of the pram, when in the bar,
As being thirsty for a jar,

Eyeing the beckoning pumps, inspecting
What's on offer, then selecting
A tasty pint of Killer Rocket,
Putting your hand into your pocket...
Discovering, as you stamp and cuss,
You've left your wallet on the bus.

So let's forget the rambling bug;
Come on and join me in the snug,
Where no rude winds roughly blow,
Where there's neither sleet nor snow.
Bring me to the Pheasant Inn,
Hark-to Bounty, Poacher's Pin,
Hunter's Lodge, or Heights Hotel,
The Bull, the Bowl, the Ball, the Bell.
In the Black Lion I would sojourn,
Rain and wind and hail a-dodgin';
In some fabled watering hole
Where the fires burn proper coal,
Where the landlord's cheeks are rosy,
Everything is quiet and cosy,
No one talks a bit of sense,
And a pint costs twenty pence.
Jokes are funny, laughter hearty,
Every day's a birthday party;
Roast beef sandwiches, of course,
Plenty of horseradish sauce.
Tabletops are wide and stout;
You can spread your maps right out.
Beer comes from a wooden barrel;
No one minds your strange apparel;
Floors are muddy, no one cares

If your boots are on the chairs;
Dogs are welcome, walkers too,
And there's paper in the loo.
Should you, by some happy chance,
Through the lamplit window glance
And see a walker limping past,
Shivering in the icy blast,
Do not pity him his lot,
Do not weep for him one jot –
Thank your stars for what you've got:
He's outside – and you are not!

Life goes to and fro – it's tidal.
Make the most of being idle.
There's no need to grasp the nettle;
Put your feet up on the settle.
Greet each stranger like a brother;
Take your time and have another,
Chase it with a warming noggin,
Open the stove and put a log in.
Start a song and sing it through;
Get the cat to talk to you.
Inspect the pictures, watch the telly,
Contemplate the landlord's belly…
Soon the hour will strike, you know,
When through those doors you'll have to go,
Into wet boots squeeze sore feet,
Don a coat against the sleet,
Scowl as though you'd Colin Firth it,
Growl and wonder if it's worth it;
Out into the storm a-stumbling,
Hat and gloves and gaiters fumbling,

Tripping over rock and boulder…
If the Devil on your shoulder
Shows you, through the haze of beer,
A handy bus stop, lurking near;
If his charming voice you hear,
Whispering softly in your ear,
'Let's give up this walking lark;
And let's get home before it's dark' –
Do not feel ashamed, my friends,
If there your expedition ends;
Do not slink with guilt away –
You can walk another day.

*

Here's to the babe in hat and gloves
Carried by the ones it loves,
Learning atop the mountain's crown
The lifelong thrill of looking down.
Here's to the child that I was once,
Who would not walk on, silly dunce,
But sat down like a sulky pup
And howled until they picked me up.

Here's to the youth who'll lace his boots
In expectation of new routes,
Of paths to bear him far away
From ordinary everyday.
Here's to the girl who hoists her pack
With jubilation on her back,
Intending to assault the peaks,
Where ravens call and magic speaks.

Here's to those of riper years,
Grinding through the lower gears
With creaking bones and wonky knees,
Still keen to sniff the mountain breeze.

And here's to the man, and woman too,
Who can't do what they used to do,
But still contrive a last hurrah
By telling whoppers in the bar.

Notes

1 Richard Jefferies, 'Hours of Spring' in *Landscape with Figures: Selected Prose Writings* (London, 2013).
2 'Online maps "wiping out history"', BBC, http://news.bbc.co.uk/1/hi/uk/7586789.stm.
3 Richard Jefferies, 'Hours of Spring' in *Landscape with Figures: Selected Prose Writings* (London, 2013).
4 Clement Scott, *Poppy Land* (n.p., 1888).
5 'Introduction', *The First World War Camps of Cannock Chase*, www.staffspasttrack.org.uk/exhibit/chasecamps.
6 Alexander Cordell, *Rape of the Fair Country* (London, 1959).
7 *Discovering Britain*, https://www.discoveringbritain.org.